MONOPOLIZED

Also by David Dayen

*Chain of Title: How Three Ordinary Americans Uncovered
Wall Street's Great Foreclosure Fraud*

MONOPOLIZED

LIFE IN THE AGE OF
CORPORATE POWER

DAVID DAYEN

THE
NEW
PRESS

NEW YORK
LONDON

Requests for permission to reproduce selections from this book should be made through our website: https://thenewpress.com/contact.
Published in the United States by The New Press, New York, 2020
Distributed by Two Rivers Distribution

ISBN 978-1-62097-542-8 (ebook)

LIBRARY OF CONGRESS CATALOGING-IN-PUBLICATION DATA

Names: Dayen, David, author.
Title: Monopolized : life in the age of corporate power / David Dayen.
Description: New York : The New Press, 2020. | Includes bibliographical
    references and index. | Summary: "From the cars we drive to what
    toothpaste we use, how a tiny group of corporations have come to
    dominate every aspect of our lives"-- Provided by publisher.
Identifiers: LCCN 2019055148 | ISBN 9781620975411 (cloth) | ISBN
    9781620975428 (ebook)
Subjects: LCSH: Monopolies.
Classification: LCC HD2757.2 .D39 2020 | DDC 338.8/2--dc23
LC record available at https://lccn.loc.gov/2019055148

The New Press publishes books that promote and enrich public discussion and understanding of the issues vital to our democracy and to a more equitable world. These books are made possible by the enthusiasm of our readers; the support of a committed group of donors, large and small; the collaboration of our many partners in the independent media and the not-for-profit sector; booksellers, who often hand-sell New Press books; librarians; and above all by our authors.

www.thenewpress.com

Book design and composition by Bookbright Media
This book was set in Minion, Fort, and Grotesque MT

Printed in the United States of America

10 9 8 7 6 5 4 3 2 1

No one may presume to exercise a monopoly of any kind . . . and if anyone shall presume to practice a monopoly, let his property be forfeited and himself condemned to perpetual exile.

—Emperor Zeno to Praetorian Prefect of Constantinople,
A.D. 483

No one man should have all that power.

—Kanye West, "Power," A.D. *2010*

CONTENTS

MONOPOLIZED

INTRODUCTION

On April 15, 2019, Salesforce.com announced a $300 million deal to buy Salesforce.org.

I'll back up if you're confused.

There's this company called Salesforce that makes "customer relationship management" software. It tracks current sales and projects future sales. It sounds to me like a shared spreadsheet, but I'm reliably informed that it's a transformative product. Anyway, at one point, Salesforce spun off an independent philanthropic arm, unimaginatively called Salesforce.org, which offers the software to nonprofits and educational groups for little or no money. As people like cheap things, that business took off. So much so that Salesforce decided to buy it.

In its announcement, Salesforce boasted that it would enjoy a $200 million revenue boost from the deal. Salesforce.org would still supply to nonprofits; it would just become a business line of Salesforce. Of course, if you give away the core product to some customers at a discount, profit *margins* fall. That's probably why Salesforce.org got spun off to begin with. On a conference call, Salesforce chief financial officer Mark Hawkins reassured analysts that Salesforce.org will "be on a pathway and convergence over time to our overall Salesforce operating margin." That's a deliberately convoluted way of saying that Salesforce.org will either jack up the price to nonprofits or "streamline areas of operational duplication," another deliberately convoluted way of saying it would make job cuts.

The larger point is this: Salesforce, which has made sixty acquisitions since 2006, according to deal tracker Crunchbase, has become either so starved for growth or so eager to please Wall Street that it has begun to buy itself. And I wouldn't bring that up, except that it feels like a trend. Within a week of the Salesforce/Salesforce acquisition, Expedia Group bought Liberty Expedia Holdings. This reconfigured a deal from the 1990s that created separate stockholder groups for Barry Diller and John Malone, two wealthy industrialists with their own empires and separate claims on Expedia, an online travel site that has spent the past couple of decades scooping up adversaries. Expedia was once part of Microsoft, then Diller's corporation owned it, and then it became its own company but Diller still had a hand in it. Now it was purchasing itself. To make things simpler.

We're living in an age where companies buying themselves offers the only respite from companies buying each other. It sounds absurd, but our era is absurd.

The capitalist economic system, whether you value it or not, relies on competition. At its best, competition keeps companies honest, narrows costs, expands the job base, sows innovation, distributes the fruits of productivity widely, and gives every member of society a chance to use their talents to earn a living. Competition protects economies, affords possibility, and allows democracy to flourish, as no one firm becomes big enough to control the corridors of power. That's the theory, at least, and historical evidence bears it out. America's best moments of shared prosperity line up favorably with eras of robust competition, when government-appointed guardians attacked efforts to corner markets.

Those attacks have been kept in abeyance for over forty years; government has abandoned its post as the guardian of competition. As a result, we toil in this age of monopoly, this age of plutocrats, this age of soaring inequality and broken democracy, this age of middle-class despair and sawed-off ladders to prosperity. The fact that fewer and fewer companies control most economic sectors today helps to explain virtually all the challenges America faces.

This book means to explain that connection. But we must also address the dissenters, the still-dominant faction of antitrust scholars, academics, and policymakers, who look at the world and see no concentration problem worth their attention. I've been to their conferences, I've heard them speak, I've read their papers. And I've read the academic rebuttals. Researchers in 2018 found increases in concentration in 75 percent of all industries over the past two decades; the Obama White House's Council of Economic Advisers found similar systematic increases in 2016.

My main advice to the naysayers is to go outside. It's not hard to identify the collections of monopolies encircling our every move through life.

(Just a note here: I'm using the term "monopolies" to refer to companies with significant market shares in highly concentrated industries. I could refer to "oligopolies" or "large companies," but "monopolies" will suffice, for ease of use.)

Some monopolies are obvious to everyone. There are four major airlines, four major commercial banks, four major companies that deliver phone, wireless, cable, and internet services. One company controls most web search; one company controls most social media; one company controls about half of all e-commerce. Handfuls of firms dominate virtually every aspect of food and agricultural production, media, military equipment, medical supply, and regional hospital management. Phrases like "Big Pharma" and "Big Oil" are ubiquitous in political discussion. In nearly all states, the top three health insurance companies take upward of 80 percent of the market.

For other monopolies, you need a decoder ring of sorts; I think of it like the sunglasses worn in John Carpenter's 1988 schlock sci-fi classic *They Live*. Carpenter himself has called the film an allegory about unrestrained capitalism in the Reagan years. When people put on the sunglasses, they see the world in its true ugliness. Political and business elites are actually skinless, bulging-eyed aliens, and advertising includes bold subliminal lettering demanding that subjects obey, consume, and submit. It's also amazing for a random, six-minute-long fight scene between Rowdy Roddy Piper and Keith David, but that's not important right now.

Put on the sunglasses, crack the code, and you uncover monopolies, ridiculous monopolies, throughout American life. There appear to be lots of dating apps out there, appealing to some cross section of the eligible bachelor and bachelorette pool. They're almost all owned by the same company, Match Group, which includes in its portfolio Tinder, OkCupid, Match.com, Hinge, and forty other sites. Match Group itself is part of a conglomerate called InterActiveCorp, owned by the aforementioned Barry Diller. The only big dating site outside of Match Group, Bumble, got bought in November 2019 by the world's biggest private equity firm, Blackstone. Maybe you like to ski in far-flung locales across the country. It turns out most of the big ones are owned by the same two companies, Alterra (a division of private equity firm KSL) and Vail, catering to 18 million skiers across North America every year. You unquestionably don't think much about plastic hangers, but the industry has been a monopoly for over twenty years, first under a division of Tyco International, and then after a 2006 acquisition through an Italian firm named Mainetti.

Enter a multiplex and see all the genres and styles of films, yet Disney in 2019 earned around 40 percent of all dollars spent at the box office, with control of Marvel, Lucasfilm, and 21st Century Fox properties, along with its existing empire. Harvey Weinstein finally was exposed as a sexual predator because his power (he cornered the market on Oscar-winning films in the late 1990s, when his company Miramax was part of Disney) started to wane, making it safer to go after him. The horrors that today's consolidated entertainment business has enabled are as yet unknown.

Walk into a supermarket and witness the glories of capitalism at work, aisles upon aisles of different products for different tastes. They're mostly the handiwork of a few giant companies, from Nestlé to Unilever to PepsiCo. Here's a fun game: pick an aisle at random at your local supermarket and check the back of every product in succession. I've done this at my neighborhood Ralphs (a division of Kroger, which also runs Fred Meyer, Dillons, Food 4 Less, Mariano's, Harris Teeter, and others). Maybe you see a lot of peanut butter brands but they're almost all from three companies. Maybe you see a lot of jelly but they're all from . . . three companies. All that toothpaste? Two companies, Procter & Gamble and Colgate-Palmolive. All those disruptive, healthier brands taking on the stodgy incumbents? Well, Naked Juice comes from PepsiCo, Larabar comes from General Mills, Kashi is part of Kellogg's, Seventh Generation is part of Unilever (so is Ben & Jerry's ice cream), and Blue Bottle coffee is a Nestlé product. This has brought the incumbents back to life. One article headline from 2018 sums up the situation: "Yogurt Is Cool, So Deal Talk Is Heating Up." Whatever people want, large companies respond by turning their cash cannon on the upstarts and buying them out.

Put on your sunglasses and you can finally see, with clear vision, the monopoly in sunglasses. Practically every lens and frame outlet in America—Pearle Vision, Sunglass Hut, Target, LensCrafters—has as its owner an Italian firm named Luxottica, which also makes frames for brands like Ray-Ban, Vogue, Prada, Chanel, Coach, and dozens more. In 2018, Essilor, a French lens maker that controls half the global market, merged with Luxottica, creating a monster supplying more than a billion lenses and frames per year. In 2019, EssilorLuxottica bought GrandVision, a Dutch company that owns For Eyes, among other retailers. It's a global glasses monopoly.

I could fill the rest of this book by just naming hidden monopolies, though my publisher would recommend against it. There's an office supply wholesaler monopoly, after Staples and Essendant, the main two national suppliers, merged. There's a sanitary napkin monopoly, as three companies absorb about 92 percent of market share. There's a font monopoly, after a private equity firm bought the company that owns popular typefaces Times New Roman and Helvetica. There's a matzo monopoly, after the merger of Manischewitz with a conglomerate that supplies a bunch of kosher foods.

The current media fascination with monopoly is incredibly focused on Big Tech, which is indeed a menace, invading our privacy, distorting our attention, serving as conduits for misinformation, and destroying start-ups. Entire books have been written about the tech behemoths, from Jonathan Taplin's *Move Fast and Break Things* to Franklin Foer's *World Without Mind*. They're good and you should read them. I'll have more on Big Tech later. But believe me when I say this: if you broke up Facebook, Google, Apple, and Amazon tomorrow, we would still have a grave monopoly problem in America. The structure of modern capitalism now favors monopoly, in the absence of government action to prevent it. Early Facebook investor and PayPal co-founder Peter Thiel, one of our foremost monopolists, supplied the words that sum up an era: "Competition is for losers."

America has habitually drifted from a country of shared abundance to a country teeming with predatory monopolists. Citizens under British rule in New England reacted to the Tea Act of 1773, which gave the East India Company unfettered control over the sale of the sought-after leaves to the colonies by tossing chests of the stuff into Boston Harbor. The Boston Tea Party, in other words, was an antimonopoly riot. And we have seen other rumblings, reactions to consolidation and control over our lives, throughout American history. Monopoly in transport of goods sparked the farmer-led Granger movement; monopoly in industrial factory work sparked the labor movement; trusts throughout the economy sparked the Progressive Era and produced the government's tools to combat market power. The push and pull of monopoly and resistance exists on the periphery of our most critical debates and conversations.

We're currently on a particularly precarious edge of that swing, a side of the pendulum rarely reached in the nation's 240-odd years, a second

Gilded Age. And if you had to find one man to thank for that, he was the same guy looking down at me, smiling, on November 9, 2016, the day after the presidential election that installed Donald Trump in the White House.

I was at Yale Law School, Hillary Clinton's alma mater, scheduled to speak to a foreclosure litigation class about my previous book, *Chain of Title*, and then address the local chapter of the American Constitution Society over lunch. The classroom discussion was fine, but Yale Law students were too grieved by the results of the election to trifle with me. The lunchtime sandwiches were still sitting there, so my contact and I went down to eat in this huge, empty lecture hall where the speech was to be held. As I looked up, a bit demoralized, I saw the massive portrait of one of Yale Law's legendary professors, sitting in front of a yellow drape and a shelf of imposing law tomes, sporting vaguely Amish-looking facial hair. His name was Robert Bork.

To the extent the popular consciousness remembers Bork at all, it's as a failed Supreme Court nominee. In reality, Robert Bork achieved far more off the bench than he might have in a lifetime of rulings. He forced an entire area of the law into surrender without firing a shot.

The ideas Bork assembled for his 1978 treatise *The Antitrust Paradox* existed for a couple of decades, through his writings and those of a group of scholars at the University of Chicago (these concepts are often described as the Chicago School of economics). But Bork released his work at the right moment, when Democrats were abandoning the New Deal framework and Republicans were coalescing around corporate conservatism. Within a couple of years of publication, Ronald Reagan would win election and put Bork's theories into practice. And the rest was history.

The Antitrust Paradox reinterpreted the Sherman Antitrust Act, the main law used to confront monopolies. Instead of an enforcement mechanism to fight market power, Bork argued, the Sherman Act constituted nothing more than a safeguard for "consumer welfare." To Bork, consumer welfare effectively meant lower prices. Therefore, if a merger made the combined business more efficient, able to earn profits while dropping prices, that merger should be approved. And to Bork, larger scale generally enhanced efficiency. The argument was completely circular. As for concerns about monopoly, Bork had an even simpler theory: whenever a dominant incumbent abused its power (by raising prices, since Bork's frame couldn't imagine any abuse beyond that), rivals would naturally arise to compete away the damage. The "paradox" of Bork's title was that antitrust enforcement made consumers worse off. So it's not just that concentration posed no problems for America; it's that concentration afforded massive benefits. You still see this attitude among defenders of the status quo today, the ones who cite the availability of a ten-pack of socks at Walmart for eight bucks and proclaim the best of all possible worlds. Monopoly is good, competition is for losers. Robert Bork, everyone.

None of this holds up even within Bork's narrow definitions. There's no real evidence that mergers make companies more productive, which would be the "efficient" part of efficiency. John Kwoka, an economics professor at Northeastern University, had the novel idea in 2015 to look back at approved mergers and do the math. Of the forty-six he studied, thirty-eight resulted in higher prices, about 7.29 percent on average. "Someone described my work as driving a stake into the heart of the argument," Kwoka told me. "It takes on the Chicago School on its own terms and describes that theory as false." A 2018 paper from researchers Jan de Loecker, Jan Eeckhout, and Gabriel Unger found a similar trend: a rise in markups (another word for profits) that began to build around 1980, just two years after *The Antitrust Paradox* was published.

The timing fits, because in 1982, a year after Reagan entered the White House, his antitrust enforcement chief, Bill Baxter, rewrote the Justice Department guidelines used to analyze mergers, contouring them to Chicago School theories. Baxter narrowed the type of mergers that would invite official scrutiny, and made sure that efficiency was among the key subjects studied to determine if a scrutinized merger could be cleared. It wasn't the only reason concentration ran amok—the influence of Bork and the Chicago School reached the judiciary as well, as court rulings started to quote *The Antitrust Paradox* directly—but altering the antitrust guidelines transformed official policy without changing a comma of the Sherman Act. As Barry Lynn of the Open Markets Institute, one of the foremost chroniclers of the age of monopoly, told me, "America could not be more different economically than it was in 1978. There's been a complete revolution."

Antitrust law was now understood solely through the inexact science of economics, and well-heeled corporations could always find someone with a chart to assert massive efficiencies from any merger. An industry grew up to tell companies what they wanted to hear: that bigger was better, that mergers would make them rich, that growth through acquisition represented a shortcut to success. We turned over protection of the public interest from democratically elected governments to self-interested economists, bankers, and consultants, using theories disconnected from everyday Americans. And over four decades, corporate power flourished. There are a few good books about this history as well, from Matt Stoller's *Goliath* to Tim Wu's *The Curse of Bigness*. (As an alternative, you can keep reading the book you conveniently have in your hands right now.)

Bork and his acolytes shrewdly confined the question of monopoly to consumer welfare, and confined "consumer welfare" even more to prices. It's easier to sing the praises of monopoly when you conveniently omit so many of the dangers it unleashes upon the world:

Monopoly steals wages. When companies talk about "efficiencies" in mergers, they typically mean that the merged company's combined operations require fewer workers to make it run. Efficiencies, in other words, equals layoffs.

But a new wave of research, previously pushed to the back burner of economic analysis, helps solve the more difficult puzzle of how we could have stagnant wages with such low unemployment rates. There's no single explanation for this, and the decline of labor unions certainly played a big role. But the technical term for part of the answer is "monopsony." In a monopoly, many buyers are faced with one seller; in a monopsony, there are many sellers and one buyer. That buyer can purchase labor or manufacturing materials. When an industry concentrates, workers in that industry have fewer places to sell their labor. And that means that companies can offer less without worrying about losing employees to a competitor.

Harvard's Nathan Wilmers estimates that buyer power accounts for at least 10 percent of wage stagnation since the 1970s. Simcha Barkai, a PhD candidate at the University of Chicago, found a 10 percent decline in the labor share of income (that is, the amount of each dollar generated in the economy going to labor) over the last thirty years, almost all of which was transferred into profits. It comes out to about $14,000 per worker per year. Researchers José Azar, Ioana Elena Marinescu, and Marshall Steinbaum discovered a 17 percent decline in wages in highly concentrated industries. Another group led by MIT's David Autor identified "superstar firms" and monopoly power translating into a lower labor share, as did the Obama

White House, with sharper declines correlated with higher levels of concentration. Corporate profits are up and wages haven't kept pace, because when you're a star, they let you do that.

Working under monopoly means that the boss sets the rules, and not in your favor. Millions are classified as independent contractors, losing benefits and hard-earned rights. To depress wages, oligopolists collude with rivals on no-poaching agreements, vowing not to hire away competitors' workers or even workers at its own franchises; the guy at the McDonald's in Dallas can't work at another McDonald's in Dallas. Job classes as diverse as summer camp counselors, doggy day-care minders, and janitors must sign noncompete agreements, preventing them from seeking the same position somewhere else. If you think businesses must stop janitors from taking their lucrative cleaning trade secrets to a competitor, you have a future as an expert witness for the janitorial industry. And if workers want to complain about this, they should check their employment contract, as they're probably bound to a mandatory arbitration agreement, which blocks access to courts and instead shuttles disputes to secret tribunals where the employer has the advantage.

Monopoly weakens economies. Contrary to assumptions that everyone in America has invented a website or an app, startup activity has plummeted since the late 1970s, as fewer new businesses open. The share of workers employed by younger firms has been cut in half. This has robbed the nation of a key engine of good-paying jobs. Many new companies' dreams extend only to getting bought out, which beats the alternative of getting crushed. High-tech startups operate in a "kill zone," fearful of being either copied or throttled by incumbents. When an entrepreneur with a great idea looks at the brick wall monopolists construct around their businesses and just gives up, we all lose. Mergers typically lead to lower innovation as well, because a monopolist doesn't have to outcompete nonexistent competition.

Your everyday capitalist likes higher profits, and for centuries capitalists achieved them through investing, whether to increase sales and productivity or to access new markets. You've got to spend money to make money, as they say. Except these days you don't. Today you sit on the market and either buy out alternatives or prevent them from reaching customers, and the profits roll in. Why invest when you can do what the landlord does: collect rent?

Indeed, pretax profits have been at historical highs, while investment remains relatively low. The incumbents don't invest because they don't have to, and would-be competitors don't invest because they're afraid to. Investors are actually stumped about where to put their money, despite enormous social and economic problems around the world. A sclerotic, low-investment economy doesn't grow as quickly; indeed, economic growth in the twenty-first century has flattened out. A monopolistic economy, in short, means a worse economy.

Monopoly degrades quality. If I sell widgets and nobody else competes with me on widget sales, what incentive do I have to make the widgets any good? You know the answer if you've ever called the customer service line of a cable company. Without choice in cable service, there's little need to invest in customer care specialists. The monopolist can tell the complainant that a technician will be at their house between 6:00 a.m. and 11:00 p.m., because what choice do the lowly customers have?

Declining quality is a feature of the age of monopoly. Air travel triggers feelings of revulsion matched only by trying to figure out what insurance your hospital takes. Boeing builds planes that fall out of the sky, and military suppliers don't do much better. Mass-produced fruits and vegetables have engineered out flavor as an optional extravagance. Technological devices wire in either planned obsolescence or deliberate degradation to force repurchases. Amazon happily ships a flood of counterfeit goods. If you're wondering why things fall apart so easily, why you seem to get less for your dollar, thank your local monopoly business.

Monopoly heightens disasters. One factor supercharging monopoly in the modern age is logistics, the ability to manufacture goods halfway across the world and bring them to a customer's doorstep just in time. Advanced logistics has created a path to centralizing production, and it renders our economy fragile, just as surely as every major financial institution piling into narrow bets on the subprime housing market created a tinderbox. Interdependent markets magnify problems.

When Amazon Web Services assumed its role as the backbone of a large proportion of the internet, random outages among its servers paralyzed users everywhere. When goods or raw materials can be accessed in only one location, disasters natural and unnatural ripple around the world. Barry Lynn traces his interest in monopoly back to an earthquake in Jiji, Taiwan, in September 1999, which disabled one industrial park from which a large amount of technology component parts emanated. A decade later, the Japanese earthquake that rocked the Fukushima nuclear reactor also damaged a Sony factory that made videotape, triggering desperation in the entertainment industry. We've seen supply shocks in flu vaccines and cancer drugs; we see them in gasoline all the time. And as you'll read, we saw it recently with a solution of salt and water—two of the most abundant commodities on the planet.

Monopoly supercharges inequality. To fewer victors go greater spoils. We have plenty of data now about the rise of inequality in wealth and income in the United States, and monopoly plays a role. Though CEO pay, now up 940 percent since 1978 while the typical worker's wages have risen just 12 percent, is completely out of control, a 2016 paper from a quintet of researchers shows that most of the variance in incomes happens *between* firms. Monopolized companies earn more, and this filters down to compensation.

The profit-extracting forces behind monopoly don't benefit workers; they shower cash on executives and shareholders, leaking out dividends in the completion of a cycle that values short-term valuations—and the economic moats that secure them—over reliable and durable products. Gifted with incredible riches, elites earn money from having money, deploying capital, and collecting rent on real estate or interest on debt. The top 1 percent holds the greatest share of overall wealth in recorded history. Jeff Bezos, the world's richest man, said in 2018 of his $131 billion personal fortune, "The only way that I can see to deploy this much financial resource is by converting my Amazon winnings into space travel." Our overlords literally shoot money into space while millions around them suffer.

Monopoly hollows out communities. Inequality has a regional component as well, as this book will demonstrate. We have superstar firms clustered in superstar cities, abandoning the rest of the country. The top twenty-five metropolitan areas are responsible for half the economic growth. This trend started around the early 1980s, a familiar date that tracks with the release of *The Antitrust Paradox* and the rise of Reagan. It has created a "geography of discontent" within America, pitting a dejected and resentful left-behind class against their more prosperous brethren, as political opportunists use immigrants and foreigners as scapegoats to explain away the inequity. This bounces off our national walls, reverberating with social and political unrest, right-wing populism and xenophobia, and a disconnection hardwired into American life. The country cannot come together because monopoly has separated us, and thrown us from power.

Monopoly screws up politics. Regional inequality mapped onto a presidential election system that dispenses electoral votes state by state creates situations like Donald Trump winning the presidency with nearly 3 million fewer popular votes than his opponent. But more than that, economic power readily converts into political power. Monopolists can more easily buy politicians, bend lawmakers and regulators to their will, get away with abuses, and obtain special favors that entrench their position and enrich their pocketbooks. When you hear from a politician that certain policies aren't "practical" or couldn't "survive" a special-interest onslaught, they are telling you that they aren't in charge of the government. It's an articulation of corruption, of a captured polity that operates on a level few can access, handing out favors to the well connected and leaving everyone else to rot.

All economies contain regulations, in the sense of rules that citizens are obligated to follow. "Deregulation" is kind of a misnomer. When we deregulate, we simply transfer authority from elected democratic representatives to corporate boardrooms and investors. And by choosing to allow consolidation, successive governments, Democratic and Republican, have kicked regulation upstairs to the C-suites. Laws already on the books can stop everything you will read in this book. Indifferent enforcers of those laws cannot. And a democracy run by plutocrats, for plutocrats, bears no resemblance to democracy at all.

This is the world Robert Bork and his fellow academics envisioned. This is the air we now breathe. And yet we don't always look at it this way. We don't boil down America's challenges to the influence of monopoly. We come up with other rationales, we make other excuses, we look to other causes. We treat concentrated corporate power as a secondary factor, rather than a primary force frustrating progress.

Do you want to protect elections from foreign interference? Facebook and Google control 99 percent of all new advertising in America and increasingly dictate what news people receive, how they communicate, and what messages they hear. Do you consider student loans a problem? The two largest private companies that manage student debt, Great Lakes and Nelnet, merged in 2018 and control a majority of all accounts, despite constantly and illegally denying borrowers options to reduce payments. Do you think the country remains consumed with race? Monopolies have over the past forty years destroyed black-owned businesses, black farmers, and black entrepreneurship, denying self-sufficiency to a downtrodden class.

How about immigration? Private companies, mainly CoreCivic and GEO Group, provide over 60 percent of federal immigration detention beds, and the entire apparatus could not exist without assistance from a collection of monopoly support services. Climate change? If you can find a way to reduce greenhouse gas emissions that meets the favor of Exxon-Mobil, Koch Industries, and Duke Energy, let me know. The opioid crisis, the worst drug epidemic in American history? Monopoly pharmaceutical companies, distributors, pharmacy benefit managers, and pharmacies counted their money, while millions of pills got shipped and sold as pain relief instead of a gateway to addiction. A broken health care system? Yes, thanks to concentrated corporate power gouging patients, creating the highest-cost care in the industrialized world.

I've already mentioned several authors, thinkers, and journalists who have analyzed this problem. We are living in an antimonopoly moment that could become an antimonopoly movement. Sometimes it's called the New Brandeis movement, in honor of Supreme Court justice Louis Brandeis, America's most determined antagonist of corporate power. Monopoly has been wrestled with outside these pages as comprehensively as I could ever hope. But beyond the intellectual arguments, the explainers, the history, the careful plotting of the Herfindahl-Hirschman index (it's a metric for measuring market concentration, and it's the last time you'll hear about it in this book), I noticed something missing: how monopoly affects people in their daily lives.

How does it affect the patient in the hospital, the sales agent on the road, the renter, the farmer, the woman in New York City or rural Tennessee? How does it affect workers on the way up, and executives seemingly already at the top? How does it affect the citizen activist, inspired by injustice to right wrongs? How does it affect the small entrepreneur wanting to contribute to the American pageant? What is monopoly actually doing to this country?

I wanted to travel around, talk to people, and find out. And because Robert Bork defined monopoly entirely on the basis of consumer prices,

I wanted to do precisely the opposite. I didn't want to parcel out whether people paid 2¢ more or 2¢ less for a soda or an air-conditioning unit. I don't think that's the sum total of America. We are more than our Amazon Prime accounts. I wanted to know about monopoly's distortion of contemporary life, what it does to our families, our jobs, and our psyche. Only by surveying these real-world impacts of monopoly can we understand what to do next.

This book tells that story.

In 2019 I came into possession of a hard copy of the Berkshire Hathaway annual report and voting form. (Thanks to the person who sent it to me; you know who you are.) Berkshire is the holding company of Warren Buffett, America's cuddliest investor, and while you can get his chairman's letters online, holding the entire report in your hands is a different experience. That's especially true because, while I've examined a fair bit of shareholder disclosures in my time, this was the first I've seen that contained ads.

"It doesn't take a genius to see that switching to GEICO is a bright idea," the copy read, above a picture of the famed GEICO gecko next to a lightbulb. (Get it?) The ad encouraged shareholders to obtain a free auto insurance quote and, while they're at it, protection for their motorcycle, RV, boat, business, home, or umbrella coverage for all of the above. GEICO is the nation's second-largest auto insurer. A second glossy ad advised shareholders visiting the annual Berkshire Hathaway meeting in Omaha that their credential entitled them to savings at the Nebraska Furniture Mart throughout the week. Nebraska Furniture Mart has two-thirds of the local furniture market in Omaha.

The annual meeting has been described as "Woodstock for capitalists." Forty thousand disciples pack into a giant arena, complete with an exhibit hall of dozens of Berkshire Hathaway products. There are also branded events sponsored by Berkshire businesses: a Nebraska Furniture Mart picnic, a Brooks Sports 5K run, a cocktail reception brought to you by Borsheims, a local jewelry store. A pair of two-carat diamond stud earrings from Borsheims on sale at the event will cost you $8,950.

Who does this? Why would any self-respecting billionaire, let alone one of the richest in the world, be such a shameless carnival barker in front of his own investors? Well, a monopolist would do this. A monopolist knows when his audience is captive and when to exploit that advantage. A monopolist sees every waking moment as a rent-seeking opportunity. And Warren Buffett, more than anything else, is this country's premier monopolist.

Buffett's gambit wouldn't work for other corporations. A Disney shareholder knows what most of the Disney products are; a GM shareholder knows how to support the cause by buying a Chevy or Cadillac. But nobody really understands the breadth of Berkshire Hathaway's business. Buffett is more renowned as an investor: he's the guy with big stakes in Apple and Coca-Cola, the guy who put $5 billion into Goldman Sachs during the financial crisis, the hoarder of blue-chip company stock.

But as a company, Berkshire is an old-school conglomerate, owning dozens of seemingly random businesses, the way you used to see in the 1960s with companies like ITT Corporation, Ling-Temco-Vought, or Gulf + Western. Berkshire subsidiary businesses include Borsheims, Nebraska Furniture Mart, and GEICO. Berkshire also owns eleven other insurance concerns, Benjamin Moore paints, Duracell batteries, Justin boots, NetJets private planes, Dairy Queen ice cream shops, See's Candies, Acme bricks, the BNSF railroad, fourteen separate energy companies, a global industrial manufacturer called Marmon Holdings that houses over one hundred separate businesses, and Fruit of the Loom. In all, Berkshire holds sixty-three different main businesses and hundreds of sub-businesses. It's the largest non-technology company in the United States by market value.

The insurance businesses make everything else run. Insurance premiums don't get immediately paid out in claims; while the cash sits, Buffett can deploy it in capital markets. This is known as "float," and Berkshire Hathaway's share has grown from $39 million in 1970 to an astronomical $100 billion today. This is equivalent to the world's largest interest-free loan; Buffett has built an empire with other people's money.

He uses that money, as he's repeatedly stated, to build moats, a cute euphemism for monopolies. "We think in terms of that moat and the ability to keep its width and its impossibility of being crossed," Buffett told the annual Berkshire Hathaway meeting in 2000. "We tell our managers we want the moat widened every year." There are other virtues of great companies; Buffett chooses to invest and buy monopolies, because government inaction presents no risk for that strategy.

Buffett likes to cheerlead for capitalism, but he doesn't mean it. Nothing in his history shows respect for what's supposed to make capitalism virtuous: competition, innovation, meritocracy. Instead of all that, Buffett believes in unearthing companies with market power and demanding that they employ it aggressively. He has driven this spectacle in corporate America of low investment and high corporate profits, a feat that would be impossible without moats. Because he is an investing icon, his preference for monopoly is constantly imitated. Morningstar offers an "economic moat" index fund of the twenty companies with the highest walls around their businesses; another money manager created a tracking fund with the stock ticker symbol MOAT. He's not a passive bystander of the monopoly trend; he's leading it.

He's also the kind of guy who hocks insurance to his investors so he can use their money twice. A true American icon.

You might see Buffett pop up once or twice in this book. It would be impossible to write a book about monopoly without him.

CHAPTER 1

*Monopolies Are Why People Keep Contracting
Deep Vein Thrombosis on Long-Haul Flights*

On December 29, 2006, Kate Hanni, her husband, Tim, and her two children boarded American Airlines Flight 1348 in San Francisco, en route to Dallas. Kate, a forty-seven-year-old real estate agent from the Napa Valley wine region, occasionally moonlighted in an R&B band called the Toasted Heads. (Tim played guitar.) Six months earlier, she told me, she had been violently assaulted inside one of her home listings, and spent the next several months working through the incident in therapy. That Christmas week, Tim set up a trip to a resort in Point Clear, Alabama, giving Kate a chance to de-stress before going back to work.

It was the first flight out, so the family got up at three-thirty in the morning to hoof it down to San Francisco. After a forty-five-minute mechanical delay, they took off. But Flight 1348 never reached Dallas; thunderstorms forced a landing in Austin. The plane was sent to the maintenance ramp and rolled to a stop. Out the window, Kate could see some of the thirteen other jets on various parts of the tarmac. This would be her home for the next nine hours and seventeen minutes.

Nobody was allowed off, not even several travelers who lived in Austin. The American Airlines ground crew never serviced the plane; in fact, they were sent home for the day. The plane was never restocked with food or water. There was some alcohol in first class, which economy-class passengers raided. But although Tim Hanni was a certified Master of Wine, the highest honorific of professional knowledge, he was also a recovering alcoholic, so drinking was out of the question. Kate saw a woman fashioning a diaper for her toddler out of a seat pocket barf bag. Others used their bags for more traditional purposes, as the smell of overflowing toilets wafted across the cramped cabin.

At about the four-hour mark, Kate reached her mental and physical breaking point. "I was having the worst reaction," she told me. "I was sweating, thinking, 'Why is this happening?'" Others were growing crazed as well: a claustrophobic passenger (whom Kate still keeps in touch with) used his phone to flash an SOS signal out the window, hoping for a rescue.

The operations manager at the Austin airport adamantly refused to allow any planes into the gates, regardless of the pleading from pilots about sick people needing to disembark. Kate would later find out that thirteen thousand American Airlines passengers were stranded that day on 138 separate flights across twenty-four airports, stuck in airplane-shaped prisons on tarmacs. "We couldn't get off because the airline was committed to not refund a portion of the ticket," Kate said. "They know if they let you off it may cost them money." American's policy, it seemed to her, was to prevent liberated passengers from escaping its grip.

Finally, at 9:30 p.m., Flight 1348 rolled into a gate. As she emerged from the jetway, Kate saw the last restaurant in the airport rolling down its door for the night. "It was like *Chariots of Fire*—I'm running toward that door, I'm trying to fly under it," she said. "I say to them, 'We've been out there for nine hours, none of us had anything to eat, the kids are starving.' They said it was too late, they're closing." All the family could access were the vending machines by baggage claim.

American didn't relinquish any bags. The family found a cheap hotel for the night, returned the next morning, and went on to Dallas. Continued bad weather and the cascade of delays tangled service at the American hub. At the gate for their connecting flight, the Hannis were told they couldn't board, even though their bags had already been loaded onto the plane. "The pilot was sitting there," Kate recalled. "We both had blue eyes. I locked onto his and I said, 'Do you understand what we've been through in the last twenty-four hours?' He said, 'I don't care if you're the Queen of England, you are not getting on this plane.'"

The family muddled through the rest of their truncated vacation, and upon returning to Napa, they found dozens of voicemail messages. That first night in Austin, Kate had jumped in front of a news camera to express her anger at the tarmac incarceration. Her performance skills and winning smile got the attention of news bookers, who were now calling to request interviews. That was the beginning of the next six years of Kate's life. Though she never wanted to become a consumer advocate, she was determined that nobody ever again would be subjected to what her family experienced.

It was going to be an uphill climb. As many as two hundred thousand travelers suffered extreme tarmac delays every year. After a similar, weather-caused pileup in Detroit in January 1999, activists demanded that the Federal Aviation Administration put in place a "passengers' bill of rights" to end the practice. But the U.S. Chamber of Commerce sank efforts to set a three-hour time limit for tarmac delays, and the post-9/11 kid gloves that regulators donned for the airlines subsequently took prominence over any rule making.

Kate wasn't deterred, putting the real estate business and singing gigs on hold and devoting her life to the mission. She appeared on dozens of news shows. She started a blog and an online petition that garnered twenty thousand signatures. She set up a hotline for other passengers to tell their stories. She founded a nonprofit organization called FlyersRights.org, which within a few years became one of the largest consumer groups in the country. She appealed to her congressman, Mike Thompson, and testified at seven different hearings on Capitol Hill. In September 2007 she led a "strand-in" on the National Mall in Washington, where she set up tents like an airplane cabin so people could feel the sensation of a long tarmac delay (even the smell; she had portable toilets brought in). She used her musical chops to rework an old Animals hit, serving up a rendition of "We Gotta Get out of This Plane."

"I had to hire someone to be my full-time assistant just to manage the media," Kate said. "We got everyone's story out there."

But despite all this momentum—a telegenic leader, thousands of fired-up volunteers, outrageous scenes of passengers being put through hell, an easy-to-understand and obvious solution—meaningful regulation took another three *years*. The airlines successfully sued to block state-level efforts, arguing that only the Department of Transportation (DOT) had jurisdiction to regulate. The DOT then commissioned a task force stacked with airline executives, who spent a year coming up with vague conclusions. Weeks before Barack Obama took over the White House from George W. Bush, DOT finally proposed a tarmac rule, with no maximum time limit for stranding passengers. It was a naked attempt to preempt the new regime, and it took another year before Obama's DOT issued the final rule on December 30, 2009, which included the three-hour limit, and requirements for provisions of food, water, ventilation, and working toilets.

The rule successfully ended airplane imprisonment—well, mostly. Five years after the rule's implementation, DOT fined Southwest Airlines

$1.6 million for sixteen illegal tarmac delays. And research indicated that airlines responded to the rule by rapidly canceling flights to avoid the fines, increasing rather than decreasing overall passenger delays. But even on its own terms, the road to the tarmac rule is instructive. From the original 1999 disaster, it took Washington nearly eleven years to agree to the modest proposition that airlines shouldn't keep passengers cooped up for any longer than the average NFL football game. And that's at least an abuse regulators were willing to address. Powerful airlines have fended off slam-dunk reforms time and again, while customers were abused and humiliated.

Airlines would only get more powerful after Kate Hanni's disastrous night in Austin, combining and merging until there were only a handful left—and, for many travelers around the country, really only one. Forty years after deregulation transformed the nature of the commercial air market, airlines have mostly been freed from worrying about competition, to the delight of investors and executives. These days, imposing suffering on travelers is not just an unavoidable annoyance; it's a business strategy.

In the First Gilded Age, the transcontinental railroad shrank America by connecting East and West, allowing people to visit friends and family and allowing farmers and manufacturers to sell products nationwide. It didn't make financial sense for railroads to lay down competing lines of track, and consequently the business quickly trended toward monopoly. Robber-baron railroad owners understood their inherent leverage. They fixed prices and gouged customers, not to mention slaughtering workers, breaking strikes, bribing politicians, fleecing investors, and neglecting safety measures.

America's grassroots antimonopoly coalition of the nineteenth century was the Granger movement, a collection of farmers incensed by exorbitant railroad storage and transport prices for grain. The Grangers won action at the state level to cap shipping rates. Antimonopoly sentiment grew in the Progressive Era, and the federal government would create the Interstate Commerce Commission to police rail company abuses. During Theodore Roosevelt's presidency, lawmakers expanded the ICC's authority to break railroad monopoly power, ensuring broad access nationwide while granting a reasonable profit for the private companies that managed the rails.

After the Wright brothers realized the genius of flight and entrepreneurs commoditized the invention, the United States adapted the railroad public utility model to air travel. In 1938 the fledgling industry came under the control of the Civil Aeronautics Board (CAB). Franklin Roosevelt's administration designated air travel a "public convenience and necessity" that every community deserved. CAB guaranteed airlines a 12 percent profit on a flight that was 55 percent full; prices could vary if fuel or other fixed costs fluctuated. More important, airlines had to serve the entire nation, with more popular routes subsidizing the less popular ones. Much like the way the postal service broadly shared access to communication, government would give Americans equal-opportunity access to the social and economic benefits of air travel.

The CAB's control was strict; airlines had to get permission to alter routes and fares, or even change uniform colors. This may have angered airline executives, but the CAB presided over a thriving commercial aviation industry for businesses and passengers. There's a myth that before deregulation, flights were restricted to a privileged few. In actuality, while only 33 percent of Americans over eighteen had taken a plane trip in 1962, by 1977 that number had climbed to 63 percent.

The demise of the CAB coincided with the 1973 oil embargo and subsequent economic malaise. There was always an exemption to fare regulation for oil costs, but enemies of the CAB could blame ticket price increases on regulators rather than on the fuel that planes required. Then-prominent consumer advocate Ralph Nader charged that airline executives had captured the CAB. But the real antagonist was Ted Kennedy. Preparing to run for president, he went searching for a populist issue to champion. His top staff aide, future Supreme Court justice Stephen Breyer, convinced him that taking on the CAB would render him a populist hero.

Market-oriented liberal economists longed to ditch the CAB and other central planning mechanisms. Alfred Kahn, then a professor at Cornell, was a leading voice, promising that deregulation would benefit everyone by making airlines more efficient. As Paul Stephen Dempsey, now a law professor at McGill University, wrote in a 1990 chronicle of deregulation for the Economic Policy Institute called *Flying Blind*, economists believed entry and pricing restrictions led to "excessive service" for passengers, while airlines were denied "adequate profits." In other words, the fliers were too comfortable and the corporations too poor. Somehow this was depicted as a pro-consumer sentiment.

"The public was being misled," Dempsey told me. "Watergate really turned the left against Washington. By the end of that, the left and right converged on a common path, viewing government control as the enemy."

Kennedy found an ally for his deregulatory aims in the newly elected Democratic president, who would later become his rival. Jimmy Carter appointed Kahn, an avowed enemy of the Civil Aeronautics Board, to run it. In October 1978 Carter signed the Airline Deregulation Act, after near-unanimous passage through Congress. "When I announced my own support of airline deregulation soon after taking office, this bill had few friends," Carter said at the signing, "I'm happy to say that today it appears to have few enemies."

But there was at least one opponent. At one of the hearings, a "mean-looking fellow with pointed teeth and slicked-back hair" approached a Kennedy staffer and told him, "You [bleeping] academic eggheads! You're going to wreck this industry!" That man was Bob Crandall, then American Airlines' head of marketing and later its CEO. "And I think they have wrecked it," Crandall, now retired, said to me in an interview forty years later. "They didn't take into account the ubiquity of the system. And there's simply no competition. Trading all that off against cheap fares is a crock of shit."*

The stated purpose of airline deregulation was to bring competing carriers into the market, driving prices down and convenience up. Competitors did rush in: People Express, Air Florida, even a small airline that served New York, Boston, and Washington called Trump Shuttle. Fares did drop, mostly thanks to a conveniently timed crash in oil markets that cut fuel prices by more than half from 1980 to 1986. Thanks to technological advances, fares were actually dropping *faster* before 1978, once you adjusted for the oil spike. At the time of deregulation, America already had the world's lowest airfares. This didn't stop deregulation's defenders from taking initial credit for price declines.

Before long, the burst of competition fizzled, as airlines engaged in price wars they couldn't manage. During the 1980s, two hundred airlines went

---

* It's hilarious for Crandall to complain about lack of competition. Just four years after deregulation, he suggested to a rival airline executive in a phone call that they collude to raise prices by 20 percent.

bankrupt, including majors like Eastern and Braniff. The Airline Deregulation Act specifically directed the government to guard against "unreasonable industry concentration" and "excessive market domination." But between 1979 and 1988, fifty-one airlines merged; the Department of Transportation never challenged a single one, eventually giving up merger oversight authority to the Justice Department. David Morris, an author and former newspaper columnist, was a student of Kahn's at Cornell. He once sent his former teacher a letter detailing problematic airline consolidation after deregulation. "His response was he overlooked the possibility of monopoly," Morris said. "It's quite something if you think about it."

Two critical bend points shaped the industry, each coinciding with economic catastrophe. First there was 9/11, which fundamentally transformed air travel and the companies that provide it. As demand plummeted and security measures increased, practically every major airline declared bankruptcy in the 2000s, primarily to shed "legacy costs," or what workers call wages and benefits.

About one-quarter of full-time airline jobs were eliminated between 2001 and 2005. Other jobs were kept nonunion, with airlines determined to keep it that way; an infamous flyer released in 2019 showed Delta advising flight attendants and ramp service workers that they could spend their union dues money on a sweet new video game system. Janitorial and catering staff remains outsourced, mostly to another duopoly (LSG SkyChefs and GateGourmet) that has so antagonized workers that they threatened strikes throughout summer 2019. Maintenance was outsourced as well, to low-cost operations in El Salvador, Mexico, and China. The head of Southwest's pilot union claimed in 2019 that 80 percent of its aircraft are maintained by nonunion mechanics. This has coincided with operational emergencies at Southwest, like a 2018 incident where a woman was sucked out of the cabin when an engine fan blade dislodged and crashed through a window.

Keeping other airline employees off the payroll and making them somebody else's problem has been a key innovation. If you ever noticed that your United or Delta connecting flight is "operated" by Mesa Airlines or SkyWest or Republic Airways, you're flying on a separate regional airline, outfitted with the logo, uniforms, in-flight magazines, and peanut wrappers of United or Delta. This saves the major carriers a boatload, because they're using the equivalent of low-cost temps for the final leg of passenger journeys, absolving themselves of responsibility for salaries and benefits.

Workers left at the majors suffered across-the-board wage cuts of 30 to 40 percent, according to Sara Nelson, president of the Association of Flight Attendants, the largest flight attendant union. Starting salaries for pilots, particularly at the regional airlines, can be as low as $15,000 a year. "The pay is not for a middle-class income anymore," Nelson told me. Reduced options due to industry consolidation left most employees with no choice.

The main targets for airline bankruptcies were pensions, with carriers shifting to 401(k) plans. United used a grueling, thirty-eight-month bankruptcy to terminate pension obligations for four plans affecting 126,000 workers in 2005. Attorney James Sprayregen, who handled the bankruptcy for United, admitted to PBS's *Frontline* that the company deliberately dragged out the process, imposing concessions gradually to prevent labor unrest. "It really affects workers close to retirement, five to ten years away, who are not able to retire," said Sara Nelson.

The second bend point—the financial crisis of 2008—represented the final transformation of the industry, with four key mergers. Bill Clinton's Department of Justice (DOJ) imposed such stringent conditions on a proposed USAir/United deal in 2000 that the parties scrapped it. But when Northwest and Delta petitioned to merge in 2008, George W. Bush's DOJ waved it through without conditions. That encouraged the rest of the industry to follow suit. "D.C. finally threw its hands up and said let the airlines consolidate," said Paul Stephen Dempsey.

Under President Obama, United/Continental and Southwest/AirTran deals followed, the latter notable because it removed a low-cost carrier that was aggressively forcing prices downward and just starting to expand. Finally, American and US Airways announced their intention to combine in 2013. Obama's Justice Department initially filed suit to block the merger, arguing that "increasing consolidation among large airlines has hurt passengers"—even though they played a major role in that by allowing the United and Southwest deals. But within three months, DOJ changed course, stunning staff attorneys working on the case. Intense lobbying from former Obama administration officials, including former chief of staff Rahm Emanuel, who signed a letter written by an airline lobbyist encouraging the deal, may have played a defining role. The airlines spent $13 million on Democratic-friendly lobbyists, in some cases personal friends of Justice Department officials. Instead of suing to block the merger, DOJ merely forced the divestiture of some gate slots at airports in Washington and New York.

Today we're down to four major carriers: United, American, Delta, and Southwest. They collectively control over 80 percent of all U.S. routes. Zooming in makes this look even worse: in ninety-three of the largest one hundred airports, either one or two airlines control a majority of all seats. You know how you can't find a nonstop flight to bunches of midsized cities, and instead you're constantly making connections through Chicago or Atlanta or Dallas? That's an intentional by-product of deregulation, which freed airlines from covering the country with direct flights. Instead they created "hubs," points of transfer for hundreds of connections. The airlines like this because it centralizes operations and saves money on personnel and equipment, but residents of hub cities often have no choices for air travel. American controls 90 percent of all flights out of Charlotte, with prices 21 percent above the national average. The industry has a term for really concentrated airports, where they've bought up all the gate slots: "fortress hubs." For competitors, it's as hard to penetrate the fortress as it is a medieval castle.

Fortress hubs aren't entirely beneficial to hub locations: most passengers just travel in and out of the airport rather than experiencing the city. The hubs add congestion at individual bottlenecks, making the system more vulnerable to delays. The environment also suffers from extra takeoffs and landings, as well as out-of-the-way detours to hub cities. But cities blessed with hubs at least enjoy reliable service, and much like with railroads, that's a potent economic development tool. You can't call yourself a major-league city and attract business investment without a vibrant international airport.

When airlines merged, they consolidated or eliminated hubs. Public officials once ensured universal access, but now corporate executives picked winners and losers among the nation's urban metros. Cities were kind of stuck; they wanted airports to bring in more competition to lower prices, but they didn't want to trigger the dominant carrier to pull away the hub.

Hub consolidation altered the fortunes of cities like Pittsburgh, Memphis, and St. Louis in the flash of a press release. Delta cut back hub operations at Cincinnati/Northern Kentucky International Airport in 2010, and passenger flights there have fallen by 75 percent since 2005, and now there is only one direct international flight, to Paris. The airport managed to survive by reinventing itself as a logistics and freight destination. But that does little for the business traveler who simply can't get to meetings in Cincinnati without a connection, if at all. Fortune 1000 company Chiquita Banana left Cincinnati for Charlotte, the American Airlines hub. Caterpillar moved its headquarters from Peoria, Illinois, to Chicago for the same reason: lack of access to flights. Other cities lost conventions and business conferences. It just isn't workable to have a multinational headquartered in a city with second-class air travel.

"I used to be from Ohio," said Paul Hudson, an aviation attorney who joined Kate Hanni at consumer advocacy group FlyersRights.org, eventually taking over the organization. "At one time we had three hubs: Cleveland, Columbus, and Cincinnati. Now there are zero. Say you live in Cleveland; sometimes you have to drive to Pittsburgh to get a flight. It's a big negative for the economy."

For smaller cities that never had a hub, the lack of a service guarantee proved an immediate hardship. Prices rose across the board, as flights shifted to lucrative population centers and the economics of supply and demand did its work. Some cities were simply cut off: a hundred cities fell off the commercial aviation map in the first two years of deregulation. By the 1980s, the only way to fly into state capitals like Dover, Delaware, or Salem, Oregon, was by private plane. The carnage has continued, with another thirty-two regional airports losing service between 2015 and 2018. The federal Essential Air Service subsidizes small community airports, but it hasn't stopped the bleeding. Inaccessibility has isolated large swaths of the country.

Kate Hanni and her husband, Tim, moved to Bend, Oregon, four years ago. Because of his wine business, Tim must travel to Canada and Asia. It can be a chore. "Almost everywhere he needs to go is an extra flight out of Redmond," Kate said, referring to a municipal airport about twenty miles away. What's interesting is that Bend is not much smaller than Napa, where the Hannis previously lived. But Napa was near enough to San Francisco that mobility was never a problem. These days, Kate notes, "it sometimes gets in the way being off the grid."

Postmerger problems cropped up almost immediately, starting on the ground. Hub-and-spoke setups inevitably lead to delays if a hub experiences bad weather or some other tie-up. The vast majority of all flight delays can be traced back to a handful of large airports—mostly in New York and Chicago—where giant amounts of air traffic flow. The subsequent delays affect travelers nearly everywhere.

Some airlines don't value getting their planes off the ground on time. "We don't necessarily believe that it's cost-effective to end up in the top quartile for on-time performance," Frontier Airlines senior vice president Daniel Schurz told Bloomberg in 2017. They simply don't want to spend the money honoring the arrival time stamped on your ticket. Many flights only reach destinations "on time" by padding the schedules to give a false impression of promptness to regulators. Planes today may be faster, but the flights are slower.

For the major carriers, scarcely a few months go by without hearing about a "technical glitch" (for some reason always that exact phrase) grounding thousands of flights. United suffered system-wide crashes in 2015 and 2017; such issues affected Southwest in 2016, Delta in 2016, 2017, and 2018, and American in 2018. In a reflection of the industry's commitment to innovation, on April Fools' Day 2019, United, Southwest, Delta, and American all experienced a technical glitch at the same time.

With so few major carriers, individual airlines service more flights, so glitches cascade through the system, causing stranded planes, missed connections, and an inability for crews to keep on schedule. This has been exacerbated by another change. Previously, passengers could take a ticket for a delayed flight to another airline, which was obligated to honor it. Now the "reciprocity rule" is voluntary. And because large carriers have so much power, they've refused to rebook customers from competitors, fearing losses on their open seats.

The classic example of the fragility of our concentrated travel system is the July 2015 United computer crash. The same day, the New York Stock Exchange also suffered from one of those pesky technical glitches. But because there were numerous competing exchanges, others picked up the trading slack, so stock volume went virtually unchanged. With United, the glitch grounded thousands of flights nationwide and caused bottlenecks for days. There were no redundancies to keep traffic moving.

As Delta's CEO has admitted, airlines do not typically upgrade their information technology (IT) after mergers, instead piling one legacy system of reservations and flight departures and crew schedules on top of another. With multiple mergers going back decades, this means that computer networks have patches lurking in them from the 1990s. A report from Diana Moss of the American Antitrust Institute has demonstrated how computer meltdowns become more prevalent after mergers. "A behemoth airline with a behemoth IT system does not work well," Moss said. Amazingly, all these mergers were sold on creating "efficiencies," specifically from integrating the computer systems that chronically glitch. Of course, in merger-speak, "efficiencies" just means saving money. As long as passengers have nowhere else to go, there's no incentive to fix a perpetually broken system.

Since few can vote with their wallet for an alternative, airlines don't have to care about customer well-being. But they have discovered that every passenger has a breaking point—and a price. There's a distinct link between how miserable airlines can make their passengers and how profitable their enterprise has become.

The hardship begins by making planes more crowded. From 55 percent targets in the 1970s, planes were 83 percent full on average in 2018, and that doesn't count crew members shuttling to catch their next flight. Airline executives want to keep it that way; at industry conferences, they explicitly talk of maintaining "capacity discipline" on flight schedules. That's code for putting fewer seats in the air; planes using staff and jet fuel cost money, and grounding more of them makes the remaining flights more crowded and more profitable, even if inconvenient schedules anger passengers.

Everything, from modern innovations to basic necessities guaranteed in any prison camp, is fairly terrible at thirty thousand feet. The seats are narrower and the distance between other passengers compressed (more on this later). Delta announced in April 2019 that they would reduce how far back seats recline by two inches—to make it easier for passengers in the next row to use laptops, they say. Passenger headroom has also been shrinking. The future could be standing "seats" that look something like tools the Spanish Inquisition had at its disposal. Airplane Wi-Fi is abominable, mainly because Gogo, the dominant in-flight internet provider, locked up long-term contracts and prevented better services from entry. Restrooms have shrunk in size by up to seven inches, freeing up room for more rows. Passengers have despaired of the contortions necessary just to get through the lavatory door. The one "improvement" inside the plane?

Privacy-sapping cameras stationed just under seat-back monitors that can spy on passengers and distribute data back to the airline; these have drawn the ire of frequent-flying politicians of both parties.

The gouging and cramping and inconveniencing were bound to manifest in cabin rage, with underpaid, inadequate flight crews on the front lines. "All domestic flights are at FAA minimum staffing," said flight attendant union leader Sara Nelson. "There's less of us to respond to passengers who are disgruntled over being squeezed into a seat and squeezed in close to other people." Flight attendants are taught to de-escalate conflicts, but frustrations have boiled over. An International Air Transport Association report showed one air-rage incident for every 1,035 flights in 2017, up 35 percent from the year before. Over a quarter of these involve passenger intoxication, and the drinking is somewhat understandable as a way to dull the now-routine pain in air travel.

The most notorious air-rage episode happened on April 9, 2017, on United Flight 3411 from Chicago to Louisville. Cell phone cameras filmed airline police brutally pulling a screaming, bloodied Dr. David Dao down the aisle after he refused to be bumped from the flight to make room for crew members who needed to be in Louisville the next day. United randomly selected Dao for ejection after not enough passengers took an $800 incentive for rebooking. The incident went viral, amid calls for boycotts and mass outrage. It revealed that even if you have a paid ticket and an assigned seat, you're not safe from airline prerogatives.

Dr. Dao ended up settling out of court for an undisclosed figure; the DOT didn't even bother to fine United. A year later, the standard practice of overbooking flights had at least slowed down. But Dao's lawyer, Thomas Demetrio, told the *Washington Post* that little had changed in the industry. "The passenger is basically expected to sit down and shut up," explained Paul Stephen Dempsey. "If you don't like it, what are you going to do about it?"

Union leader Nelson stresses that passengers and flight crews get exploited simultaneously by the same corporate behemoths, and the results reflect a kind of societal trend in miniature. "As Elizabeth Warren would say, the game is rigged," she said. "The great American experiment is happening on our plane with the door closed, hurtling through the air, and with no way to call for help."

If you want a way out, a safety valve to earn sweet relief, the airlines have trained passengers to pony up for it, the way laboratory mice learn how to press a button to get a food pellet. Practically everything you used to get for free on a plane now costs you: a hot meal, a comfortable seat, checked baggage, changing flights. And most carriers put the merchandise on display—in this case, basic human comfort—when you board a flight. "You should always load a plane back to front," said Kate Hanni. "That would save money and time. But they really want you to take that perp walk through first class. They want everyone to see how good it is up there."

A first class seat will cost you dearly: three times as much for around 45 percent more space, by one calculation. But worsening economy-class experiences have expanded demand for first class. Moreover, ancillary fees have become a growing profit center, allowing the airlines to boast that they consistently drop fares, which don't account for any of the extras. Fees and other charges represented a little over one-tenth of all revenue in 1995; today it's over one-quarter. The top ten airlines hauled in $29.7 billion in ancillary fees in 2017 alone.

According to industry consultant Mark Gerchick's book *Full Upright and Locked Position*, the ancillary fee gurus at IdeaWorks once ran a weekend "ancillary revenue training camp" to brainstorm additional revenue streams. We're now seeing the fruits of those bull sessions. Airlines have been known to add fuel surcharges and keep them on even after oil prices drop. In 2011 they famously raised base fares when Federal Aviation Administration (FAA) authorization lapsed and federal taxes could not be collected temporarily, pocketing the difference without passengers' knowledge. Increased revenues from loyalty credit card fees, which typically entitle cardholders exemptions from checked-bag fees or other burdens, has outpaced overall sales growth (this is why flights have become one long advertisement for credit cards). Some airlines impose a new "gate service" fee, in case passengers can't find room for a bag in the cabin and have to leave it at the top of the jetway. Others have passengers bid against one other for prime seat assignments: it's like eBay, only for what you thought your ticket entitled you to. Still others, according to a UK government study, use algorithms to deliberately split up families traveling together, so they have to pay to change seats. Airline lobbyists call it "giving customers more choice," but for passengers it amounts to a stickup: give us your money or suffer the consequences.

The combination of drudgery in the cabin and ancillary fees play on travelers' behavioral responses. For instance, checked-bag fees give passengers incentives to bring roller bags on board. That makes getting on first to find space in the overhead bin a priority. So airlines started charging for preboarding. Plus, if everyone's their own baggage handler on the plane, that means fewer baggage handlers to pay on the ground. Eliminating meals in the main cabin enabled airlines to reduce the size of the galley, opening more space for seats. The personal entertainment device on the seat back seems like a new amenity, until you realize it allows airlines to isolate and charge for viewing in ways they couldn't with a communal screen.

Fee structures like this work only if there's no competition to lure passengers away from being nickel and dimed. Virtually all airlines uncannily follow one another, like with increased baggage fees in fall 2018. If anything, the low-cost carriers like Spirit Airlines are worse, charging for seat assignments, online booking, blankets, a soda, and any carry-on larger than a purse. Sending Spirit a text on WhatsApp will set you back $25. An incredible 46.6 percent of Spirit's revenue comes from ancillary fees. United and its legacy colleagues have taken their cues from Spirit with "basic economy" fares, which entitle you to little more than a seat belt. For now.

In 2014, JetBlue decided it would zig while the industry zagged. CEO David Barger declared that his company would be the quality airline, with roomy, comfortable seating, free checked bags, and fast Wi-Fi. For Barger, the announcement aligned JetBlue with its founding principles: he had been there from the beginning, helping design the company's "service-oriented" culture. "I think you can be profitable without gouging the traveling public," Barger told a local paper.

But stock analysts hated the idea. They beat up Barger for being "overly concerned" with customers rather than shareholder returns. And they eventually ran him out of town. Two months after Barger stepped down, JetBlue rolled back the legroom and raised fees on baggage and Wi-Fi. Analysts parceled out the "improvements" to the penny. Charging a baggage check fee would add 26¢ a share; charging for Wi-Fi would add another 9¢. Springing fees on customers "might hurt JetBlue in the media," wrote Cowen and Co. analyst Helane Becker in a research note, but "the revenue benefit to the company would probably trump any customer push back."

The episode reflects how, after government deregulation, Wall Street has taken control of the airline industry and demanded oligopolistic conformity. Airlines were once seen as financial poison. The world's premier investor, Warren Buffett, joked in a 2007 investor letter: "If a farsighted capitalist had been present at Kitty Hawk, he would have done his successors a huge favor by shooting Orville [Wright] down." By the end of 2018, Buffett held roughly 44 million shares in American Airlines, 65.5 million in Delta, 55 million in Southwest, and 22 million in United, for a total investment of over $10 billion.

Buffett's bet is not predicated on any single airline prospering. As America's proudest monopolist, he's confident that a concentrated air travel market is permanently lucrative, and Wall Street joins him in that faith. In a 2014 research note, Goldman Sachs highlighted airlines as part of its "dreams of oligopoly," counseling investors to "look for opportunities created by disruptive consolidation" that generates "greater . . . pricing power with customers due to reduced choice . . . stronger leverage over suppliers, and higher barriers to new entrants all at once." Translation: customers, suppliers, workers, and rivals will feel a pinch, but executives and investors will be overwhelmed with sacks of money.

Institutional investors have piled into airline stocks. Buffett, asset management firms BlackRock, State Street, and Vanguard, and hedge fund PAR Capital Management are all among the top ten investors in the four major airlines. BlackRock, Vanguard, and PAR also hold large shares in the next two biggest airlines, JetBlue and Alaska. Even the normally pliant business press has raised concerns about this. "If you're building up such a significant stake in all the major players, is that anything that's, like, monopolistic behavior?" CNBC's Becky Quick asked Buffett in February 2017. "Is there any concern to think that you would say something to the airlines to make them make sure that they're not competing on prices?" Buffett responded that he's just a passive investor with no say in management.

But a growing body of research suggests that common ownership from large investors may make a difference. Martin Schmalz, José Azar, and Isabel Tecu wrote a research paper in 2017 showing that airfares on the average route are 3 to 7 percent higher among companies with common ownership than they would be under separate ownership. There's some logic to this; if a few "passive" firms own the whole market, what's the motivation for alleged rivals with the same owner to compete? "Buffett has explicitly said he likes investing in oligopolistic industries," said Schmalz, an associate professor at Oxford University's Saïd Business School. "It's not crazy to think that the CEO of Delta has figured out that Buffett doesn't like it all that much for him to compete with United."

Investors aren't even particularly quiet about their intentions. Public earnings calls are filled with laborious discussions of specific routes. Schmalz, Azar, and Tecu's paper cites one portfolio manager criticizing "growth initiatives out of LA [and] Seattle" and warning that "adding capacity into other airlines' hubs diminishes your shareholders' confidence and jeopardizes [your stock price]." Another investment manager is quoted as saying, "I'd like to see [Southwest Airlines] boost their fares but also cut capacity." Stock analysts write reports longing for airlines to "rein in supply growth." They complain when airlines manage to reserve a few pennies for employees. "This is frustrating. Labor is being paid first again. Shareholders get leftovers," groused Citi analyst Kevin Crissey when American announced some modest raises in 2017. Not only did American's stock price tank, so did that of every other major airline, as investors punished the whole industry because one of its leaders dared to side with employees.

Airlines have an entire high-tech system designed to prevent them from competing. The Airline Tariff Publishing Company (ATPCO), owned outright by the companies, delivers real-time information on every published fare across the United States. Large teams of airline number crunchers monitor ATPCO daily for fare changes and copy the competition's movements. A sort of nonaggression pact can emerge, where one airline agrees to not pressure another's main sources of revenue.

The Justice Department sued the airline industry over ATPCO in 1992; the case settled with few restrictions, and use of ATPCO went on. More recently DOJ opened an investigation into airlines colluding to reduce flight schedules, crowd cabins, and raise fares, backed with plenty of evidence from the lawsuit against the merger of American and US Airways. But the investigation quietly closed in 2017 with no action taken.

The battle over the measurement of passenger legroom, known as "seat pitch," further demonstrates the economic and political power of the modern airline industry. Before deregulation, seats were on average 18 inches wide, with 35 inches between rows. By 2016 the width had dropped to 16½ inches and the seat pitch to 31 inches. On Spirit Airlines, ever the innovator, seat pitch is 28 inches. Thanks to the uniquely American regimen of diet and exercise, travelers squeezing into these smaller seats get bigger every year. This discomfort has become a primary source of tension in the air, as knees are wrecked when seats recline.

For the airlines, the formula is simple. Every inch removed between rows equals more rows of seats that can be added to the back of the plane, and six or more potential fares. Less padding makes the plane lighter, saving on fuel costs. Plus, the uncomfortable quarters lead many to cry uncle and pay for "preferred" seats, which mostly have the same seat pitch that was standard ten or twenty years ago. "If you don't want to give yourself deep vein thrombosis, we're going to make you pay," said Kate Hanni.

The public health aspect is legitimate. In addition to tiny seats exacerbating arthritis and back injuries, deep vein thrombosis (a blood clot) affects one in six thousand passengers on flights over four hours, according to the UN World Health Organization. Hanni notes that medical professionals have a nickname for it. "In the ERs they call it 'economy class syndrome.' That's the first thing they ask: 'Did you have a long-haul flight?'" Studies show that potential for dangerous blood clots grows for frequent fliers. "The majority of people feel the effect and it goes away," said Paul Hudson, now the president of Flyers Rights. "In a minority of people, it stops the transfer of oxygen to the blood supply. There are cases where people walk off the plane and drop dead." Tennis great Serena Williams was treated for a pulmonary embolism, the medical term for a blood clot that reaches the lungs, in 2017. It's unclear whether Williams's schedule of frequent travel led to the embolism, but NBC News correspondent David Bloom did die from this condition in 2003, right after traveling overseas to embed with troops in Iraq.

After years of warnings, in 2015 FlyersRights.org formally petitioned the FAA to create a minimum requirement for width and seat pitch, making the case on the grounds of health, comfort, and safety. The FAA rejected the first two out of hand, claiming no jurisdiction on health grounds and no responsibility to ensure comfort. But the agency had to account for safety; that was its core mission. Based on a previous regulatory order, all passengers had to be able to evacuate a plane in the event of an emergency within ninety seconds. FlyersRights.org maintained that the evacuation rule, which went into effect in 1990, was now impossible with the newer, narrower seats.

The FAA rejected FlyersRights.org's request, claiming that industry-run tests showed that the public would be able to evacuate in time. When asked for the tests, officials refused to release them. FlyersRights.org took the agency to court. And in July 2017, the DC Circuit Court of Appeals ordered the FAA to reconsider taking action. "This is the case of the incredible shrinking airline seat," wrote Judge Patricia Millett. It was a vindication of years of work for Hudson, who got into aviation safety after his daughter died on Pan Am Flight 103, which was blown up over Lockerbie, Scotland, in 1988.

Judge Millett's ruling, however, only committed the FAA to reconsider the matter. Airlines for America, the industry trade group, saw "no need for the government to interfere" with corporate decision making on seat pitch, a signal to the FAA to back off. And the regulators listened. A year later, the FAA informed FlyersRights.org that there was "no evidence that there is an immediate safety issue" with tighter seat pitch that would affect evacuations. It denied that passengers climbing out of the diminutive seats would be a factor at all.

The FAA unveiled several video tests to prove its case. "You can see these tests, the people are fairly physically fit," Hudson said. I checked out the videos, made by each of the major airplane manufacturers: Embraer, Airbus, and Boeing. There weren't any professional athletes among the evacuees, but everyone seemed to be in their thirties, nobody looked particularly obese, and not a single passenger had any trouble sprinting down the aisle. In the Boeing video, I saw one woman holding what looked like an infant-shaped doll; no children were involved in the simulation. It wasn't exactly a representative sample of the populations I've seen on flights.

The fact that the manufacturers run the test without FAA input is a bit of a giveaway. "The manufacturers never fail anything. I've been on committees involved in this since 1993," Hudson said, adding that he believed the tests were rehearsed numerous times. "If you have rats in a maze, if you give them twenty times, they will find their way through." Nevertheless, FlyersRights.org's attempt to appeal the FAA's decision failed.

Congressional reauthorization of the FAA did include a requirement for seat regulations. But airline consultants consider it unlikely that the new regulations will lead to more legroom, and they actually could lead to less. Nothing in Congress's order stops regulators from making a 28-inch seat pitch, already approved for travel on Spirit Airlines, the de facto minimum. That same FAA authorization bill initially included stronger oversight of ticket change fees, with regulators empowered to determine which are considered reasonable. "It is our top priority to ensure that this . . . does not become law," said an Airlines for America lobbyist. And it didn't; the provision magically disappeared. Thirty-five other congressional mandates have simply gone unanswered. Even extreme tarmac delays, the one thing regulators seemed to get right, are having a renaissance, more than doubling in frequency between 2016 and 2017, while enforcement fines have nearly stopped.

When I talked to Paul Hudson, he told me about one of the worst new planes in the U.S. fleet. It included thinner padding and lower seat pitch than the planes that most major carriers purchased. Originally it was all the way down to 29 inches until public outcry pushed it back up to 30. It had only three bathrooms for over 150 passengers. The aisle was so narrow "a larger person has to walk sideways," Hudson alleged.

The plane was known as the Boeing 737 Max, and by March 2019 the whole world knew its name, after 346 people died in two fatal crashes less than five months apart, revealing serious deficiencies with the aircraft's automated flight-control software. The jets that failed, in Ethiopia and Indonesia, lacked two warning indicators that Boeing sold as optional extras. (After the crashes, Boeing decided to make one of them standard.) It was later revealed that Boeing outsourced some software engineering to fresh-faced temp coders from India earning as little as $9 an hour.

As Max planes were grounded worldwide, people started wondering how they were ever approved for commercial use. It turned out that Boeing approved them. FAA managers delegated most of the safety assessments directly to the manufacturer, to help meet tight production schedules. This has been the norm for decades: a 1993 government report shows that the FAA delegated 95 percent of the safety certification to Boeing for its 747 jumbo jet. In the case of the Max, the assessments came back flawed, particularly for the flight automation system, the catalyst of the crashes. The FAA waved them through anyway; the office "defaulted" to Boeing, according to former officials. Lower-level employees lived in fear of calling out Boeing for errors and being dressed down by superiors; several of them called an FAA hotline to confidentially report issues with the 737 Max. Still nothing happened.

Pressed for answers, acting FAA administrator Daniel Elwell told the Senate that it would take $1.8 billion in federal funds and ten thousand new employees for the government to certify aircraft. In other words, outsourcing safety determinations to monopoly corporations—Boeing is the only major manufacturer of commercial aircraft in the United States, making it in many respects too big to fail for America—is a budget-saving feature, not a courting-disaster bug.

As the government investigated the breakdown, Boeing assigned its general counsel J. Michael Luttig as its point person. Luttig, once a federal judge, personally hired dozens of law students as clerks who are now seeded throughout the government, including Christopher Wray, the FBI director. Meanwhile, Attorney General William Barr worked for Boeing's longtime law firm Kirkland & Ellis, as did the deputy attorney general and the head of the DOJ's criminal division. The web of connections is borderline obscene.

"The airline industry is an abusive industry," Hudson said. "They're exempt from all consumer protection regulations; they've essentially bought off Congress with special privileges that don't apply to anyone else. There's a point where you say this should not continue."

Kate Hanni never did reach her ultimate goal as a consumer advocate. "I was going to be the mother of airline reregulation," she said. "I wanted to take on every issue. But we almost lost our house." As an unpaid volunteer for FlyersRights.org, Hanni traveled dozens of times to Washington, DC, and elsewhere on her own dime. It was unsustainable. "I couldn't afford to continue being an advocate. Eventually, my family said, 'It's either Flyers Rights or us.'" She handed over the reins to Paul Hudson in 2013. Today she works at a nonprofit music school as a development director.

Never in the history of corporate America has a lobbyist grown concerned that she wouldn't be able to survive financially doing advocacy work. Never has a lobbyist needed to hit up friends for cash to get to Washington to speak to a senator about how to boost United's profits. Airlines for America and individual corporations in the aviation sector spend over $85 million a year on lobbying. There's a severe imbalance between those who defend monopolies and those who defend the public's rights. The former thrive on the latter's inability to fund their own advocacy.

"Reregulation" is almost a misnomer, however. Regulation still exists in the airline industry: it's just been put in the hands of a handful of CEOs and Wall Street investors. We merely converted regulation by and for the public into regulation by plutocrats, who now rule the friendly skies in their own interest. "In the nineteenth century, when railroads were the source of transportation, they had an expression: people were being railroaded," said Paul Hudson. "Today with the airlines as the sole source of long-haul transportation, we're being airlined."

I reached the check-in counter at Enterprise Rent-A-Car, next to baggage claim in the Des Moines International Airport. The agent was Iowa nice, and we interacted in the usual way sales personnel and their customers interact. I initialed the eighteen different places you have to initial, and I was all set. That's when the agent said, "Hold on one moment, I'll see what cars we have."

I assumed she was headed into the back office until I noticed that, in this small airport, there was no back office. No, the agent left the Enterprise counter, walked over behind the National Car Rental counter, rummaged around in a little drawer, and pulled out a set of car keys. Then she returned and handed them to me.

I wondered if it would have been easier on everyone if I'd just gone to the National counter first. When I found the designated parking spot with my car, the sign painted on the ground said "National Emerald," which refers to the company's loyalty program. I guess National Emerald Club is so exclusive that it's Enterprise. At least in Des Moines.

That National and Enterprise keys sit in the same drawer isn't just a function of a smallish airport. National and Enterprise are owned by the same corporate parent: Enterprise Holdings, to be precise. Alamo and Zimride also fit under the Enterprise umbrella. Together, firms in the Enterprise family control about 27 percent of the total rental car market in the United States, according to a study from the Open Markets Institute. Another 15 percent goes to Hertz, which also runs Thrifty and Dollar. And 8 percent more is in the hands of Avis Budget Group, which is behind the brands Avis and Budget, the car-sharing network Zipcar, and several brands in South America, Europe, and Australia. If you restricted the snapshot of the market to rental cars on site at U.S. airports, the concentration numbers would be far higher. For example, in that Des Moines airport, you have National, Enterprise, Alamo, Avis, Budget, Hertz, Dollar, and Thrifty. It sounds like a lot of options, but it's actually just three companies.

Few people, even informed ones, seem to know this. A 2018 article from The Hill contained this lead paragraph: "Three top car rental companies are ending their discount programs for National Rifle Association (NRA) members, becoming the latest businesses to cut ties with the gun group." But the three companies were National, Enterprise, and Alamo, which all belong to Enterprise Holdings.

If National and Enterprise want to keep their keys in the same drawer, what business is it of mine? For one thing, National and Enterprise want customers to think they're different businesses. According to Enterprise Holdings' CEO, the brands cater to unique markets. National is for business travelers, Alamo for vacationers, and Enterprise the affordable choice for cost-conscious shoppers. But if they're all using the same pot of cars, intermingled in the same drawer of keys, how are they distinct in any way? Enterprise Holdings may be slicing up the market based on which customers they can and cannot overcharge, but that's just a false segmentation.

To test my assumption that the keys in the same drawer don't go for the same price, I ran a search on rental cars in Des Moines. I did this using Kayak, which asked me if I wanted to compare its results with the prices on Priceline, Hotwire, Expedia, and Orbitz. That also sounds like a lot of choice, but it's really two companies. Kayak is owned by the umbrella group Booking Holdings, which also owns Priceline, Booking.com, Agoda, RentalCars.com, and OpenTable, the restaurant reservations service. Expedia Group owns all the others, including Hotwire, Hotels.com, Trivago, CarRentals.com (not to be confused with RentalCars.com), home rental companies Vrbo and HomeAway, and Orbitz, which it purchased in 2015. So when Kayak asked me if I wanted to compare its price to those at Priceline, Hotwire, Expedia, and Orbitz, really it was Priceline asking me to compare its prices to Priceline's and Expedia's.

But I'm off track.

Anyway, Kayak quoted me a week's rental of the same Nissan Versa for $233 on Enterprise and $294 on Alamo. Prices on the other services were similar. So that's a $60 difference for the same car from the same company. Interestingly, I couldn't find a price quote from National Car Rental. Maybe its entire role at the Des Moines airport is to hold on to the keys.

CHAPTER 2

Monopolies Are Why a Farmer's Daughter Is Crying Behind the Desk of a Best Western

Large bodies of water in Iowa aren't entirely out of character for the upper Midwest—neighboring Minnesota is the "Land of 10,000 Lakes"—but Clear Lake, sprouting out of the heartland with yellow-sand beaches, boating piers, and resort hotels, did take me a second to get used to. Clear Lake's lovely midcentury music hall, the Surf Ballroom, played host to twenty-two-year-old Buddy Holly's final song before his plane crashed on the way out of town. Don McLean called it the day the music died, in that famously endless tune of his.

The population of Clear Lake swells when the marinas fill with tourists, but this was a blustery night in October, after the vacationers had emptied out. The main street (actually named Main Avenue) was mostly empty by 6:30, save for a couple of bars and the VFW, which doubles as a tornado shelter. Clear Lake's population has been declining since 1990, and as I trudged along the lakefront, a decision I immediately regretted as the winds picked up, I thought about how I could have unrolled a sleeping bag and lain down in the road without being disturbed.

Clear Lake at least has a summertime attraction, so it isn't *always* this quiet. The rest of northern Iowa sometimes gives off the sensation that a comet ripped through and vaporized the population. You don't see a single animal grazing by the side of the road, a startling absence given that this is farm country. Mostly you pass corn and soybean fields, and in the distance some silos. The old towns look like places you pass through on a journey, rather than a destination.

The next morning I headed a few miles south, past a bunch of those corn and soybean fields, to Chris Petersen's place. Chris is sixty-five, a third-generation hog farmer of Irish and Danish stock, who constructed all the barns and sheds on his farm by hand. He answered the door in the classic farmer's uniform: a beat-up old trucker's hat, flannel workshirt, canvas coat, and blue jeans. We talked at his kitchen table, where prominent senators, governors, and even presidents have sat over the years. Chris is active in Democratic Party politics, and in Iowa that gives him a certain access to power, at least once every four years.

Chris's grandparents came through Ellis Island, traveled west until they reached Iowa, and saved up for a plot of land. His dad farmed ten miles southeast of Clear Lake; his wife's family farmed five miles north. "I owned pigs when I was a junior in high school," he told me, his eyes narrowing until they almost appeared closed. "All I wanted to do was farm."

But that tradition is ending. Petersen's operation these days is small and a bit niche, and he knows he's the last in that line. "After how many dozens and dozens if not hundreds of generations, back in Denmark and Ireland, all farmers, this is it. I'm it. This is the dead end. You know, it's sad." The way of life of the independent family farmer has been supplanted by mammoth agribusinesses: industrial-sized confinement lots, ruthless livestock companies and seed merchants, monoculture crops stretching for miles. Our monopolized food system has made the Chris Petersens of the world obsolete and unsure of how to survive. It has destroyed communities, both environmentally and socially. It has occasioned a great leakage of wealth and opportunity out of rural communities and farm states, creating a dynamic of regional inequality that historically leads to social unrest. It has implications for every farm family, but also for a profession and a region, and ultimately for our politics and our world.

Chris's voice starts to crack a bit as he tells me about his daughter, Becky, a farm kid who grew up wanting to carry forward her father's legacy. She loved helping out with the pigs and chickens; Chris thought of her as his right hand. But she ran into the solid wall that agriculture has become for anyone who's not an agribusiness executive. Becky moved on; when she was only nineteen, she got a job managing a Best Western Holiday Lodge in Clear Lake. "She called one day," Chris said. "And I could tell something was wrong. I said, 'What's up?' 'Oh, Dad, what a day. This person didn't show up for work, and this food was not prepared right for a wedding. I need to fire this person, I don't have the heart to.' On and on. She started crying. Then the words came out of her mouth that I'll never forget."

Chris paused, trying to collect himself, his face reddening. "She said, 'Dad, I just wish I could come home and farm.'"

He wiped his eyes. "Made the old man cry."

The life of a farmer has forever been precarious, always one bad season or bum crop from ruin. As agriculture in America moved from subsistence to commodification, new threats emerged. Railroads gouged farmers on shipping in the nineteenth century, and farmers fought back. Even before the Great Depression, farm country experienced a depression in the 1920s, due to post–World War I price collapses and mechanization increasing yields, which reduced the need for so many farmers. Vertical combination and price manipulation by meatpackers, who also owned warehouses, stockyards, and wholesalers, also distressed farmers and ranchers. The 1929 stock market crash increased the pain, with financiers pursuing over two hundred thousand farm foreclosures. As the Depression raged, desperate Great Plains farmers cultivated grasslands that weren't appropriate for agriculture, and Dust Bowl drought conditions blew the topsoil clear away, deadening the land and scattering farmers from the region.

When farmers constituted a larger and more politically influential voting bloc, government periodically intervened. The Interstate Commerce Commission, strengthened throughout the early twentieth century, placed restrictions on railroad price predation. Woodrow Wilson's administration busted up the meatpacking trusts, and the Packers and Stockyards Act of 1921 sought to prevent market manipulation. After the Depression, states enacted mortgage relief and moratoria on foreclosures. New Deal crop production controls, known as "price parity" adjustments, guaranteed a decent profit from annual harvests. "That saved family-farm agriculture," said Chris Petersen. "My grandpa wouldn't be alive without that."

The next crisis hit in the 1980s, as overproduction and a grain embargo against the Soviet Union rocked commodity prices downward. Interest rates soared in the early 1980s as Federal Reserve chairman Paul Volcker vowed to tame inflation; this directly affected farmers whose land, supplies, seeds, and machinery are purchased almost entirely on credit. Farm debt doubled from 1978 to 1984 as farmers dealt with rising input costs, higher interest payments, and bottoming prices. Farm income reached $92.1 billion in 1973 and fell to just $8.2 billion a decade later. As foreclosures spiked, the farm credit system sustained its first major losses since the Depression. And under Reagan, government proved slow or even unwilling to react to the suffering. The 1985 Farm Aid concert, spearheaded by the likes of Willie Nelson, Kris Kristofferson, and Neil Young, arguably provided more for family farmers than the government that year. By the time Congress intervened, it was too late; ghost towns and abandoned farmhouses were already fixtures of the rural landscape.

The 1980s were Chris Petersen's formative years in farming. Somehow he survived, working night shifts full-time at manufacturing plants to afford his sows. He rented most of the land, built pens on the cheap to house the hogs, and used the proceeds from selling them to buy more. By the mid-1990s Chris was able to quit the night shift; at his peak he owned three thousand pigs. "We were doing four hundred acres," he said. "We didn't have a life. That's how committed I was to farming. I had pigs on six different farms. I'd sleep two hours and work all day. I lived on Coke." After a couple of years of six-figure incomes, the Petersens started to think big. "The wife and I talked, and I said, 'My God, we're this close. We're going to be able to send these kids to college. If they want to farm, we can make it happen. We're going to be able to start buying land. This is the dream.' And within two years—gone."

The tipping point was 1998, when hog prices dropped from $46 per hundred pounds to $17 within a year. That was around the time agribusiness pioneered the use of concentrated animal feeding operations, or CAFOs. Big Ag huddled thousands of hogs in warehouse-sized feedlots, giving the animals no sunlight and barely enough room to move. Centralizing operations under one roof saved money, but the increased scale spiked the supply of hogs, sending prices downward. Only the big boys could prosper. The major catalyst to CAFOs came from ultralow feed prices, a relic of the 1950s, when Eisenhower stripped out price parity adjustments. Corn was cheap enough to sustain thousands of pigs, and smaller farmers couldn't compete. "They were getting under-the-cost-of-production corn to feed their damn hogs," said Chris. "If a family farmer wanted to raise livestock and own the pigs, the corn costs more for him coming off his farm to produce than what the industry is getting out of the market."

Curiously, prices didn't drop for pork buyers in 1998 the way they did for hog farmers, leaving middlemen meatpackers with fat profits, effectively cross-subsidizing their factory farm operations. But the crisis took Chris out. He lost tens of thousands of dollars in a matter of weeks, and ultimately entered bankruptcy. Many of his colleagues suffered the same fate; more than 70 percent of hog farmers have gone out of business since the mid-1990s, including a 25 percent decline just from 2007 to 2012, according to the U.S. Department of Agriculture. In 1997 there were over 18,700 hog farms and 27.3 million hogs in Iowa; by 2017 there were only 6,200 farms but 60 million hogs. The CAFOs had taken over.

The top four hog firms now control two-thirds of the market. The largest is Smithfield Foods, which directly and indirectly raises one-quarter of all U.S. hogs, processing 32 million per year. Smithfield owns hog farms, slaughterhouses, warehouses, and distribution trucks, the full journey from farm to table. Independent producers simply cannot compete with vertically integrated rivals.

Smithfield and other agribusinesses either directly own hogs or lock family farmers into ten- to twelve-year contracts, which dictate the design of the barns and pens, the type of feeders and fans, and the prices paid. Almost no prices are negotiated on the spot market. The processors locate their plants far from each other, giving farmers little choice of where to sell their meat. Farmers and ranchers even pay part of their profits into a government fund called the "checkoff" program for promotion and advertising, but the money is funneled to industry trade groups, which use it to fund lobbying campaigns that maximize Big Ag profits. So farmers pay to have their own interests undermined in Washington and in state capitals.

"The system now is no better than the collective communist farms of the USSR," Chris said. "There it was run by the government, here by corporations. They turn the farmer into little workers with hardly any say over their future."

In 2013, Chinese conglomerate WH Group purchased Smithfield from its U.S. owners. At the time it was the largest-ever Chinese acquisition of an American company. WH Group is now the world's largest meatpacker; the company's chairman earned $291 million in 2017. Price supports, crop insurance, and other farm subsidies, intended to keep family farmers alive, flow to Smithfield and others at the top.

Donald Trump has funneled $28 billion in two separate bailouts of farmers, after his trade war with China led to high tariffs on U.S. pork and other agriculture imports. In 2018, during the first bailout, Smithfield qualified for purchase contracts of its surplus for food banks and school lunch programs. This would have compensated a Chinese company for Trump's intended punishment of China. After initially taking $240,000, Smithfield bowed to public pressure and rejected the contract. But the second-largest pork company in the United States, Brazil's JBS, is also foreign-owned, and it received $78 million in bailout funds, even while it was under Justice

Department investigation for bribery. In all, over half of the farm bailout money went to the richest 10 percent of farmers, according to a study from the Environmental Working Group. The top 1 percent of farmers averaged $183,000 in payments; the bottom 80 percent averaged $5,000. The Trump administration found protecting family farmers challenging in a factory system dominated by multinational giants.

CAFOs also produce disastrous side effects for farm communities. Typically, CAFOs funnel waste through slatted floors into giant open lagoons as big as a football field, making nearby areas nearly uninhabitable from the odors and flies. "You can't stand to be outside," Chris Petersen said. "The wife can't hang clothes on the clothesline, the inside starts to stink, you get in a car that stinks, you open your suitcase and smell confinement. It's an infringement on individual rights." In election years, Chris likes to take visiting politicians on factory farm tours, advising them to bring an extra suit, because the CAFO smell will stick to their clothes. Concentrated farm operations are also vulnerable to disease outbreaks: a bird flu epidemic in Iowa in 2015 led to the killing of 26 million chickens. The healthy ones weren't segregated from the sick; the operations were so vast that it was easier to just kill them all.

Outside of Iowa, the biggest hog state is North Carolina, with 9.7 million hogs and 10 billion gallons of waste per year. In 1999, Hurricane Floyd flooded hog manure pits, running pale pink slurry into nearby rivers and trapping thousands of pigs atop CAFO roofs. The state reached agreement with Smithfield to invest millions of dollars into researching and implementing more environmentally stable alternatives to the lagoons. But changes to the system were deemed not "economically feasible." So in 2018, after Hurricane Florence, fifty-seven more lagoons flooded, breached, or overtopped. That waste contaminated rivers with excrement, leading to algae blooms and fish die-offs. And the region has a high water table, putting the waste runoff into contact with drinking water.

The major response from the swine industry during Hurricane Florence was to frantically increase lagoon capacity by spraying waste in the fields, which got washed into tributaries anyway, and to truck the hogs out of the barns, avoiding the bad visuals of stranded animals. "They pulled their commodity out of harm's way, and left all the waste in the coastal plain," said Will Hendrick of the Waterkeeper Alliance, an environmental group in North Carolina. Even still, thousands of pigs and over 3 million chickens drowned, buried en masse in close proximity to groundwater.

CAFOs in North Carolina are disproportionately located near communities of color, and they create harms even without a hurricane. Multiple studies have correlated living near CAFOs to public health problems, like improper lung function, shortness of breath, and trouble with balance. A Duke University study found higher mortality rates from anemia, kidney disease, tuberculosis, and septicemia. Prospective home buyers aren't blind to these concerns, and real estate prices have dropped as a result, shackling residents to unhealthy homes. After Hurricane Florence, a couple of lawsuits awarded CAFO neighbors compensation for these hazards. The industry reacted by getting the North Carolina legislature to limit legal exposure and damage awards for CAFO suits. Agribusinesses also often use shell companies under different names to hide the identity of CAFO ownership, making it harder for rural communities to hold them accountable.

Life is no better for those working inside processing plants, who also happen to be mostly people of color, with nearly a third born outside the United States. Average annual salaries for food processing workers hover around the poverty level, despite the terrifying risks: sharp knives, wet floors, hazardous equipment, high assembly-line speeds, and constant pressure to keep moving. Smithfield had to destroy over fifty thousand pounds of meat in 2018 after a production worker was filmed urinating at the assembly line. Sixty-five percent of production workers report being injured on the job, though many fear telling their bosses; worries about deportation work wonders as catalysts for subjugation.

This is almost certain to get worse. In 2019 the U.S. Department of Agriculture (USDA) lifted most limits on assembly line speeds, while cutting government inspectors by 40 percent and shifting inspections to plant employees. The same people afraid to report ailments or take bathroom breaks will probably not stop production if they find a diseased or infected pig. Even before these changes, pig slaughterhouses were a hygienic nightmare: inspectors had all of three and a half seconds to verify the health of the carcasses flying past them. Cutting that time down will not improve the food you eat.

On top of all this, the factory farm process degrades food quality. The hogs are shot through with antibiotics, so animals fatten up more quickly. Waste and runoff leach higher levels of bacteria into the surrounding soil, affecting fruits and vegetables. Consumption of this meat could lead to antibiotic-resistant "superbugs" in humans. "It's also just shitty meat," said

Austin Frerick, an Iowa native and former Treasury Department staffer who now works at Yale Law School. "There's actual flavor in Chris's pork chops."

The Petersen farm raises around five hundred Berkshire Gold hogs, and the high-quality meat fetches a robust price, even in this suppressed market. The farm also is home to a hundred chickens who lay brown and turquoise eggs ("It's Easter all year round," Chris tells me) and a small home garden with tomatoes, potatoes, watermelon, and cantaloupe. The hogs live in an open-door pen, with plenty of room for grazing and running around. "When I wake up, I know if it's a good or a bad day by listening," Chris said as we walked by hogs frolicking in the slop. Usually it's quiet, unlike at the CAFOs, where noise is only one of the sundry pollutions. A quiet pig is a happy pig.

Chris's wife sells eggs out of the house; his daughter raises a handful of broiler chickens. But better taste and humane treatment go only so far. "You gotta have other income," he said. "That's what they've done to the family farmer. Thirty, thirty-five years ago, what was called mainstream agriculture back then, it's now called alternative or niche. That's what they have done."

Hog farmers are hardly the only agricultural players enduring the consequences of increased concentration. In fact, monopoly power lurks everywhere you turn in our food production system. It's the main reason that farmers and ranchers have lost a significant share of the retail food dollar, from 37¢ down to only 15¢. The monopolists lap up the excess.

The meat industry is more concentrated now than during the time of Upton Sinclair's muckraking epic *The Jungle*. JBS, Tyson Foods, Cargill, and National Beef control roughly 85 percent of the beef industry. The days of independent cattle ranchers selling into competitive feedlot auctions are nearly over. Big packers own most of the feedlots and slaughterhouses, either directly or indirectly. A proposed 2019 merger between independent cattle company Iowa Premium and National Beef (like JBS, National Beef is also a Brazilian company; I guess the "national" in its name refers to the nation of Brazil) would eliminate one of the only cash markets left in America. When the entry of Walmart as a direct purchaser of cattle is seen as a ray of hope, you know it's a heavily concentrated industry. (Walmart is also now processing its own milk.)

Most cattle ranchers work exclusively for a specific packer on what is called a "forward contract." If you can sell to only one buyer, and that buyer controls what cattle it purchases, where it goes to get slaughtered, and how it moves along to retail outlets, the economics of supply and demand become irrelevant. Like with hogs, beef packers enjoy high margins that don't filter down. Independent operators alleged in a 2019 lawsuit that the Big Four would close slaughterhouses strategically, stop buying live animals, or artificially depress farmer pay. All of this conspired to make ranchers more desperate to sell cows cheaply. Many find it impossible to survive; seventeen thousand have tapped out every year since 1980. It's not great for shoppers either, with chronic recalls as the big packers cut corners. Twelve million pounds of ground beef possibly tainted with salmonella in 2018 emanated from one JBS plant that allowed sickly cows onto the production line. In an age of monopoly, one bad decision has a magnified impact.

If anything, the situation for chicken farmers is even worse. The industry has four giants: Perdue, Pilgrim's, Sanderson Farms, and market leader Tyson Foods, which has scooped up dozens of competitors in the past twenty years. Over 90 percent of the industry involves contract farming: chicken farmers are given feed and chicks, and are told how to house the chickens, nourish them, and inject them with medicines to fatten them up. "Farmers are nothing more than babysitters if you're a chicken grower," Frerick told me. They bear all the costs of securing land and equipment, building chicken houses, performing company-mandated upgrades, and carrying out the labor, but they don't own the chickens and cannot ensure a price that covers expenses.

Chicken farmers operate under the tournament system, a particularly grisly novelty of late capitalism where they compete to supply the major processors and are docked if their chickens come in too thin. It's not true competition because the purchasers have rigged the system: demand rises and falls, but the input prices never change. In 2018, the Small Business Administration determined that chicken farmers were so indentured to Big Ag that they could no longer be considered independent businesspeople.

A manipulator is a manipulator, and the big chicken firms treat supermarkets and restaurants accordingly. In 2016 it was revealed that companies provided inaccurate information that led to an inflated "Georgia Dock" benchmark price estimate that virtually all retail chicken buyers use. That translated to billions of dollars in ill-gotten gains for Tyson and friends. In 2019 the Justice Department intervened in a separate price-fixing case, pursuing a criminal investigation. Other supermarket chains and food distributors sued as well. Collusion is simple because a subscription service called AgriStats gives any meat processor instant access to prices throughout the industry. (Fish aren't exempt from this either; there's a price-fixing scandal in the tuna market.) The airline industry has ATPCO, Big Ag has AgriStats, and the goal is the same: exploiting information advantages.

A 2013 Pew report noted that 71 percent of all chicken farmers earn incomes below the poverty line. Farmers get anywhere between 5¢ and 6¢ a pound for their product. "Those farmers have not seen an increase in pay for twenty years," said Joe Maxwell, a Missouri hog farmer who served as the state's lieutenant governor from 2000 to 2005. "They've spent a million dollars to raise chickens, have hopes and dreams, and they're stuck." When farmers complain about these practices, the chicken companies retaliate by giving them smaller chicks and lower pay, if the tournament system doesn't lead them to bankruptcy first. We've gone from 1.6 million independent chicken farms in the 1950s to just 25,000 today. Even beyond the penury, the tournament system sows community mistrust. "This is dividing communities, breaking the fabric of those communities," Maxwell said. "It should be criminal, in America it's called good business."

Dairy farmers are in total crisis in the United States, as prices for milk have plummeted since 2014, well below the break-even point needed to turn a profit. Around 4,600 dairy farms close every year, and that number is expected to accelerate. "There's just nothing in dairy farming that makes any money right now," Wisconsin farmer Emily Harris told the *Milwaukee Journal-Sentinel*. But some folks are making money: the giants who milk animals on confined lots, as anyone driving between Los Angeles and San Francisco and encountering the sea of cows and the smell of manure in Coalinga can testify to. The average number of cows per dairy farm has doubled since 2004, and factory farming has expanded overall production even as total farms have decreased. Agriculture secretary Sonny Perdue read the eulogy for family dairy farmers in 2019, brazenly questioning whether they could survive: "In America, the big get bigger and the small go out."

The problem, once again, is the purchasers. Dean Foods processes about a third of all U.S. milk; its bankruptcy filing in November 2019 had farmers worrying who would buy their goods. Another processor, Grassland, was the sole buyer for hundreds of Wisconsin dairies, and when it slowed its purchases in 2017, it put farmers out of business. Companies like Grassland love overproduction because it reduces their costs, but it destroys the family farmer.

In the past, dairy cooperatives owned by the farmers themselves would protect their interests against consolidated buyers. But modern dairy co-ops include monopoly giants like Dairy Farmers of America (DFA), which "represents" thirteen thousand farmers producing 30 percent of the raw milk supply. As a hybrid producer and buyer, DFA can dictate terms to farmers in areas where there's no alternative. They also own or partner with milk processors and marketers, meaning they make *more* money when prices to co-op members drop. DFA's profits never get shared with members. When Dean Foods filed for bankruptcy, it quickly turned to DFA for "advanced discussions" about a merger, which would create a behemoth that could further squeeze farmers and fatten profits. Dean Foods and DFA have been accused in the past of colluding to keep down prices; with a merger, that would be merely an internal business decision.

Other co-ops turned monsters include Land O'Lakes, the butter people, and Ocean Spray, which has been accused of tanking the independent market for cranberries, while increasing supplies so much that enormous amounts of cranberries have been either frozen for storage or buried in the ground. The Capper-Volstead Act of 1922 gives an antitrust exemption to farm co-ops, which made sense when they weren't effectively multinational corporations in their own right. Now it just gives farmers no recourse.

A series of mergers in 2017 and 2018 left four companies in control of over 60 percent of the global seed market: Bayer, which purchased the notorious Monsanto; Corteva, created from a merger between Dow and DuPont; ChemChina, which took over Syngenta; and BASF. Bayer now is the world's largest seed company for vegetables and cotton, as well as the largest seller of herbicides like Roundup, which successive jury trials have judged to be cancer causing. Nevertheless, the EPA has continued to authorize Roundup's use.

In a practice that elicits gasps when explained to the uninitiated, farmers do not own their own seeds, and it's often illegal to save seeds and replant them the next season, as has been done for thousands of years of human history. In some cases, seeds are bred to not produce progeny after one harvest. This allows big seed companies to extract money from farmers annually; prices have skyrocketed over threefold since 1995, while yields have not increased at the same rate. The system also makes farmers dependent on pesticides that pair with the seeds. For instance, Bayer's Xtend soybean seeds have been modified so that dicamba, an herbicide, doesn't kill them. But when dicamba is sprayed, it blows onto nearby farms, and if those farmers don't use dicamba-resistant seeds, their crops wither. So Xtend now holds three-quarters of the market, simply because every farm in a community has to switch soybean seeds if one of them does. Farmers filed an antitrust lawsuit over this in 2018, and they may need another: Bayer got approval for a dicamba-resistant corn seed in 2016 and could roll it out soon.

This commodification of seeds, a foundation of life on earth, has taken variety out of the market. An astonishing 99 percent of iconic Iowa corn won't reach your kitchen table, instead rerouted to ethanol (used in gasoline), livestock feed, and even packaging and fabrics. As with corn, biodiversity has evaporated from wheat, soybeans, and virtually all other crops. Not only does monoculture eat up tons of available farmland, it makes farmers vulnerable to one blight wiping out the whole crop. "Farms before had three or four things growing, so if one didn't do well, you weren't screwed," said Austin Frerick. "Now everyone gets the same tomato bred in the same part of Baja or California." And it's usually a tomato of the rubber-ball variety, bred to survive long, carbon-intensive trips to all corners of the continent. Flavor and distinctiveness are secondary concerns.

Food safety hazards proliferate with market concentration. The largest recall of 2018, affecting dozens of grocery chains, hundreds of products, and 99 million pounds of food, all came out of one plant in California operated by McCain Foods, which supplies ingredients for frozen food products eaten around the world. Contaminated romaine lettuce largely came from a single *E. coli* strain in Yuma, Arizona, that got distributed nationwide.

Wait, there's more. Two companies, Deere & Co. and Dutch firm CNH Industrial, sell about half of all tractors and other farm machinery, and they prohibit farmers from fixing them by restricting access to the embedded software needed to facilitate repairs. This funnels thousands of dollars in service costs to manufacturers and their authorized agents every time there's even a minor breakdown. You could miss a harvest and lose your farm just because you can't fix a locked machinery circuit. An entire network of underground hacking and a "right to repair" movement have emerged to fight the tractor monopoly. The industry has spent millions to block both, with Deere even asserting that when farmers buy a tractor, they merely own a "license to operate the vehicle." (Warren Buffett had a major holding in Deere for years, but he sold it all in 2017.)

For years, big farm companies like Monsanto, Syngenta, and DuPont have scooped up farm technology firms, prying open a Big Data trove of crop yields, soil fertility, and machine efficiency. The data can be leveraged to personalize pricing, market better practices to neighboring farms, speculate on crops, or go toward dozens of other uses in the interests of the corporation rather than the farmer. Such information used to be estimated in government reports; now it's locked up on corporate mainframes.

Farm credit companies have been merging into conglomerates; since the farm crisis of the 1980s we've gone from nine hundred lending associations through the Farm Credit Service, a quasi-governmental enterprise that backs loans, to only eighty. Many rural community banks have vanished as well or were sucked up into larger regionals. The top agricultural lenders are megabanks Wells Fargo and Bank of America, Dutch giant Rabobank, French-owned Bank of the West, and John Deere, which has gotten into the business of financing farmers, who then buy or lease things like Deere machinery.

Borrowing from big banks (and tractor companies) puts farmers in a far different position with their lenders than what has historically helped them survive. "The farmer and the banker used to have a close relationship based on trust," said J. D. Scholten, whose grandfather sold seeds in Iowa. "Now it takes a week to hear from the banker. The banks are looking at the bottom line, and with no personal relationship, they're not going to give out the loans." Scholten, a Democrat, ran a spirited race for Congress in 2018 against Republican Steve King, coming up just a few points short in a red district; he talked incessantly about farm monopolies in that campaign, and he's trying again in 2020.

Finally, the companies who distribute, sell, and prepare food are all consolidating. The reasoning makes sense: fewer players on one side of a transaction pressures companies on the other side to team up to keep their purchasing power intact. There's no formal name for it, but many antitrust reformers call it "concentration creep," and we see it across the food sector. Four corporations dominate grain trading. Three companies manage nearly all the large-scale cafeteria services in hospitals, stadiums, and government buildings. Four chains sell nearly half of all groceries. Nestlé alone sells over two thousand brands.

In 2018 Dr Pepper Snapple merged with Keurig Green Mountain; you can forgive yourself for thinking that separate companies manufactured all four of those product lines. Later on in the year Keurig Dr Pepper (that's the name they settled on) merged with Core, which makes bottled water and sports drinks. And that's not the whole story, because Keurig Dr Pepper is a wholly owned subsidiary of a coalition of private equity companies, 87 percent of which is in the hands of a secretive European firm called JAB, which has majority stakes in or outright ownership of Caribou Coffee, Peet's Coffee, Intelligentsia Coffee, Stumptown Coffee, Mighty Leaf Tea, Einstein Bros. Bagels, Noah's Bagels, Panera Bread, Bruegger's Bagels, Krispy Kreme Donuts, Au Bon Pain, Paradise Bakery and Café, and Pret A Manger. Asked about its control over giant segments of America's breakfasts, lunches, and coffee breaks, a straight-faced JAB chairman Bart Brecht responded: "The consumer wants choice."

The consequences of this monopolization are etched into the For Sale signs in front of farmhouses, scrawled through the loose dirt lying fallow, burned onto the face of a scared family calculating savings through sobs at a kitchen table, uncertain of the future and their place in it. Midwest farm belt bankruptcies soared to higher levels in 2017 and 2018 than during the Great Recession, according to the Minneapolis Federal Reserve, whose analysts didn't think the number had reached its peak. Bankruptcies in most other farm regions have also increased. It's great for lawyers, but that's about it. The USDA estimates that more than half of all farm households are losing money.

What does that look like on the ground? I crisscrossed Iowa for several days before the 2018 midterms, from Des Moines to Sioux City and several points in the northwest corner, listening to farmers, policymakers, journalists, and residents. Fifty years ago Iowa had seven congressional districts; today it's down to four. In parts of the state you can feel that depopulation. "I can show you cornfields where there used to be viable family farms. I can show you farmhouses that are falling down," said Chris Petersen. "I think of that farm family trying to make it. All the blood, all the sweat, all the tears, all the hope. I can't handle it."

The congressional district J. D. Scholten contested now represents 40 percent of Iowa's landmass. Scholten bounced around minor-league baseball as a pitcher before his grandmother told him to get back to Iowa and take care of the family farm. He felt compelled to return, but despite his education and relative youth viable employment options proved hard to find. "I looked for a job, and the best I could find was $15 an hour with no benefits," he told a town hall in Spencer, the seat of Clay County, population 16,170. "I had my twentieth high school reunion. The kids I grew up with are doing amazing things but not doing it here." That was the moment he decided to run for office, to help give people like him better reasons to stay in Iowa.

The crowd nodded; their kids were probably among those Scholten was talking about. The average age of a farmer in America is fifty-eight. In Iowa, 60 percent of all farm owners are over the age of sixty-five; just 1 percent are thirty-four or younger. More than half of all Iowa farmland is rented out, and the startup costs of land, machinery, and other inputs are a huge barrier to entry. A substantial number of farm owners are elderly widows who inherited the land. As they pass on, Iowa could be transformed. "They'll sell to the highest bidder, probably a corporate ag group who doesn't give a crap about the land or small towns," Scholten told me as he drove his Winnebago, nicknamed "Sioux City Sue," from one town hall to the next.

In a state like Iowa, where agriculture and related industries are still responsible for 30 percent of the economy, a farm crisis triggers a broader malaise. The grocery stores that stocked food for farm families, the restaurants that cooked them dinner, the banks that lent to them, the hair salons and hardware shops and watering holes—none of them have as many customers, or in some cases any reason to exist. So the towns downsize, the Main Streets shrivel. Communities scramble to consolidate school districts and public services. Hospitals close up. The only new business you see in most towns is a Mexican restaurant, a nod to the immigrants who work in the CAFOs and slaughterhouses.

The farmers sticking it out in Iowa, with two farms operating on their rural road instead of a dozen, feel isolated and adrift. Chris Petersen remembers a town not too far from Clear Lake called Swaledale, which in the 1960s and 1970s had a fully operational central district. "You'd come to town, late afternoon, it was a gathering community place, a social place," he said. "Main Street was alive. That's all gone. Big Ag has bypassed all these towns. They don't need it anymore." The social fabric deteriorates in line with the abandoned farmsteads. Rural life becomes lonelier.

Those trying to stay in the game bear tremendous pressure. They sell off unnecessary equipment or bits of land. They take off-farm jobs to make it through lean times. And some seek a tragic form of relief. Farmers commit suicide at the highest rate of any U.S. occupation, even twice the rate of veterans, which we often think of as its own epidemic. Life on the farm has always been stressful, but a slow-motion crisis with no end in sight just ratchets that up; feelings of failure, humiliation, and alienation long for an outlet. Dairy co-ops have begun to include a list of suicide prevention hotlines in the envelope with their checks.

Mike Rosmann, a psychologist who counsels farmers and ranchers, hears from more and more desperate folks every day. He told the *New Republic* that the suicide epidemic is a symptom "of their economic well-being . . . the entities that control farm prices largely have to do with business interests that lobby heavily at the state and federal levels. If the behavioral health state of farmers is poor, you can bet those lobbies are winning."

When those lobbies win, they carry rural wealth out of the community and into corporate treasuries. This transfer is responsible for a pernicious phenomenon of the Second Gilded Age—regional inequality. Hillary Clinton stumbled upon it during a speech in Mumbai, India, in 2018. "I won the places that represent two-thirds of America's gross domestic product," she boasted, referring to her popular-vote victory and Electoral College defeat in the 2016 election. "So I won the places that are optimistic, diverse, dynamic, moving forward." It's true that the counties Clinton won, mostly on the coasts and in big cities, contributed 64 percent of U.S. GDP in 2015. Since the election, that trend has likely grown; a Brookings Institution study estimated that metropolitan areas with populations over one million accounted for 72 percent of U.S. employment growth since the financial crisis. We have winner-take-all cities, the same way we have winner-take-all firms.

That's not a good thing. It means that the economic life has been sapped out of a large section of the country, fomenting anger at establishment neglect. It means that the millions of people stranded in those areas have no hope of building a business where they were born, or seeing their kids stay close to home. It causes a bifurcation in the American idea, and not just red state versus blue state. Upstate New York and the Central Valley of California align with North Carolina and Iowa, with Alabama and Arkansas, and even with abandoned blue-collar towns like Dayton, Ohio, in open defiance of the few counties lucky enough to serve as America's winners. Those looking in from the outside feel powerless and forgotten, socially and economically.

Regional disparities correlate heavily with the rise of right-wing populism in the United States and Britain. This was Clinton's *downfall*, not some consolation prize. Declining metro areas in Pennsylvania, Ohio, and Michigan accounted for her loss. Electoral College imbalance connects directly to regional inequality, tilting victory away from presidential candidates who earn the most votes. A similar dynamic is at play in the composition of the Senate, where Democrats represent 56 percent of the population but only 47 percent of the votes. This threatens the institutional legitimacy of our politics.

On a broader level, regional inequality stirs up debilitating factionalism and tribal disgust. And concentrated corporate power is at the heart of it all. The Economic Innovation Group (EIG), a bipartisan policy research organization, has been sounding this alarm for several years, starting with a 2017 report that expressed some painful truths: "Americans are less likely to start a business, move to another region of the country, or switch jobs now than at any time in recent memory." EIG calls this "dynamism in retreat," with only a few metro areas saved from this lack of vibrancy. Just 20 percent of rural counties added businesses from 2007 to 2016, and five metro areas (New York, Miami, Los Angeles, Houston, and Dallas, the latter two from a coincidental oil boom) produced more new businesses than the rest of the nation combined. Regions lacking dynamism see lower wages and declining opportunity.

When all the economy's gains go to a few cities, ecosystems develop to feed off that wealth. Startups cluster close to the source of workforce talent and multinationals that can one day buy them out. New services and innovations cater to this creative class. The rest of the country is stuck in a different era, unable to afford or even witness the march of modernity. Health care grows more expensive as rural hospitals close. Public transportation is nonexistent because the nodes are simply too far apart. Air travel is arduous. Major corporate headquarters have escaped. Chain stores, rather than local businesses, dominate the landscape. Civil society barely exists. Despite people being surrounded by fresh food, obesity increases amid sedentary lifestyles and unhealthy eating habits. Opioids are a coping strategy. "Deaths of despair" are an identifiable trend.

"It goes a long way to explaining economic anxiety and political angst," said John Lettieri of EIG. "People are tired of hearing how great the recovery was when the reality is not reflected in their own communities." The aggregate statistics in news stories lauding an economic boom, reflected against rural desperation, triggers understandable cries of fake news. A few cities and a few corporations have simply hoarded all the wealth. And everyone else is unhappy.

"We're the grunts of America," Chris Petersen explained. "The family farmer, the construction worker, the teacher, the people who built this country with their hands. We're the grunts. We're getting screwed. It's ruining America as we know it and as it should be."

Iowans have reason to feel frustrated. The past decade in politics has seen an unending series of broken promises. Talk to enough people in Iowa and at least one will tell you that Barack Obama won the 2008 caucuses, and thereafter the presidency, on a promise to bust up agricultural monopolies. After the election, his Justice Department convened five public workshops around the country to discuss agricultural issues and antitrust enforcement. This was considered a prelude to real action to help farmers.

Chris Petersen testified at one of these meetings, in Fort Collins, Colorado. He sat right next to Tom Vilsack, the former Iowa governor whom Obama named secretary of agriculture. Petersen had helped Vilsack get elected; their wives were friends. Vilsack asked each speaker in Fort Collins to name one thing that would improve life for family farm agriculture. Petersen got up, explained his operation and the slow death of independent hog farming, and said, "If we want to start to solve this problem, ban the packers from owning livestock, period." Raucous applause followed. "Everyone stood up and cheered and clapped, and Vilsack's eyes got real big," Chris said.

The meetings were thorough, informative, and practically the last word from the Obama administration on the subject. Though farmers risked retaliation for speaking out, the Justice Department conducted no enforcement actions to weaken the power of Big Ag, claiming dubiously in a report that antitrust laws made it impossible to bring a case. Mergers went through, largely without incident. And though Congress had demanded in 2008 that the USDA revise rules for the Grain Inspection, Packers and Stockyards Administration (GIPSA), which would have formally banned Big Ag retaliation against farmers and given farmers stronger legal tools to prevent abuse, Vilsack hesitated before finalizing them. After taking over in 2011, the Republican House issued a rider preventing enforcement of updated rules, which stayed in place until 2015, when HBO's John Oliver shamed them into removing it after a long segment on his television show. Only in the Obama administration's final days did Vilsack complete a full suite of GIPSA rules, and even then in weakened form. Vilsack is now a lobbyist for the dairy industry's trade council, whose members have contributed to the agricultural crisis and gouged farmers. He goes around Iowa warning Democrats about getting too tough on Big Ag, his personal money machine.

For the most part, the Obama administration went silent on farm monopolies. Big Ag took the timidity as a signal to continue its predatory practices.

Donald Trump also promised rural voters that he would end "American carnage." He said he would use his dealmaking skills to rewrite trade laws destroying the country. In reality, Trump's tariffs made things worse for farmers. Exports slowed to a crawl and meat lay frozen in storage. The administration proposed bailouts to tide over some of those struggling, but assistance for corn growers amounted to an almost insulting penny per bushel. And the trade war had nothing to do with the real economic forces damaging farm communities. If farmers aren't profiting from what they produce, beneficial treaties do nothing for them.

On this point, Trump's team sided aggressively with Big Ag. His secretary of agriculture, former Georgia governor Sonny Perdue (no relation to Frank, though the former's ties to chicken industry interests might throw you off), delayed and then withdrew the GIPSA rules that Vilsack had finalized a month before the inauguration. One of those rules would have reformed the tournament system for chicken farmers; Perdue's donors in the industry wanted no part of that. Trump's GIPSA administrator acknowledged the withdrawn rule would have granted "broader protection and fair treatment" for farmers, but said agency savings from not having to enforce the rule outweighed the societal benefit. Even Iowa's Republican senator Chuck Grassley had to admit that Trump was "pandering to big corporations."

The Organization for Competitive Markets, a bipartisan group formed by rancher Joe Maxwell and other farmers (Chris Petersen is on the board), sued the USDA over killing the GIPSA rules, bringing farmers to rally outside the U.S. Court of Appeals in St. Louis. But the court dismissed the case. Then, after promising to revisit the rules in 2019, Perdue actually eliminated GIPSA entirely, folding it into the Agricultural Marketing Service, a PR agency that Maxwell's group calls a satellite office for the meatpackers. Enforcement of the few remaining laws yielded fines at less than 10 percent of the level under Obama. "To date, this administration has not fulfilled their promises nor any vision toward rural America and family farmers," Maxwell told me. "The sustainability for the future of rural communities and a safe and secure food system lies in the viability of the family farmer."

Maxwell sees the death of the family farmer as existential for America. "This country is not founded upon common faith or where your ancestors came from," he said. "We share one thing in America—that's the hope of opportunity. The idea of liberty and justice, that I can take my toil and work and have an opportunity. Because we lack the economic justice that fair and open markets provide, we destroy that hope."

An entirely new group of politicians trudged through Iowa in the 2020 presidential cycle, eating corn dogs and convening roundtables, again promising the world to farm country. Some of the ideas were pretty good: reforming commodity checkoff programs, placing a moratorium on agriculture and food mergers, enacting a national right-to-repair law, even breaking up agribusinesses and returning to price parity mechanisms to ensure that any farmer can make a decent living. But even the most optimistic farmers have had most of their hope snuffed out by now. Some analysts predict megafarms will dominate all food production within a generation. Nobody on the ground sees another path.

"Rural America is being mined," Chris Petersen told me at his kitchen table. "Big money is gaming the system. I believe, in the future, we'll either wake up and turn the *Titanic* or it's the dead end, the system will fail. And then what? How will we feed ourselves?"

Tony Hoehner's dad loves the Oklahoma City Thunder; he never misses them playing on TV. But Tony wanted to give him a bigger thrill for Christmas: two tickets to a game in person. It was a nice gesture. Or at least it was before Tony discovered that he had to purchase the seats through Ticketmaster. Then it became a form of torture.

Ticketmaster offered Tony two ways to deliver the tickets. He could have them sent directly to his father via mobile app. The mobile tickets could not be printed or emailed, so they would have to go right to his dad. "My father is more than seventy years old and doesn't use a smartphone," Tony told me. "This is not an option."

As an alternative, Ticketmaster would mail the tickets out. But they would only mail them to the purchaser's billing address. Tony was buying the tickets, and he lives a thousand miles away from Oklahoma City, in Arlington, Virginia. Ticketmaster gave him no way to send the tickets to his father directly, even though he lives just ten miles from the arena. The option of leaving them at will-call wasn't even available.

Fortunately, there was a phone number on the website, so Tony gave that a try. A message informed him that "all agents are busy," but he could try automated assistance at a different number. Tony did so, and attempted to buy the tickets there. But for automated purchases, the billing address had to be in the vicinity of Oklahoma City. That's not the address on Tony's credit card, so it was another dead end. By this point, Tony was an hour into making this simple transaction.

"As best as I can tell, my only option is to keep calling the number and hope that at some point all agents won't be busy," Tony said, exasperated. "This has been the most frustrating, soul-sucking experience you can imagine."

You might be wondering whether some other ticket broker would be able to work with Tony to get the tickets over to his father. But of course you would never wonder that, because everyone who's ever attended a concert, sporting event, or practically anything requiring a ticket knows that all venues work with a single agent, usually Ticketmaster or Live Nation. And the smarter of you know that Ticketmaster and Live Nation are the same company, after a 2010 merger created a monopoly with an 80 percent share of the ticket market.

So why exactly would Ticketmaster make it easier for Tony Hoehner to get the tickets he wants? It serves as the gatekeeper between fans and events; people like Tony have nowhere else to go. That's also why Tony and everybody else endure giant charges for the privilege of using Ticketmaster's inconvenient, unyieldingly bad service. That includes your service fee, order processing fee, facility fee, and delivery fee, even if the delivery isn't going where you'd like. The Government Accountability Office estimated in April 2018 that fees average out to 27 percent of the face value of a ticket; those fees make up about half of Live Nation's total revenue.

Even the most disruptive of disruptions probably can't dislodge this empire, because Live Nation owns over two hundred venues and promotes over five hundred major artists, which it leverages to guarantee Ticketmaster as the exclusive broker for those sites and musical acts. Indeed, Ticketmaster is the only ticket seller for the home of the Oklahoma City Thunder, Chesapeake Energy Arena, whose leadership presumably wants to keep hosting Ariana Grande or Taylor Swift at their location.

Incidentally, it was obvious at the time that the Ticketmaster–Live Nation merger would create an unaccountable anticompetitive giant—complaints about Ticketmaster exploitation date back to Pearl Jam in the 1990s. But I confidently assume that the presence of Ari Emanuel on the Live Nation board helped matters. Not because he was the model for Ari from Entourage, *but because his brother, Rahm Emanuel, was serving at the time of the merger as White House chief of staff.*

However, you say, there's another option! What about the newly vibrant online resale market for tickets? Well, sure. Half of that market belongs to StubHub. The number two seller is . . . Ticketmaster, through its website TicketsNow.com.

The secondary resale market exists because individuals, usually through robot programs, capture a stack of tickets and then capitalize on the desperation of entertainment seekers locked out of the initial sale, jacking up the price and larding on fees. The Canadian Broadcasting Company reported in 2018 that Ticketmaster recruited resellers for partnerships to sell overinflated tickets to customers, even though the resellers acquire tickets only through gaming Ticketmaster sales. Ticketmaster even partnered with artists to transfer to them tickets to sell at inflated prices on resale sites. Ticketmaster has settled cases with the Federal Trade Commission over allegations of steering customers to tickets above face value on TicketsNow.com without disclosure. Concertgoers have also complained of being led to believe they were buying directly from a venue when they were actually buying an overpriced ticket from a Ticketmaster-linked reseller.

The government could solve this problem by separating ticketing from promotion and artist management, breaking up the ticketing monopoly. But that would require a willingness to fight concentrated power.

In the meantime, Tony Hoehner bit the bullet. He bought the tickets, had them mailed from Oklahoma to his house in Virginia, and then mailed them back to Oklahoma to his dad. It wasn't the biggest deal in the world, just a minor annoyance and a pointless tax on his time, a typical day in our age of corporate power. "Absolutely ridiculous," he told me. "But Dad enjoyed the game."

CHAPTER 3

Monopolies Are Why Hundreds of Journalists Became Filmmakers, then Back to Writers, then Unemployed

Jamie Pearson (whose name I've changed at her request) didn't understand the text: "I heard the news, is everything OK?" She was at a doctor's appointment at the time, but this former co-worker wouldn't have any knowledge of that. Then Jamie realized it probably had something to do with Mic, the millennial-focused digital news company where she had worked for the past two years.

"She said that rumors were going around that Bustle bought Mic," Jamie told me. "I went through social [media] and saw nothing." Bustle was a digital news site that catered to young women, and it had been picking off smaller publishers throughout the year, including the hollow shell of the once-popular blog Gawker.

Jamie raced back to the office, on the eighty-second floor of the One World Trade Center complex in lower Manhattan. It was the Wednesday after Thanksgiving, 2018, and the newsroom was pretty empty, as it had been for the past few months. Leadership was never really around, some staffers were off making videos, and attrition plus rounds of layoffs made even a full building look uninhabited. "We had another company renting out space in our office—that emphasizes how much room we had," Jamie said. But that day, the Mic journalists on hand were freaking out, pacing back and forth. Many were frantically calling their union local, NewsGuild of New York (Mic employees had just voted to unionize earlier that year). The union didn't have much information to offer, but late that afternoon Recode broke the news publicly: Bustle was in talks to buy Mic.

Two months earlier, Mic's CEO, Chris Altchek, himself only thirty-one, had acknowledged that the company was seeking a buyer. Since then Mic had lost a video series deal with Facebook called "Mic Dispatch," worth up to $5 million in revenue. That pierced Mic's viability and made obtaining venture capital money, its main source of funding, challenging. Teaming with Bustle wasn't a bad match, in theory. But there was one passage in the Recode story that leaped out: "Mic employs more than 100. . . . Right now, it looks like Bustle would consider bringing in half or less of the Mic staff." Upper management never emailed that day, as they had in the past, to knock down the rumors.

By the time Jamie left the office the mood was grim. She thought about the coat she kept at work for whenever the building got cold. That next morning, despite the November chill, she decided not to wear a coat to the office, because she had a feeling she would be taking that office coat home.

"We had a nine-thirty meeting of editors. Usually that was six or nine people," Jamie said. "But everyone was at the meeting. They said if there's stuff you want to publish, get it out in the next few hours." It dawned on everyone that this would be their last day at Mic. Jamie's section of the website had a huge project scheduled to launch the following Monday, and she spent the morning helping to methodically publish some of the dozens of pieces they'd been holding back.

At ten o'clock Chris Altchek made the tearful announcement in the kitchen: Mic was being sold, and almost everyone was being laid off. Staffers were told they had to leave by two o'clock; after that, all computers and internal networks would be switched off. One of the more than one hundred people being fired had started work only that Monday. As news of the layoffs trickled out, many said goodbyes on social media. "The time I spent at @mic was the best of my career," tweeted Colleen Curry, the managing editor. "Hire my amazing colleagues," wrote reporter Emily Singer. Erin Evans tweeted a combination farewell/résumé: "I'm a great manager, line editor and can think big around entrepreneurial projects." Jamie described it as "an incredibly strange feeling," with plenty of emotion, hugging and crying, and a healthy dose of alcohol. "People started drinking all the booze," she said.

What happened here? How could a company that had raised $59.5 million, with the most recent round coming in only five months before the sale to Bustle, flame out so spectacularly, with a value at acquisition of only $5 million? The answer, bluntly, is Facebook, which enabled and purged a digital media revolution in short order, based only on whims about where to direct its army of 2 billion users. Upstart media sites had no choice but to ride the Facebook wave if they wanted meaningful traffic, accepting whatever the social network dictated as its engagement strategy. And while Facebook zigged and zagged, Mic—and bunches of others—crashed.

"They became very dependent on Facebook and they went all in on it, and they got burned," one insider told Recode.

That left journalists, many of them at the start of their careers, on the unemployment lines, joining grizzled veterans at local dailies across the country, whom Facebook (and Google) also put out of work by this and other means. The digital advertising duopoly has sucked up practically all the revenues from the news business, threatening the survival of dozens of independent media outlets. In just the first few months of 2019, 2,400 journalists lost their jobs. "Journalists are trained to not talk about ourselves. We're uncomfortable to make ourselves the story," said Laura Bassett, who was laid off after ten years at *Huffington Post*. "But not enough people are talking about how Facebook and Google are strangling journalism."

It's not just because I happen to be a journalist that I mention its presence as one of the small handful of professions named in the U.S. Constitution. The Founders saw journalists serving as a check on power, a function worthy of protection. But the Constitution guarantees only press freedom, not the press's existence. When state capitols have nobody to watch policymakers in the public interest, when news deserts spread across America, who fills that silence, and what agendas do they have? When an entire class of young professionals must struggle to establish their careers, when their jobs are fragile and livelihoods uncertain, do we lose a generation of reporters, and with what consequences? And why should Mark Zuckerberg get to decide what kind of media we must live with?

America's founding newspapers were full of political bias and fake news. Thomas Jefferson midwifed the *National Gazette* in 1791 as a vehicle for discrediting the ideas of Alexander Hamilton. The *Gazette of the United States* had the opposite goal, as a mouthpiece for Hamilton's Treasury Department. There was a Federalist press and an anti-Federalist press. In the election of 1800, each posted scurrilous lies about the other side, from stories about John Adams preferring a hereditary kingship to tales of Jefferson fleeing a guard post near Monticello when the British approached during the Revolutionary War. A political cartoon depicted Jefferson attempting to burn the Constitution on an altar.

Biased house organ papers were the norm throughout U.S. history, and media owners were able to influence, rather than just report on, world events. In 1876 the western branch chief of the Associated Press (AP), former Republican operative William Henry Smith, plotted to snatch the Republican presidential nomination for his friend Rutherford B. Hayes. Glowing dispatches about Hayes's attributes were placed into newspapers nationwide. Hayes took the nomination, and though he lost the popular vote to Samuel Tilden, three southern states representing the margin of victory in the Electoral College were too close to call. As a congressional commission investigated the results, the pro-Republican Western Union leaked telegrams from Democratic officials to the AP, which were forwarded to Hayes's campaign so they could anticipate Tilden's moves. With the AP as his personal Fox News, Hayes eventually took office, to the delight of what critics called the Hayessociated Press. Democrats created the *Washington Post* in 1877 as an antidote to the AP, mostly to troll Hayes; the paper invented the nickname "His Fraudulency."

William Randolph Hearst's yellow journalism pushed the nation into the Spanish-American War in the 1890s, after baselessly charging that Spain sank the battleship *Maine*. In 1964, a more professional and objective media regurgitated Johnson administration lies about the Gulf of Tonkin, facilitating another pointless war. Forty years after that, the professional and objective media planted false stories fed by Dick Cheney about weapons of mass destruction in Iraq, leading to . . . you get the picture.

All that being said, throughout most of American history, competition in journalism allowed readers to judge the quality of the news for themselves. Most major metro areas had multiple newspapers, in morning and evening editions. By the 1970s some newspaper owners sought local monopolies as their end goal, including a guy from Nebraska named Warren Buffett. Some of his first investments outside of the insurance industry were newspapers, including the 1977 purchase of the *Buffalo Evening News*. Buffett immediately targeted the only rival paper in Buffalo, the *Courier-Express*, by launching a Sunday edition. By 1982 the *Courier-Express* was out of business, and Buffett's local monopoly became his largest single investment. As Buffett told the Financial Crisis Inquiry Commission in 2010, "If you've got a good enough business, if you have a monopoly newspaper or you have a network television station, your idiot nephew could run it."

The internet is often held responsible for the news business's decline, but that take needs to be refined. At the outset, the ability to access news instantly from anywhere in the world, mostly for free, was a great resource. So were desktop publishing tools that allowed anyone to become a citizen journalist, posting opinions and insights from their living rooms. (Full disclosure: I was part of that digital revolution, starting my own blog in April 2004, after the disaster in Iraq sent liberals searching for escape from an increasingly right-wing, Islamophobic, war-hungry media.) Bloggers combined niche expertise and an unwillingness to uncritically accept official government talking points. They weren't objective—bloggers were akin to Revolutionary War–era pamphleteers—but they did elevate and democratize the press in the early 2000s.

Self-appointed news guardians, of course, hated the blogosphere. It was too partisan, too opinionated, and not deferential enough to media expertise. Reporters also accused bloggers of stealing the work of "real" journalists and using it for their own devises. Bloggers customarily quoted a couple of paragraphs of a news item and then supplied a link for the rest, a courtesy that was rarely reciprocated in Big Media articles that cited "a blogger" while appropriating their scoops. But the idea that bloggers were parasites ruining the business model of journalism was quite prevalent, even more so when *Huffington Post* premiered in the spring of 2005. It used scores of unpaid bloggers to produce op-eds, and also engaged in plenty of aggregation, rewriting stories from other news outlets and optimizing them for searches to grab traffic. "We were seen as the problem from the beginning," said Laura Bassett, who would start working for *Huffington Post* in 2009. "We were the pernicious force that was killing newspapers. Everyone hated us." But blogging was never the problem on the internet; only the platform monopolists annihilated journalism's revenue models.

Many point to the establishment of Craigslist in 1995, which began as Craig Newmark's email newsletter listing music and art events in San Francisco and grew into a free classified listing empire with 50 billion page views a month in seventy countries, as the reason for the media's downfall. (Full disclosure: I bought a couch on Craigslist when it was still a San Francisco–focused site, in 1998.) One study estimated that Craigslist cost newspapers $5 billion in classified ads from 2000 to 2007, and classifieds were responsible for around 40 percent of industry revenue.

Of course, somebody was going to use the web's convenience to list things for sale; it just happened to be Newmark, who has since repented by donating at least $50 million to journalistic enterprises. Craigslist is practically the one ad-free, subscription-free useful site left on the internet; it'd be weird to slander it as bringing forth the apocalypse. And you could always go further back to find causes of declining news circulation, from broadcast television in the 1950s to twenty-four-hour cable news in the 1980s to Fox News Channel in the 1990s.

The real accelerant to journalism's demise was the rise of Google and Facebook. Not only did they commandeer the digital ad market, snatching most of the new revenue stream news sites had just tapped to make up for the loss of classifieds, but their vast referral networks became a distorting lens through which editors and writers chased audience share. "What we get exposed to and discover is very much driven by the rules which the major platforms determine," said Jason Kint, CEO of Digital Content Next, a trade group for online publishers.

Like Craigslist, Google fulfilled a need: to organize the internet and help people navigate it. Unlike Craigslist, it sought to monetize its work through advertising. It worked out: $400 million in revenue in 2002 grew to $136 *billion* by 2018. Craigslist evaporated $5 billion in ads from the news business over a period of eight years; the News Media Alliance estimates that Google took about $4.7 billion in advertising just in 2018, as much as the entire news industry's digital advertising take that year, and over *seven times* the annual loss imposed by Craigslist.

While Google has long held a monopoly on search, two major purchases enabled it to spin gold. In 2006, Google bought YouTube, which had launched only a year earlier as one of the web's first digital streaming sites, bringing unique ad inventory to the company. The 2007 purchase of DoubleClick added back-end ad technology.

Josh Marshall, creator of the venerable online news site Talking Points Memo (TPM), aptly described on his website the way Google currently lords over publishing. DoubleClick provides TPM's ad software, while Google's AdExchange auction site finds and places advertisers. Google Analytics collects the site's data so it can track traffic. TPM's internal website search also runs off Google, and the company email is provided through Gmail. "It's a bit like being assimilated by the Borg," Marshall writes. "You get cool new powers. But having been assimilated, if your implants were ever removed, you'd certainly die."

This is extremely normal. (Full disclosure: my magazine, *The American Prospect*, uses Gmail for email, Google Docs for word processing, Google Drive for storage and file-sharing, and so on.) Publishers employ Google tools, allowing Google to harvest their site's data, and run advertising through Google's ad network. This extends Google's reach well beyond its own websites, enabling it to model audiences and track them around the web. As Jonathan Taplin, in his 2017 book *Move Fast and Break Things*, explained, "Google treats all content as a commodity against which it can place ads." You might say, to both publishers and web surfers, "If you don't like it, just don't use Google." But the ubiquity of the system makes that nearly impossible.

For decades in media advertising, sales reps generated research about their audience that might attract sponsors. If the *Wall Street Journal* has high-income, well-educated readers, many of whom are business executives, advertisers would want to reach those valued potential customers. That specialness means nothing now. By accumulating billions of data points, Google can serve up a carefully modeled audience to any advertiser. If you want to advertise to a young woman who likes sports and recently searched for a watch, no problem. And that ad will follow them around, no matter what website they visit. "There is no differentiation between NYTimes.com and a porn site," Taplin wrote. Suddenly that cultivated, highly sought after *Wall Street Journal* audience is mostly irrelevant, and the ad space built around them mostly worthless. Newspapers cannot possibly compete with the trove of information Google has on its users. This drives websites to pick up scraps of ad money by using Google ad tools, accelerating the company's dominance.

The month before Google bought YouTube, in September 2006, was the month Facebook opened its site to all users with a valid email address. Facebook became as essential in social networking as Google was in search, organizing the connections between people rather than information. And the network now boasts 2 billion users worldwide, which advertisers covet.

Like Google, Facebook mines every inch of knowledge about you to serve up targeted ads. Like Google, Facebook grew through swallowing competitors, including Instagram in 2012 and WhatsApp in 2014. Like Google, the combination of Facebook's surveillance and ad targeting printed cash by the billions; global digital ad spending outpaced ad spending on television globally by 2017, and reached $100 billion in the United States for the first time in 2018. Facebook and Google have accounted for 99 percent of all digital ad revenue growth. These are effectively not tech firms but junk mail companies.

I should say here that targeted digital ads don't work as well as everyone

thinks. They certainly should work: data companies combine browsing and
search history, app usage, email communication, social media likes and
shares, metadata, smart TV and smart home device streams, credit card
purchases, voter registration, geolocation, and even information on your
friends to segment you into one of thirty thousand profiles. You're tracked
on apps after you shut them off. You can be tracked even in encrypted messages. This should build a pretty detailed picture.

But while targeted ads can be personal to the point of creepiness, vehicles for age and racial and gender discrimination, methods to capture
the attention of children, shady scam attempts, or just obvious invasions
of privacy like when law firms target ads based on knowing the user is
sitting in an emergency room, we've all had the experience of buying a
pair of shoes online and then being served an ad for the same shoes ten
minutes later. Targeted ads are slow to react; they show Mother's Day ads
long after people's parents have died, and parenting ads after children pass
away. They make inferences that don't always pan out. A 2018 study found
that data brokers assumed the correct gender on a targeted ad, a seemingly
easy task, only 42 percent of the time. It should tell you something that
the world's biggest advertiser, Procter & Gamble, cut its digital ad budget
in 2018 by $200 million, because it didn't see the value in it. P&G esti-
mated that the average viewing time for a mobile ad on Facebook was just
1.7 seconds.

Tech platforms have repeatedly been caught lying to advertisers about
the reach and effectiveness of their ads. "The numbers are all fking [sic]
fake, the metrics are bullshit, the agencies responsible for enforcing good
practices are knowing bullshitters enforcing and profiting off all the fake
numbers and none of the models make sense at scale of actual human
users," said Aram Zucker-Scharff on Twitter at the end of 2018, and let me
assure you I'm not quoting a random Twitter egg by noting that he's the
director of ad tech for the *Washington Post*. And he has the data to back his
claims up: fake users, fake engagement, fake ad impressions, et cetera. As
an example, Facebook has misreported audience measurements to advertisers for years, from time spent reading to referral traffic to video views,
and even the definition of a "minute" of video viewing, which under its
calculations didn't have to be consecutive.

Most advertisers don't examine such things too closely, and Google
and Facebook certainly don't give them any clues. So they continue to

pay handsomely in an effort to target audiences. But the middlemen have stolen all the money. A groundbreaking 2019 study found that publishers earn just 4 percent more for enabling targeted ads than untargeted ones, or $0.00008 per ad. The market is completely opaque, and even the research authors are at pains to decipher where the money goes.

The history of selling advertisers on the basis of opaque statistics is long and storied: some used to call it "Nielsen ratings." But in this case, that hustle leads to Google and Facebook reaping the rewards of targeted ads at the expense of everyone else. And if investors invest on fake numbers too, and publishers make editorial decisions on fake numbers, and journalists get assignments on fake numbers, then what you're building is a house of cards. And it won't take much for it to come crumbling down.

Mic started under the name PolicyMic in 2011. Altchek, a former Goldman Sachs analyst and intern for George W. Bush's White House, and his more liberal co-founder, Jake Horowitz, were high school buddies who wanted to develop a space for twentysomethings to debate important issues. At the time a host of pathbreaking sites were coming online, primarily on the strength of venture capital (VC) funding. Outlets like BuzzFeed, Vox Media, Vice Media, and Refinery29 sucked up investor dollars, promising to attract large, diverse, desirable audiences. It was something of a digital media bubble.

PolicyMic got incredibly lucky out of the gate—an unsolicited query from David Dietz, an American writer living in Tunisia, led to exclusive reports from the first stirrings of the Arab Spring uprising. Altchek and Horowitz kept hitting jackpots, and leveraged millions of page views to grab nearly $15 million in VC funding by mid-2014, and another $17 million a year later. "We want to become the most important news and media company for our generation," Altchek humbly told CNN. Profitability was not a major concern; like other VC-backed startups, the first mission was to gain audience.

When Jamie Pearson arrived at the company's offices, everyone was in their mid- to late twenties and fairly enthusiastic. "You got to know people really fast," Jamie said. "Everyone was really happy to be there, excited to do good work." The staff was small, but savvy enough to know what young readers would click on. By 2014, PolicyMic was hitting 14 million unique visitors per month, a figure that rose to 30 million the next year. At least half of those readers were referred over from Facebook and other social networks, and this played deeply into the editorial direction. "You asked yourself, who is sharing this story," Jamie said. "And even before that step, why it's important for the world."

Article headlines drove a lot of the traffic; Mic even kept a template for headline styles that fell into a formula, either stoking curiosity, highlighting injustice, or promising a list. (Full disclosure: I have no idea why, but people love lists.) This tactic itself represented a digital media shift, from chasing eyeballs on Google to chasing them on Facebook. "With Google headlines you needed keywords," said former *Huffington Post* writer Laura Bassett, describing the strategy of search engine optimization. "If it was about John McCain running for president, you would have to get 'John McCain president' in the Google headline. That changed to viral Facebook headlines: 'This woman thought XYZ, and you'll never guess what happened next.'"

At Mic, rebranded to minimize the importance of policy in 2014, a balance between earnestness and tactics drove page views. Stories were built to generate conversation. They were sometimes aggregations from other sources, sometimes editorialized hot takes intended to provoke, and sometimes deep and meaningful reporting. Like at *Huffington Post*, Mic found thousands of bloggers to submit work (unlike HuffPost, it paid them), increasing its frequency and reach. Mic also monitored its competitors' Facebook and Twitter feeds, judging what stories did well and quickly publishing something that piled on. The site fed an instantaneous news cycle where culture was politics and politics was culture. But there was a kind of focus: on social justice, on moral clarity, on cutting down bullies. The young staffers believed in raising marginalized voices, in diversifying who media served and listened to. There was a certain nobility in the concept.

By 2015, Mic was professionalizing. Former NPR executive editor Madhulika Sikka came in to run the newsroom, whose ranks swelled to well over one hundred. (Sikka would leave just seven months later, which was a red flag.) Bloomberg, *New York Times*, and *New Yorker* executives were brought in as outside advisors. Funders included WarnerMedia, the parent company of CNN. The site scored a one-on-one interview with President Obama. It split up into specialized sections (known as "verticals") and developed a team to optimize stories for search. And it dipped its toe into monetizing content, as its investors desired. This started with "native

advertising," sponsored stories penned by Mic writers that resembled reg-
ular news items. Brand partners included Grey Goose vodka, Microsoft,
General Electric, and McDonald's. And a lot of the sponsored content was
filmed.

The last bit was an industrywide trend that even had a name: the pivot
to video. In mid-2014 Facebook announced it was getting one billion video
views per day on the platform. As any ad sales executive salivating over a
television-sized media budget knows, video offered a rich potential vein
of profits. Facebook's problem with video was that YouTube had the early
advantage and all the stars; Facebook users would instinctively link out
to YouTube for their video fix. Facebook's algorithm muted that by prioritizing video from Facebook's native player. (Upworthy, a website whose
entire model was based on serving YouTube content to Facebook users, lost
nearly half its traffic as a result.) But Facebook needed plenty of inventory
in that player to keep users engaged.

In a short January 2015 blog post that no longer exists but can be viewed
through the Internet Archive, Facebook informed "content creators" that
they were seeing a shift toward video on the platform. The post was a basic
how-to for websites to get videos noticed on Facebook: make sure they
stand out from the rest of the News Feed and grab viewers from the jump.
"Whether you're a journalist in the field or a public figure sharing a part
of your life, post raw videos that are compelling, shareable, clips that no
one else will have," the disembodied voice of Facebook wrote. A year later,
Mark Zuckerberg told the Facebook developer conference that before long,
"video will look like as big of a shift in the way we all share and communicate as mobile has been." He added that Facebook would be mostly video
within five years.

The implication was unspoken but clear: Facebook would give more
care and attention within its algorithm to native video. Facebook "views
links to outside pages as a problem to be solved," said media critic John
Herrman of the late, lamented website The Awl. "Facebook has made a
great deal of money selling ads against links to media originally published
elsewhere . . . [but] the new vision, in which Facebook not just theoretically
but practically constitutes the entire internet, is potentially *more* profitable. Publishers, in Facebook's view, are middlemen."

The financial proposition for publishers was a bit unclear—though
Facebook would eventually dangle money to sites that produced video

consistently—but any website desperately seeking eyeballs was all but told that the only available road map to success lay in becoming video makers. So they began to pivot. BuzzFeed and Vox added video teams. NowThis decided to operate without a website and go all in as a video producer. Mashable fired its editorial writing staff to double down on video; so did Vocativ. MTV News, which had invested deeply in reporting resources, fired all of them a couple of years later to complete the pivot. Jamil Smith, who lost his job in an overhaul at the *New Republic*, got to MTV News and his boss was fired a week later. "I was on two pivots in a row," he told me. (He's at *Rolling Stone* now.)

Mic caught the pivoting fever, developing reams of programming for Facebook, from original series like *Flip the Script* to daily programming from its vertical teams on Facebook Live. "They said, 'You need to spend X hours a week on Facebook and come up with something interesting,'" recalled Jamie Pearson. The live hits derived from high-pressure brainstorm sessions, with executives demanding viral victories. The whole thing had a bit of a slapdash quality. "It was just a box to check," Jamie said. "Every now and then your video would take off, and that would be exciting. But mostly it felt like the only people watching were my mom and my co-worker's mom."

Mic's video strategy included "Mic-ros," short videos designed to capture attention. There were op-ed contributors on video, correspondent pieces on video, and video annotated with words, designed to be watched on mobile with the sound off. Some videos featured an advertiser logo in the corner. The branded-content teams produced videos linked to specific advertisers and pushed them out on social media. There were hard quotas for brand videos, up to three a week. It was sometimes hard to judge whether Mic was a news outlet or an ad agency.

Even during the Facebook drive, Mic was also pivoting wildly in other directions, Jamie explained. Google brought to Mic a slideshow project called Stamp, for which Mic built proprietary technology. Google never went forward with the project. Mic learned Instagram was hot, hired an Instagram team, and summarily fired them within a couple of weeks. "We wasted a ton of hours," Jamie said. Elsewhere at Mic, teams were thrown together, new hires paired with older writers trying to learn new skills. Writers were implicitly told to scrap entire subjects, like health care, that didn't promise to reel in millions of readers. Video initiatives were planned, scrapped, and planned again, for one streaming platform and then another. Mic formed a TV studio but then farmed out video production to outside companies.

Executives clearly marked video as the future. "We're in the very early stages of an evolution—of the visual revolution," publisher Cory Haik wrote in Recode. Mic laid off twenty-five employees in August 2017, which Altchek justified because "visual journalism already makes up 75% of the time that our audience spends with Mic." In all-staff meetings, Altchek and his colleagues would always briefly nod to editorial content as the foundation of Mic, and then move to whatever white whale they were chasing that day.

Writers and editors put their heads down and tried to tell good stories; one about the opioid crisis, produced in partnership with *Time* magazine, even won an American Society of Magazine Editors award. But the focus on video was clearly cannibalizing the rest of the site. Traffic on Mic fell from 20 million users a month to 4 million as content traveled to Facebook and beyond. And the jokey videos Mic was prioritizing over the editorial team's work—the double entendre "#69TheVote" was a particular low point—just exhausted them. "It was so rushed and thoughtless," Jamie said. "I think a lot of the editorial team was sort of flailing and didn't have a point for their existence."

And then came the bombshell: those video stats Facebook touted, the pot of gold driving websites to transform staffs and editorial directions, were based on lies. Facebook was massively overcounting video viewing by dropping out any views that lasted for under three seconds, which inflated the average watch time. The entire reason websites piled into video was because Facebook had seemingly cracked a code to keep users watching, but none of it was true. Internal documents showed Facebook was aware of the issue for over a year before disclosing it to advertisers. Eventually it was revealed that Facebook's stats were inflated by as much as 900 percent. This ad fraud was nothing new for Facebook, which in 2017 claimed its ads reached 25 million more young people in the United States than existed at the time.

Like a fickle teen flipping through an Instagram feed, Facebook then changed its mind. It stopped paying publishers to make videos. It announced plans to show more posts from families and friends through its algorithm. Facebook's algorithmic fickleness had always given media fits, but "audience teams" would tweak metadata or headlines and stanch the bleeding. This was a different matter: the de-emphasis of video wiped out entire business models in a click.

After the shift, Mic's short-run video views on Facebook dropped by 90 percent in twelve months. Executives put on a brave face. In 2018, Facebook picked up a twice-weekly news program from the company called *Mic Dispatch* for $5 million. It was the final pivot, the last shot to salvage the company, and Mic leaned into it hard, hiring video makers while freezing editorial hiring. The show found an audience of about one hundred thousand per episode, which Facebook deemed not good enough. *Mic Dispatch* wasn't renewed.

It's clearly a terrible idea to bank your entire business on a dalliance with Facebook. As Columbia Journalism School professor Bill Grueskin told the *Washington Post*, Mic was sold to Bustle for only about one-twelfth of what it had raised over the years. "Most newsrooms have come to regret making hiring and investment decisions based on the whims of a company that really doesn't care much about journalism," he said. And he's correct. But companies like Mic also didn't have a choice. That's what monopoly does: it restricts any path but that through the monopolist's networks. The eyeballs lived on Facebook, and to prosper and thrive, digital media had to kowtow to Facebook's wishes. It was obviously a losing game, but the only alternative was not playing.

Mic's demise came in the middle of a digital apocalypse. Media companies cut 15,474 jobs in 2018, the most since the Great Recession, and another 7,200 through September 2019. Some publishers, like Little Things, shut down. Others, like Vox, laid off video teams. BuzzFeed dropped two hundred people. Vice Media let go 10 percent of its staff, as did Refinery29; eventually Vice bought Refinery29. *Huffington Post*, Yahoo, and other media outlets owned by telecom giant Verizon lost eight hundred journalists. At the time she was fired, Laura Bassett was helping an acquaintance get an internship at her outlet, *Huffington Post*. The friend got the internship the day she was let go. "I told her congratulations," Bassett said. "She said, 'What am I supposed to think? What future am I going to have in this industry?'"

The hammer didn't just fall on digital news. Local media were also devastated by Facebook's pivot away from outbound links; many outlets disclosed referral drops of 80 to 90 percent. This accelerated a systemic decline, because with Google and Facebook dominating digital ad revenue there weren't many revenue opportunities left. The Cleveland *Plain Dealer* went from 340 journalists to 33 in the past two decades. The New Orleans *Times-Picayune* was folded into a competitor, ending a 182-year run, with the staff let go. The Youngstown *Vindicator*, America's best-named newspaper, closed after 150 years in operation. Gannett, owner of *USA Today* and the nation's largest print publisher, cut four hundred jobs from its suite of local newspapers.

Gannett's experience reflected one of several new models to keep journalism alive: Wall Street ownership. In August 2019, GateHouse Media, which owns around 400 papers, announced a merger with Gannett's 215, combining the nation's two largest newspaper chains. GateHouse's parent company is operated by private equity firm Fortress Investment Group, which should strike terror in Gannett employees, because Fortress's strategy involves relentless cost cutting. The companies immediately announced an expected $300 million reduction in annual expenses, which likely means journalist and support staff salaries. A separate private equity firm, Apollo Global Management, is financing the deal with a high-interest loan, which will also certainly put pressure on costs. In all, private equity firms own about 1,500 newspapers.

Alden Global Capital, a hedge fund, carries fifty newspapers, including the Denver *Post*. It also thrives on ending journalists' careers; its twelve unionized outlets have one-third the staff that they did in 2012. Often Alden combines operations and produces daily editions remotely, profiting off the real estate. Helpfully, Alden also owns real estate affiliates that specialize in selling and redeveloping newspaper offices and printing facilities. The news looks to be a secondary concern to gaining control of the buildings. Wall Street has picked up digital media as well, like private equity firm Great Hill Partners buying the parent company of Gizmodo, Deadspin, Splinter, and *The Onion*. Splinter has since been shut down.

Another journalism survival strategy has been to find a rich benefactor: Jeff Bezos and the *Washington Post*, Patrick Soon-Shiong and the *Los Angeles Times*, Salesforce CEO Marc Benioff and *Time* magazine, Laurene Powell Jobs (Steve Jobs's widow) and *The Atlantic*. But in a monopolized world, there are only so many billionaires willing to lose money, and not all of them are benign actors: casino magnate Sheldon Adelson's initially secret purchase of the *Las Vegas Review-Journal* had the clear intent of protecting him from negative coverage. Individuals also change their minds; Sara McCune decided to end philanthropic giving, and that rapidly spelled the end of *Pacific Standard* magazine.

A bright spot has been the rise of paywalled subscriptions, which received a boost after the 2016 presidential election and Donald Trump's attacks on journalism. But only big brands like the *New York Times* and *Wall Street Journal* have really capitalized with major conversions to paid readers, and most of those have displaced local subscriptions. Paywalls also restrict the free flow of information to those with the means to access it; the democratizing force of the internet is now putting up gates and creating monopolists, because there's no other sustainable revenue model.

Tech firms have talked a good game about lending a helping hand, promising $600 million in funding. But they also had their own interests in mind. Google promised to help publishers, in part by allowing users to unlock subscriptions with their Google passwords. This would "simplify" the process but also open more data for Google to harvest. In addition, Google blocked "intrusive" ads from its market-leading Chrome web browser, making the only acceptable ads the ones Google serves. And it is using Chrome to block third-party cookies, the way users get tracked across the web, disabling publishers' ability to track in the name of privacy while maintaining its own tracking power.

Other platforms just held up desperate publishers. Facebook created a digital patronage model so people could solicit donations for their work, but it took a 30 percent cut. Apple's subscription-based service, News+, was an even worse deal: Apple would take 50 percent of the revenue. "The experience is great but the economics are terrible," said Jason Kint of Digital Content Next, some of whose members, desperate for eyeballs, succumbed to the Apple service anyway. "Apple is the platform, offering a news app that competes with other news apps. If you don't play, will a competitor get traffic from notifications on the iPhone?"

Some digital sites have floated the idea of banding together through partnerships or even mergers to gain leverage over the Google/Facebook ad duopoly—another case of concentration creep, monopoly begetting monopoly. Reducing choice doesn't serve anyone, and if eight companies can't realize a profit because they rely on platforms for distribution, it's unclear how two will.

The full picture reveals an unfolding disaster. According to a 2018 study from the University of North Carolina, 1,300 communities across America have totally lost local news coverage. Overall, 1,800 newspapers have closed since 2004, and since 2012, circulation has dropped on average by about 40 percent. When Facebook unveiled an initiative to feed more local news to readers, it discovered that it couldn't find enough. Amazingly, news deserts correlate with the spread of infectious diseases, as epidemiologists rely on local articles to track outbreaks.

A generation of young journalists have no proving ground to get their career started, and a generation of veterans have no place to ply their trade. E. Scott Reckard, the *Los Angeles Times* reporter who broke the important story about Wells Fargo's fake account scandal, was out of journalism by the time federal regulators fined the bank. Two Pulitzer Prize winners in 2015 left the industry for public relations jobs. Even Warren Buffett, the wily monopolist, cashed out, turning over his newspapers to a separate management company. Newspapers are "toast," Buffett said in 2019. "They're going to disappear."

Who fills the gap when so many communities lose news? Television is full of national conglomerates and local monopolies with an agenda, in particular Sinclair Broadcasting, which pushes out its right-leaning local newscasts to 193 stations, often relying on the same scripts and coverage. Toxicity on YouTube competes for attention, and its algorithms seem to prioritize conspiratorial and provocative content; it was a major factor in radicalizing the nation of Brazil. Just-the-facts writing from robots is being honed, which might at least impart information to the public but destroy the livelihoods of thousands more. Conservative political operations pose as local websites, serving up fake news under the guise of objective reporting. Even the cleaned-up Facebook News Feed privileges lower-quality, hyperpartisan news, and Google favors established giants, offering no room for independent voices.

But the biggest beneficiary of the gradual decline of local journalism has been an old-media standby, which has also seen tremendous consolidation in recent years: talk radio.

Brad Friedman parlayed his success as a liberal blogger, where he focused on election security, into some guest spots and then into guest-hosting gigs on radio. He liked the freewheeling style and the immediacy of the medium. And he built a following, enough to start his own daily program. But

Friedman came to the exact wrong place at the exact wrong time: after talk radio had consolidated and wired itself for promoting a right-wing agenda. "I'm not terrible at this," Friedman told me. "But it's impossible for anyone to be able to make a living doing this on radio if you're not on the right."

Liberal talkers point to several critical moments in radio history. In 1987, Ronald Reagan's Federal Communications Commission (FCC) repealed the Fairness Doctrine, ending the requirement for political balance within broadcasts on public airwaves. In 1996, a Republican Congress and Democratic president passed the Telecommunications Act, which lifted restrictions on media ownership. "The combination of the two left ownership groups with no real constraints," said Peter B. Collins, another liberal talker. "They followed the money and their own biases."

In the late 1980s, Collins came on after the right-winger Rush Limbaugh on KNBR in San Francisco. After a couple of years, they dumped Collins for a sports show. Limbaugh and an army of syndicated fellow travelers surged across the country, picked up by giant ownership groups with huge station portfolios, like Clear Channel and Cumulus Radio. People spending hours in their car mostly had one choice for news talk: an unfiltered stream of aggressive conservative invective. "I never met a station manager who carried Rush who didn't agree with him," Collins said.

Liberals explicitly tried to counter this with Air America, a station birthed to coincide with the 2004 presidential election. Air America spent tons of money for carriage, often on Clear Channel stations. But financial mismanagement was evident from the start: Air America went dark in Los Angeles and Chicago weeks after launch when checks to the affiliates bounced. Even when it scrambled its way back on the air, Clear Channel, which in 2008 got bought out by Mitt Romney's private equity firm Bain Capital, put its thumb on the scale.

"For example, in Los Angeles, they put it on a 'short stick,' a station no one could hear," Friedman said. Air America's Los Angeles affiliate, K-Talk, broadcast from the same studio as right-leaning KFI, the top talk station in the area. But KFI had billboards and a strong signal, while K-Talk could barely be heard after sunset. After Friedman pointed this out, not on a K-Talk show but on a podcast, word got back to the station's program director, who also programmed KFI. Friedman used to guest-host at Air America for a liberal named Mike Malloy, and he would run it out of the KFI/K-Talk studio in Burbank. "The program director told me they just wouldn't have room to do the Malloy show out of there," Friedman told me. That effectively ended his gig. K-Talk eventually went off the air, becoming K-EIB, short for "Excellence in Broadcasting," the slogan of Rush Limbaugh's show.

Collins got passed a leaked memo from one station, with a list of advertisers who did not want any of its commercials playing in Air America programming. "It was a blacklist," Collins said. This combination of advertiser reticence, financial negligence, and a fairly tame and uninspiring product would eventually sink Air America, and by association the entire concept of liberal talk radio. At the time Collins had built a syndicated network, angling to fill up second stations in liberal bastions, behind Air America. "That was problematic, because Air America wasn't successful enough for anyone to say 'We want a second,'" Collins said. "After the bankruptcy, radio management had the evidence they needed to say liberal talk doesn't work, nobody cares."

Collins now runs a daily podcast, off the radio airwaves. Friedman's show appears on about thirty stations across the country, which to his disbelief makes him among the top five progressive talkers in the country. Meanwhile, dozens of conservative talkers acquire hundreds of affiliates practically out of the gate. The business model makes it impossible for smaller operations. Syndicated radio talkers are not paid by the stations where they air; instead, they get a portion of the commercial time. So you need to be big to be able to sell ads to a national audience. With thirty stations, Friedman has found that his ad time is relatively worthless; he's entirely funded through listener donations, and on some stations he's prohibited from asking for them. "I can say 'I want to thank you for donating to help me stay on the air,'" he said. The trickle of revenue makes him more of a subsistence farmer than a radio personality.

Clear Channel (which changed its name to IHeartMedia) filed for bankruptcy in 2018 to reduce the debt load its legacy private equity owners placed upon it. But it exited Chapter 11 with 849 radio stations nationwide. This could grow worse; the National Association of Broadcasters has proposed the elimination of the remaining, relatively weak media ownership rules. And if you think podcasting will restore balance and a marketplace of ideas, consolidation from Spotify and others has only just begun. Just ask bloggers—if you can find any left—how independent, free-form media works out.

Podcast technology aside, millions of Americans still flip on their radio and listen for hours every day. The reach of Sean Hannity on Fox News—an impressive 3.5 million viewers—is no match for his 14 million weekly radio listeners. That under-the-radar cultural force has a decided impact, Friedman believes. "These are our public airwaves, they are owned by the people," he said. "Good luck finding any voice that is not a right-wing, corporate-supporting voice. When people hear some crazy thing on Fox, that's one thing. But radio is an incredible medium—just you in the darkness, you in the car, listening to this voice telling you things. Everything that we have seen in this country at least for the past fifteen years has been supported by that. I see this as the monopoly that makes all other monopolies possible."

The news deserts created primarily by the dominance of Facebook and Google and by the crippling of the media business model have grave implications for democracy. A 2018 study of over 2,900 counties found that Donald Trump outperformed his Republican predecessor Mitt Romney in areas with the smallest number of news subscribers. It was enough of a boost to decide the election in tightly contested states. The *Washington Post* sometimes gets mocked for its slogan "Democracy Dies in Darkness," but it's undeniable that corruption spreads, conspiracies are fostered, and truth is obscured where journalism is absent.

The initial method of dealing with this will make everything worse: deputizing tech companies to separate truth from fiction. With advertisers and politicians at Facebook's and Google's throats, those companies have begun throwing broadcasters off their platforms and setting up "fact-check" services (frequently in partnership with conservative websites, which seems problematic) to prescreen news. In theory, these are private websites with their own terms of service, well within their rights to restrict membership. But in a world where Facebook and Google are the dominant newsstands of our time, enabling them to censor what information people receive is bound to cause trouble. Simply put, Mark Zuckerberg shouldn't decide what Americans get to hear and what speech gets distributed. When Facebook banned hundreds of small publishers it claimed to be "ad farms" that spammed users, several alleged that they were legitimate political activists being punished for the crime of being antiwar or for expressing dissent against the government. Conservatives have also complained of unfair treatment from the tech giants, and the work-the-refs debate of who's being suppressed more misses the point. The fact that Facebook and Google have arrogated so much power to themselves that access to their systems can have magnified effects is itself the problem.

The digital ecosystems these companies have built are too vast to moderate. Facebook reacted to Russian infiltration of political ads by blocking an ad for gay-themed send-ups of fairy tales while still allowing ad purchases purporting to be from ISIS. Google continues to wave through ads paid for in Russian rubles but shuts down innocuous article pages for advertising. Josh Marshall's Talking Points Memo explained how Facebook dropped ads from its site's news reports *about* Dylann Roof's 2015 mass shooting attack in Charleston, South Carolina, claiming those reports violated hate speech guidelines. The platforms are simply too big to make these calls in anything approaching an equitable fashion. No company should be empowered to act as a private government.

But this is the consequence of giving the keys to a free press to two private tech conglomerates. People value news and want to read more of it. But the companies who create the news aren't getting paid; they bear the costs of producing investigative and accountability journalism but enjoy little of the profits. "Google and Facebook are using our content and making it hard for us to survive," said Laura Bassett. "Journalism is in the midst of an existential crisis."

Mic is still alive, churning out articles on mostly inoffensive topics like family budgeting. It appears to be coming from nonunion writers, even though Mic unionized. That was probably the point of the mass layoffs, to rid Bustle of the need to keep union workers on staff. Many ex-Mic'ers landed on their feet. Jamie Pearson is still freelancing but also landed a full-time job outside the industry. There's a human cost to hiring scores of journalists, setting them on a mission to seek truth and expose injustice, and then just snuffing out that mission because a monopolist changed its mind. As entry-level jobs in journalism disappear, training for the next guardians of a free press grows uncertain.

Jamie admits that the experience at Mic sapped her enthusiasm for journalism. "The people hired were optimistic people who thought they could make a difference," she said. "We'll work the hours because our voices will get heard. I would hate watching new people get hired at the end. You might want to change the world, but you won't change shit."

I waited for a bus outside the Bank of America Plaza at Zuckerberg San Francisco General Hospital. Whenever the cars cleared I could see the boarded-up Victorian house directly across the street, the attic stuffed with old furniture and trash. I was on the way to the Richmond district, my old neighborhood on the western end of the city, wedged between Golden Gate Park and the Presidio.

I moved to San Francisco at the height of the first dot-com boom in the late 1990s. Even then, longtime residents would mourn how the city had fundamentally diverged from its bohemian past. The ex-hippies and Beats made a nostalgic fetish of the Summer of Love, but their wistfulness carried more than a kernel of truth. I remember walking out of my office once and seeing a Ferris wheel on the median strip; some company, fattened with VC money, decided to throw a launch party in the middle of the road.

That spirit died down after the stock market busted and 9/11 hit. But Big Tech would claw its way back to San Francisco, and subsume it. One out of every 11,600 residents here is a billionaire. The average home price is $1.6 million. There are few children and even fewer African Americans. On the other side of the divide, 45,000 gig workers prowl the streets of San Francisco for Uber and Lyft, over 8,000 residents are homeless, and five members of city government work full-time finding human shit to clean off streets and alleys.

The "San Francisco's not what it used to be" confessional narrative has almost become a cliché. And on the bus to the Richmond, a working-class, heavily Asian residential neighborhood, I was determined not to privilege my memories. The truth is, as I walked down Clement Street, the way I did practically every day when I lived there, a lot of it was exactly the same: the family-run Asian restaurants, the crazy fish and produce markets, the catch-all discount supply stores, the converted bank that hosts kung fu classes, the signature bookstore Green Apple Books, the signature ice cream shop Toy Boats. I could have told myself it was 1998 again.

Of course, there were also a few incongruous notes: the sushi place with the $135 omakase menu two doors down from my old apartment; the fancy dark-wood restaurant with a co-working space inside it; a menu headlined with the name of the executive chef. But more than that, there was just less of everything. The building that used to house Q, the funky breakfast place and avatar of gentrification during the first dot-com boom, whose large table in the back had a tree sticking out of it, has been empty for years. So has the *former location of Busvan for Bargains, where I picked up a lot of my furniture back in the late 1990s. The store windows now have nondescript art displays, but there's nothing else inside. Half of a city block near one of the produce stands is vacant.*

Life under monopoly in San Francisco is a life where everyone outside of the billionaire class has trouble making rent. It permeates the city's economy, its personality, its culture. There are company towns across America, but San Francisco's tech revolution came with stock options, and anybody without them is out of luck.

My friend Sean, who's lived in the city for nearly two decades, recalled a moment when every art gallery in the previously hardscrabble Mission District just went out of business. These days they survive as pop-ups, opening for only a few days at a time. Venerable and not-so-venerable spots close up without warning: it's a genuine challenge on some blocks to find something other than a bistro, luxury gift shop, or Google Home display showroom. Some small businesses have taken to asking customers for donations just so they can make rent. Others append surcharges to their bills to cover employee pay. The cost of living subsequently rises, pricing out the very workers supposed to benefit. Waitstaff, clerks, and hotel housekeepers, cogs of a commercial economy, cannot find housing inside the city limits. There's a mural in the Mission that lists the names of artists and community activists and the dates they were evicted. In the Hayes Valley neighborhood, now more upscale than I remembered it, I saw a mural with a quote from Coretta Scott King about the importance of community next to a notice for the filming of an internet commercial.

This is the curse of bigness in San Francisco, a city so teeming with money that nobody can afford to open a store to take it. There's an endless fight here about the need for more housing, which is acute. But the truth is that the San Francisco Bay Area is the nation's second-most dense, behind only New York City. Big money has created a vicious spiral: a winner-take-all city keeps accumulating vacant lots, dead-eyed commuters drive for hours to their barely affordable homes, landlords must keep rents astronomically high to cover their own astronomically high loans.

The concentration of extreme wealth isn't just bad for the losers in depressed counties and towns. It's bad for the winners.

CHAPTER 4

Monopolies Are Why Students Sit in Starbucks Parking Lots at Night to Do Their Homework

Dave Horowitz of Lenoir City, Tennessee, had started to sweat at the desk in his home office. He felt like he couldn't keep his head upright, like everything was happening in slow motion.

His wife, Carolyn, was busying herself in the kitchen, unaware of the nearby emergency. Fifteen minutes later, her phone began to vibrate. Dave, a diabetic, uses a wearable Bluetooth monitor that tracks his blood sugar level. Carolyn looked down at her phone. There was a gap in the data consistent with a drop in Wi-Fi connectivity. Once it came back online, the monitor showed Dave's blood sugar dipping below the level that would have alerted Carolyn. She grabbed a bar of chocolate and dashed into the home office, finding her groggy husband in time to revive him. But a few more minutes might have been too late.

"It was long enough for him to pass out and die," Carolyn told me. "People take for granted that a stable home Wi-Fi attached to a cable connection is there."

The threat of Dave's life-saving device going on the blink is something the Horowitzes have to live with in rural Tennessee. Their part of Lenoir City does not have broadband access. The couple makes do with two wireless hotspots and a sketchy satellite internet hookup. It's not reliable, a fact that in this case turned almost deadly.

The couple bought their house in 2015 with the promise of available broadband, which was necessary for both of their jobs. Dave works as a high-level IT professional for a media company and needs strong internet on a daily basis. Carolyn is a controller for thirteen manufacturing plants across the country, dealing with suppliers in India, South Africa, and Europe; she frequently teleconferences around the world.

The promises of broadband ended up being a mirage; no company has been willing to build out service to their sparsely populated area. So for years now, the Horowitzes and their neighbors have found themselves on the wrong side of the digital divide. "It makes me so mad," Carolyn said. "It's so infuriating to think that we have this entire segment of the population that's completely cut off, as digital have-nots."

About ninety miles down the road from Lenoir City, this persistent problem has been largely solved. A decade ago, Chattanooga, Tennessee, developed a way to offer publicly run, universal, affordably priced high-speed broadband. Originally labeled "The Gig" because of its one-gigabit-per-second (1 Gbps) upload and download speeds, today Chattanooga's network hits ten times that, delivering some of the fastest broadband speeds in the world. The Gig serves more than half of Chattanooga's homes and businesses, improving health and education services, spurring local entrepreneurship, boosting the economy, and pioneering a model for extending high-speed broadband to all Americans.

The Gig was so successful, in fact, that the nation's largest telecom companies reacted with a strategy to hem it in, the way doctors might formulate an antibiotic that prevents a disease from spreading. After all, the monopolistic telecom industry thrives on limiting choice; attacking public broadband was a natural fit. And that's why, when you travel just a few minutes outside the Chattanooga city limits, you find yourself in the same place as Dave and Carolyn Horowitz—a digital desert.

The Gig owes its existence to an earlier initiative to modernize rural America's critical infrastructure: the Tennessee Valley Authority (TVA). Designed under Franklin Roosevelt as an economic development engine for the rural South, the TVA supplied low-cost electric power to areas pummeled by the Great Depression and left behind even before that. In 1935, only about 10 percent of rural areas had access to electricity; twenty years later, that number was over 90 percent. Ten million Americans still get electricity from the TVA.

The initiative was a blessing to places like Chattanooga, a town of about 177,000 nestled beneath the Appalachian mountain chain and bisected by a sweeping bend of the Tennessee River. Halie Forstner was one of the TVA's first employees in Chattanooga, and at the age of 107 she told the local paper about getting electricity for the first time: "When you hadn't had anything and then you had electric stoves and electric heaters and other appliances—it just made so much difference. . . . Businesses grew from TVA and just the availability of electricity opened so many doors. And that prosperity spread out across the Valley."

Access to electricity bolstered Chattanooga, which had the railroad and river access to serve as a transportation and manufacturing hub. At one point it was known as the "Dynamo of Dixie." But the array of manufacturing plants in a town set into the hills took its toll; in 1969 Chattanooga was named the dirtiest city in America. Globalization finished things off, as jobs fled to Mexico and the Pacific and residents left to search for opportunity. By the end of the twentieth century, Chattanooga had the look of a postindustrial Rust Belt city, despite being located in the growing Southeast.

In the 1990s and early 2000s, local leaders plotted a renaissance, with the mission of making Chattanooga the best midsized city in America. Plans included restoring the riverfront, commissioning an arts district, and opening an aquarium with a pyramid-shaped glass roof. The TVA-run utility, known as the Electric Power Board (EPB), contributed to this rebirth with a proposal for an advanced smart grid that could reroute power supplies when part of the system experienced problems. Sensors would read meters every fifteen minutes, searching for trouble. The goal was to reduce outages by 50 percent, a not-inconsiderable benefit for a city in the heart of "Dixie Alley," which has a high frequency of tornadoes.

EPB decided to upgrade using fiber optics, strands of cable not much thicker than a human hair. Light moving across fiber-optic cables can be converted into electricity; EPB's team saw it as the most modern and durable solution. It wouldn't be cheap, but it did offer versatility. Fiber can also transmit virtually unlimited amounts of data, including voice or video or bits of information to load websites.

After experimenting with supplying telecommunications service to select commercial sites for a few years, EPB wrote a business plan in 2007 for a communitywide fiber network, using the same cable as the advanced smart grid. Like many telecom companies, the utility would offer a bundle of internet, TV, and phone service to every home it supplied with power. Over time, revenues from the bundle would help pay off the financing for installing the network. The city approved the "fiber to the home" concept and put up $219.8 million in bonds.

The idea alarmed Comcast, at the time the dominant internet provider in the region. It sued EPB in state court, alleging an illegal cross-subsidy of ratepayer funds to finance the venture. The judge didn't buy it—EPB had committed to repaying any funds with interest—and dismissed the case. But this would not be the industry's final salvo.

All litigation cleared by early 2009. "As it turned out, our timing was somewhat impeccable," said J.Ed Marston, EPB's bespectacled marketing guru. Rarely does anyone refer to the global financial crisis as "impeccable," but the federal stimulus response signed by President Obama that February earmarked money for shovel-ready infrastructure projects, including smart grid and broadband technology. "We were already digging the trenches for fiber," Marston said. Chattanooga got a $111 million stimulus grant to accelerate fiber deployment; a ten-year planned build-out of nine thousand miles of fiber could now be accomplished in two years.

The city launched The Gig in the fall of 2010, becoming the first city in the United States wired for gigabit internet, both upstream and downstream. As soon as the cables passed by a potential home or business customer, EPB would flip the switch. The $70 per month cost (discounted for residents in lower-income neighborhoods), with no data caps or traffic throttling, came in lower than any private-sector rival, whose speeds weren't nearly as fast.

"The initial reaction was real pride," said Andy Berke, at the time the state senator for the area; in 2013 he would become Chattanooga's mayor. "Being the first Gig city was something that we had not thought was possible for Chattanooga. We didn't think of ourselves as a tech city."

The takeup was immediate, and it got another boost five years later, when EPB ramped up to 10 Gbps service, more than five hundred times the national average internet connection speed. At the end of 2018, The Gig signed up its 100,000th customer. That's well over half of the 160,000 homes and businesses in the service area. Revenues from The Gig paid off the bonds twelve years earlier than expected, and produced spillover revenue that has allowed EPB to drop home utility rates. The cross-subsidy, in other words, went in the opposite direction than Comcast predicted. Electricity customers didn't finance The Gig; The Gig financed lower costs for electricity.

When the service launched, Chattanooga leaders reached out to big tech firms and venture capitalists, dangling reliable and superfast internet as a reason to relocate. But very little relocation actually took place. Instead, local residents realized that fast internet could allow them to bring their own ideas to life. The entrepreneurs formed a community, using The Gig to expand their imagination of what was possible. And the city capitalized on this fervor.

Accelerators began popping up to cater to these young entrepreneurs, like Gig Tank and the INCubator, the latter of which has graduated over 550 companies alone. "We tried to build the base to get the attention of larger firms, and then we realized that the base was the important part," said Mayor Berke, who created the city's innovation district, putting start-up companies and services within a five-minute walk of one another in downtown.

The "front door" of this district is the Edney Innovation Center, a reno-vated ten-story building that stands out among the old redbrick structures in Chattanooga's modest downtown. The first floor belongs to CO.LAB, a nonprofit accelerator that advises would-be startups. On my visit, opera-tions coordinator Erroll Wynn, an Atlanta native and former football player for the University of Tennessee–Chattanooga, showed me around. Wynn has launched two startups of his own.

"This is a 3-D printed shoe," he told me, pointing to a display case. The shoe looked pretty comfortable; recycled polymer plastic curved around in ribbons that appeared to be stitched on top of one another, with a small sole at the bottom. The company that created it, Feetz, customizes each pair. Customers upload their measurements through an app, the numbers get inputted into the printer, and the shoe components are extruded out in a matter of minutes. The manufacturing process uses no water and gener-ates no waste.

Everybody in this part of town seemed to be 3-D printing something; the files are so massive that fast broadband service is a necessity. A Gig Tank product, Branch Technology, which is the brainchild of Alabama archi-tect Platt Boyd, 3-D prints housing materials with plastic and carbon fiber, allowing for unique curves and shapes with radically smaller construction costs. "They are in the process of producing the first 3-D printed house, entirely," EPB's Marston said, beaming. Another 3-D printing concern, Collider, develops production-grade rubber, plastic, and even metal, which can be used to make gaskets, cell phone cases, custom valves, and more.

Other startups capitalized on Chattanooga's historical role in logistics, due to its easy access to rail lines and interstates and close proximity to Atlanta, Nashville, and Birmingham, Alabama. WorkHound rolled out as an anonymous feedback platform for truckers; FreightWaves is an analytics engine for logistics firms. International Maritime Security Associates, which designs risk management software for water-bound shipping companies, shifted operations from south Florida to Chattanooga, even though the city is nowhere near an ocean.

The Edney Innovation Center features a co-working space, a community classroom, corporate offices for CO.LAB graduates, and a group called the Enterprise Center that sort of connects everything together. The Edney has event space as well, hosting networking meetups, courses, and hack-a-thons. Chattanooga has also become a testing ground for scientific research. One study links autonomous automobiles together, allowing vehicles to effectively see around the car in front. Another test involves a miniature scanner that examines subterranean spaces before any infrastructure digging, to check for obstructions or needed repairs.

As local tech businesses grew successful, they began to fund successor startups, nurturing the community building up around The Gig. National organizations have taken notice: an e-sports-focused TenGIG Festival came to Chattanooga in 2017, as well as two successive Alexa Conferences in 2018 and 2019, for developers of Amazon's smart-speaker apps. It's not normal for a random midsized city in the Mid-South, thousands of miles from Silicon Valley, to harbor this kind of reputation. "The fiber served as a platform, a calling card, an asset that no one else could claim," said Marston.

Non-entrepreneurs benefited from The Gig as well. Subscribers can download full-length movies at home in less than a minute, and watch streaming video without glitches or interruptions. Super-fast internet can increase productivity for workers and help students learn. The Gig operates on the same fiber-optic network that's constantly metered to prevent outages. In 2018, *Consumer Reports* named EPB the top-rated internet service provider in the country for value, speed, and reliability.

The Gig has also spurred direct improvements for local residents. Mayor Berke credits it with bringing tech jobs to Chattanooga and lowering the city's unemployment rate. Landlords include gigabit-speed internet connections in monthly rents of new properties downtown. Telemedicine services have expanded access to doctors. At the Enterprise Center offices, Mary Stargel, one of the directors, fired up a video for me of one of its projects, where local high school biology students remotely control a superpowered microscope equipped with a 4K camera typically used on film productions. The microscope used to be located at the University of Southern California, but now it's stationed at the Chattanooga STEM (science, technology, engineering, and math) school, and linked to three other public schools in the county, including two in low-income areas. The setup enables high schoolers to study fine-grained images of microorganisms that previously were accessible only to graduate-level researchers; without The Gig, the remote networking simply wouldn't work. "We're using tech to improve the lives of Chattanoogans," said Stargel. "It's not just about creating unicorn startups; it's about tech as a lever to benefit the community."

Two other initiatives have broadened the benefits of The Gig across the socioeconomic spectrum in Chattanooga, where one-third of the population is African American, and 31 percent of them live in poverty, compared to 13 percent for the city's white residents. A program called Net Bridge enables a few thousand families, including anyone on free or reduced-price lunch, to get 100-megabit-per-second (100 Mbps) service in their homes for $26.99, well below the standard rate (state law prevents Chattanooga from giving broadband to residents for free). Another program, Tech Goes Home, teaches internet skills to the community. These two digital equity initiatives in Chattanooga attack an important divide: even if broadband is available, it's often not affordable to those who need it. But the digital divide separates Americans by geography as well as by race and class.

The Federal Communications Commission's 2019 broadband deployment report estimated that 26.4 percent of rural Americans remained unable to access high-speed internet. But their measurements are generous, relying often on self-reporting from the telecoms rather than discrete analysis of residential access. Gains in 2019 that the FCC touted were apparently due to a small internet provider named Barrier Free erroneously claiming that it wired up 62 million users in eight states overnight. Even without these self-reporting errors, under the FCC's standards, if one building in a census block has broadband, it incorrectly assumes that entire block to be wired. And merely claiming to offer broadband doesn't mean the speeds customers pay for are being delivered; the FCC stopped reporting results of speed tests ever since Ajit Pai became chair in January 2017. A Microsoft study from December 2018, using data from its hundreds of online apps and services, estimated that 162.8 million Americans do not use broadband internet speeds.

Lots of internet dead zones are in rural areas. For example, according to a 2016 study of Tennessee by two broadband consulting groups, only 2 percent of the state's urban residents lack access to 25 Mbps internet, while 34 percent of rural residents do.

The Horowitzes found this out the hard way. Like millions of Americans, they were refugees from the foreclosure crisis, losing their shirts on a home in central Florida purchased at the peak of the housing bubble in 2006. When Carolyn Horowitz's company took over a plant in the Knoxville area, they asked her to relocate. About twenty-five minutes from downtown Knoxville, they found a five-acre plot with an old farmhouse built in the 1870s, giving them room to raise their show dogs. "When you get away from the interstate, you get into the country really fast," Carolyn said. "We can have horses and chickens, people in my neighborhood shoot in the backyard. Everyone keeps to themselves."

With Carolyn and her husband, Dave, reliant on internet access for their careers, broadband availability was a top priority. They sought out fiber; it wasn't available to the home. They asked about cable DSL service; one carrier said that was possible, and they closed on the home on that belief. But when the technician came out to install, he couldn't get a tone on the copper wire. Carolyn called the carrier, all the way up to the office of the president, and got assurances that someone would come back and install it. But after she flew up to Lenoir City a second time—they were still living in Florida at the time—the technician again said he couldn't do it.

"I'm thinking, 'I just closed on a house. This is going to cost me a fortune,'" Carolyn said.

The couple managed to make a deal for two wireless hotspots and satellite internet. But it didn't give Dave enough reliability to perform his IT work. They found what Carolyn described as a combination dress shop and gun shop near the interstate, and they pay $500 a month to rent an office in the back of the store. Anytime Dave needs to work on a hard-core project, he trudges out to the dress and gun shop. Carolyn's office is about a half-hour drive away, in a mixed-use development in Knoxville, and her work requires her to head in at all hours. "I drive into the office at three in the morning to do Skype calls with India" in order to walk through PowerPoint slides, she said—something she can't do at home.

The satellite service offered 100 gigabytes of data a month for free, and the couple mainly used it for email and web browsing. In the summer of 2018, they went on vacation in Amsterdam. During a power outage or some transition—the Horowitzes aren't sure—Dave's computer disconnected from his employer's cloud network, connected to the satellite service, and started to upgrade itself, as it normally does in the background. Near the end of the vacation, Carolyn got a bill from the satellite service for $6,000. "We had used 7,000 gigabytes of data," she said. "We negotiated to take $1,000 off." After that debacle, the couple switched to an unlimited data plan, but they still see slowness on the line.

The reason Carolyn and Dave cannot simply buy the broadband service they want and can afford is simple: large telecom companies don't want to shoulder the expense of upgrading to high-speed service in areas with low population density. This resistance to infrastructure deployment was the original impetus for rural electrification projects and the Tennessee Valley Authority, and it persists to this day.

"The private sector has profit as its overriding objective," said Chattanooga mayor Andy Berke. "We didn't ask ourselves, 'Will it makes sense financially to put fiber in this neighborhood?' Ultimately you have to decide, is broadband a luxury or infrastructure? In the 1950s, Eisenhower built out the highway system, to connect people up, improve the quality of life, allow businesses to transport goods and services. That's like the internet today."

Six companies—cable providers Comcast and Charter, and former telephone companies AT&T, CenturyLink, Frontier, and Verizon—provide nearly all the broadband internet service in America, and anyone who has ever moved into a new house or apartment knows that it's never the case that all six are an option. The telecoms have carved up the country, giving the impression of many nationwide players while running a near-monopoly virtually everywhere. According to a comprehensive 2018 study of the telecom industry's broadband deployment, Comcast and Charter (a Nebraska-based investor named Warren Buffett owns 3 percent of the latter) are the only internet service providers for 68 million people in their networks.

Meanwhile, internet service providers like AT&T and Verizon have effectively stopped running fiber to homes. Rural America would be happy to have a monopoly provider at all. "The companies are doing much worse than we realized," said Christopher Mitchell of the Institute for Local Self-Reliance, which ran the study. "We did not see evidence that public policy encouraged AT&T and Verizon to invest in high-quality broadband. Co-ops have invested far more than the four biggest telecom companies."

Government has tried to sweeten the pot, with middling success. Despite $1.5 billion in federal subsidies for rural broadband since 2015 through the Connect America Fund, part of a collection of annual FCC subsidies for rural connectivity totaling at least $4.6 billion, there has been precious little expansion for rural residents. CenturyLink, one of the Connect America Fund recipients, has received half a billion dollars per year to wire 1.1 million homes and businesses, but the company only needs to promise that download speeds reach 10 Mbps, which doesn't even qualify as broadband service under the FCC's generous definition.

Even after President Trump's FCC reversed the Obama-era net neutrality order in 2017, which telecoms argued was freezing infrastructure investment, capital expenditures went down slightly the following year, with more reductions planned thereafter. The dominant broadband companies have proven that they will never spend the money in places where they face no real competition. And even where they do, they pick and choose deployment. "Cleveland is a good example," said Deb Socia, who in 2019 became the CEO of the Enterprise Center in Chattanooga. "AT&T upgraded the more affluent parts of the city and not the less affluent, even though the cost of service is not that different." Socia called it a digital form of redlining.

Monopoly telecoms—which include phone, cable, and internet services offered mainly by the same handful of companies—engage in plenty of old-fashioned price gouging. For example, prices for U.S. cellular phone service add $50 billion per year to the telecoms' bottom lines relative to what they charge in Europe, according to research from economists Mara Faccio and Luigi Zingales. One example is comically absurd: a Texas customer of Frontier Communications bought his own router, and Frontier still charged him a $10 per month "rental fee" on it. But beyond capturing rents and nudging up fees, monopoly also allows telecom and cable companies to continue their worst-in-class customer service programs while retaining subscriber bases. In a 2018 survey from the American Customer Satisfaction Index, cable and internet service providers (which most of the time are the same company) tied for last in customer satisfaction ratings.

Major cell phone providers AT&T, T-Mobile, and Sprint were found to have sold real-time customer location data to marketers and shady third-party data brokers; the news outlet Motherboard purchased the location data on one phone for just $300. This information, equivalent to installing a GPS device in someone's pocket, can pinpoint whereabouts to within a few meters. Hundreds of bounty hunters and bail-bond firms routinely purchased such data to track down their targets. Law enforcement has been found to use the information. Even stalkers and domestic violence abusers were able to obtain locations of their victims from the black market. Big Telecom pledged to stop selling location data in January 2019, but of course that doesn't mean they can't find willing buyers for all sorts of other data they collect. And if you don't like it, what exactly are you supposed to do, given the few available options for phone, internet, or cable service?

The antidote to all this is competition, which we know works in telecom. In 2017 the FCC declared that the wireless telephone sector in the United States was competitive for the first time since 2009, owing largely to the Justice Department blocking a proposed merger between T-Mobile and AT&T. With consolidation stymied, T-Mobile tried something novel: offering better service at a lower price. The ensuing flock of subscribers forced the rest of the industry to up its game by offering unlimited data plans. The virtuous circle was great for phone customers, as the companies were forced to bargain for their business and take a little less profit home.

Community broadband could serve that function throughout rural America. In fact, it happened in Chattanooga. Nine years after suing to block The Gig, Comcast returned to the area with gigabit fiber-to-the-home service, something it offers in very few other locations. Just years before, Comcast swore that no normal internet user needed speeds of 1 Gbps or more, only to roll it out themselves after EPB proved them wrong. Hilariously, Comcast claimed in an ad campaign that it was "introducing" gig-speed internet to Chattanooga, which it had to clarify later. And the service matched The Gig's $70-a-month price only if customers locked themselves into a three-year contract. But the point is that Comcast wouldn't have offered anything if The Gig hadn't stolen its customer base. A similar dynamic has played out in a handful of cities with Google Fiber, which led to incumbents trying to improve their services (yes, Google can foster competition in businesses they don't already dominate). In all of these cases, competition spurred telecom giants to provide higher-quality alternatives.

But a decade before The Gig rolled out, dominant telecoms had already made provisions to inhibit rivals.

The most prominent building in the skyline of Nashville, the state capital of Tennessee, has the letters "AT&T" emblazoned on it. It stands out like a Big Telecom bat signal, a monopolist keeping watch over the city. That hints at the long-standing political power of the telecoms in the Volunteer State.

In 1999, when rumblings about city-owned broadband service began to percolate, AT&T and other industry lobbyists got Tennessee to pass a law restricting any city that operated public internet networks from expanding beyond its electrical service area. For EPB, that meant that it couldn't extend its fiber network and deliver The Gig to outlying areas, where it was arguably needed the most. Amazingly, EPB could offer phone service over the same fiber-optic cables to anyone statewide, but not broadband.

Tennessee is not unusual in this regard. In fact, laws in twenty-five states either ban municipal broadband outright, place onerous regulations on it, or restrict it to a predetermined service area. Big Telecom started this movement in the days of the noisy, whirring modem: Texas banned community internet service back in 1995. Over the succeeding twenty-five years, millions of dollars have been spent harassing cities with lawsuits (it took Lafayette, Louisiana, three years to beat them back), lobbying cities and states to put shackles on community broadband, and showering politicians with campaign donations to cement these shackles in place. "It's insane that, in 2019, states are still trying to limit investment in better networks," said the Institute for Local Self-Reliance's Christopher Mitchell.

In the Trump era, Big Telecom has also enlisted federal regulators to their cause. In 2017, the FCC eliminated price caps for business broadband services under a new standard, which defines local markets with even one broadband provider as competitive. And in an October 2018 speech, Republican FCC commissioner Michael O'Rielly directly intervened in the debate. He called community broadband an "ominous threat to the First Amendment in the age of the internet," insinuating that Chattanooga enforces "speech codes" that prohibit users from posting certain types of content. This was based on a telecom-industry-funded study that invented the charge out of thin air.

Mayor Berke was at pains to explain to me the telecom industry's vendetta against community broadband. "They say it's not the place of government, this is for the private sector," he mused. But it's not like Comcast or AT&T or CenturyLink want to restrict the spread of community broadband so they can link up the nation with high-speed internet instead. They resist upgrades wherever they have a virtual monopoly. It seems more like the industry just doesn't want any threat out there, so politicians don't get the bright idea that their communities can have nice things.

There are nine publicly owned fiber communities across Tennessee, and many, including Chattanooga, have longed to expand service in some form. For years, lawmakers from both parties have sought to reverse the limitations embedded in state law, most notably in 2014, under the leadership of Janice Bowling, a Republican from Tullahoma. AT&T's lead lobbyist threatened to sue the state, and support for the measure evaporated. A second effort in 2016 went nowhere. AT&T lobbyists warned that cities using debt to deploy broadband gives them an unfair advantage over private-sector companies, as if a behemoth like AT&T has no access to capital and no resources gained through, well, their unfair advantage of monopolizing an entire industry.

Mayor Berke kept hearing from neighboring counties just outside the city limits, where residents were subsisting on dial-up and paying hundreds of dollars a month for the privilege. Even in some of the most conservative areas of the state, these communities were desperate for The Gig and appealing to Berke, a Democrat. "We're aligned on this issue, because it's not theoretical, it's practical," he said. "People down the street have a ten-gig connection and we don't."

Stuck at the state level, Chattanooga decided to go national. Berke traveled to Washington to meet with Tom Wheeler, the chairman of the FCC at the time. Wheeler had previously lobbied for the National Cable and Telecommunications Association and the Cellular Telecommunications and Internet Association, the principal trade groups for the broadband industry. But he was nevertheless receptive to the plight of those living tantalizingly out of reach of broadband. Universal high-speed internet access is part of the FCC's mission under the Telecommunications Act of 1996, which instructed the agency to "remove barriers" to deploying broadband "to all Americans in a reasonable and timely fashion."

So Wheeler encouraged Berke to petition the agency to preempt state law. Chattanooga did so, asking the FCC to give the city the ability to expand The Gig beyond its service area. In the meantime, Wheeler gave a speech in Washington that September decrying the sorry state of broadband deployment. "Three-quarters of American homes have no competitive choice for the essential infrastructure for 21st century economics and democracy," he said.

Five months later, in February 2015, Wheeler's FCC struck down the state laws barring community broadband expansion in Tennessee and North Carolina, on a party-line vote. It was a moment of promise for the concept of a public option, wiring parts of the country where telecoms feared to tread. No community would be left behind, just as none was when the U.S. Postal Service obligated itself to universal service at the founding of the country, or when the TVA and other projects ensured universal access to electricity.

The telecoms couldn't stand it. So a month later, they got the state of Tennessee to sue the FCC over the preemption order, in effect demanding that the FCC not permit the state's own residents to obtain better internet service. "The FCC has unlawfully inserted itself between the state of Tennessee and the state's own political subdivisions," read part of the short appeal, which called the FCC's action in excess of the commission's authority contrary to the U.S. Constitution, and in violation of the law. In other words, Tennessee rhetorically threw everything it had at the FCC's order. And some of it stuck. The case went before the Sixth Circuit Court of Appeals, which in August 2016 reversed the FCC's preemption order. While agreeing that broadband expansion served the public good, the three-judge panel decided the language in the Telecommunications Act did not bestow a "clear statement" of authority for the FCC to act. A few weeks later, Wheeler declined to appeal the court ruling. States' rights had won out, ironically preventing cities from doing what they wanted.

The defeat struck rural Americans hard, in the Chattanooga area and around the country. Some rural residents can't even reliably receive incoming phone calls, and now they would have to survive on whatever miserable internet speeds telecom companies deigned to offer them. That has a demonstrable economic as well as social impact. Lack of broadband correlates with lower median incomes and higher inequality, which makes sense if you think about how important internet access has become to the modern economy.

J. Ed Marston, of EPB, cited several stories he heard in communities living without reliable broadband. "I talked to one woman, she had a customer service job, and the company transitioned from a call center to working at home," he said. "She wasn't able to get adequate connectivity and she lost her job." Christopher Mitchell related a number of complaints from parents. "I talked to a family in Minnesota, they farm, fifth generation on the same land. They told me they were worried they would have to leave that farm because they were actively harming their children without access to broadband. I'm a small-*c* conservative—the idea of a family moving because they lack broadband is devastating."

FCC commissioner Jessica Rosenworcel estimated in 2015 that 70 percent of teachers assign tasks to their students that require internet access for either researching material or accessing study tools and instructional videos. Many teachers demand that students turn in homework to a cloud-based dropbox every night. Children with no broadband at home—one in six, according to the Pew Research Center—fall into the "homework gap," as Rosenworcel called it.

If kids need the internet to complete their homework, they hit up libraries or stay after school in the computer lab. They do research on their phones in the one corner of the house with a decent signal. They drive with their parents for miles, night after night, to a Starbucks or McDonald's parking lot, piggybacking off the Wi-Fi, rushing to finish everything before closing, when the signal gets shut off. Sometimes kids get kicked out of the parking lot for "stealing" Wi-Fi, or are forced to go in and buy something to use the internet.

And it's not only children in those parking lots. "We go to Starbucks to use internet service," Carolyn Horowitz told me. "We have people with no cell phone service trying to run a business." These journeys for a reliable hotspot have become a fact of life in rural America, and lack of access creates not only hassle but also danger. During significant flooding in Carolyn's area in spring 2019, she worried about the public safety implications of spotty connectivity. "Wireless hotspots are not workable solutions during bad weather," she said. "Without landlines and wired internet, how do you call for help?" That fear travels both ways, as many rural governments and hospitals run off the same copper telephone wires as their residents. Delivering messages to constituents or transmitting medical records over the internet can be a chore even in good weather.

The frustration grows even more acute for Carolyn whenever she looks outside her window. The Lenoir City utility board, also a TVA affiliate, has been exploring running fiber across their service area for two years, and they've already done so for commercial customers. "I'm in the line of sight of it, I can see the box from my house," she despaired. "People are literally across the street from each other, my neighbor gets 3-gigabit ASDL, and I have no tone. It makes me want to break things. It's like not having water on your property."

After the flood, Carolyn and Dave began to talk about moving on from their old farmhouse. The damages included a partially collapsed foundation. The couple had already sunk money into home upgrades after purchasing it in 2015; more fixes would cost tens of thousands of dollars. But the catch-22 is that without high-speed internet access, a house's resale value dips. Carolyn's seen it when flipping through the real estate listings: houses with fiber get bid up, and ones without are avoided.

"I'm paralyzed about whether to put more money into it," she said. "But what happens if we try to sell it? Will we end up taking another hit?" The situation reminded Carolyn of the nightmare she endured in Florida during the Great Recession. As her home value plummeted 75 percent within five years of purchase, she and her husband found themselves trapped, unable to sell and unable to extract their home equity. The anxiety and uncertainty came rushing back, all because of a slow internet connection. "It's exactly the same feeling," Carolyn said.

But she didn't want any pity. "Dave and I are very well off. We can absorb that. But I have neighbors who aren't."

Despite numerous barriers, community broadband has flourished: over 750 cities and towns have some form of it. But with state restrictions in place, supporters must wage the fight one community at a time. Fortunately for them, the public is on their side. In Fort Collins, Colorado, a state telecom trade lobby whose members include Comcast spent almost $1 million to stop a ballot measure to establish a city-owned broadband service; though citizen supporters contributed just $15,000, they won with 57 percent of the vote. Comcast offered to hook up nearly all of the 1,300 residents of Charlemont, Massachusetts, with high-speed cable internet if the city kicked in $462,123 toward the installation cost, but the town's voters rejected the offer, instead opting to build a publicly owned gigabit fiber network, which will cost $1 million more but maintain community control.

Local officials know this is a slog that puts them in open combat with a powerful industry, something no ambitious politician desires. The relentless pushback creates its own barrier, even if community broadband sometimes wins. "The first few years we had tons of people come in and look at our system," said Chattanooga mayor Andy Berke. "The overwhelming response was, this is awesome, but I don't see how we get it done. Politically, legally, I don't see a way for us to do it." Just the time it takes to fend off lawsuits and lobbying and statewide preemption makes it arduous for municipal governments to think about. As Berke concluded, "You really have to want it."

In addition, to get community broadband accomplished, in many cases local electric companies have to buy into the concept, and not all of those are publicly owned. Three-quarters of Americans get their power from investor-owned behemoths like Duke Energy, Exelon, Pacific Gas & Electric, and Edison, which have been disinclined to distribute telecommunications services. This has produced the notable dynamic of one concentrated industry protecting another. "If you're in Tennessee with municipal electric, there's a path to broadband that requires a fight," said Chris Mitchell. "Without a muni electric, you just can't do it."

In Tennessee, the final indignity came in 2017, when the state legislature committed $45 million in grants to the telecoms to subsidize the buildout of fiber-optic broadband in rural areas. Utilities like EPB could have expanded at no charge to the state, but lawmakers opted to shower the telecoms with cash instead. The companies would not even have to guarantee fast speeds in order to qualify for the grants—it could be as low as 10 Mbps per second, 99.9 percent slower than Chattanooga's 10 Gbps service. Local cooperatives did snag some of the grants, but most of the unnecessary subsidy went to large, highly profitable companies.

Telecom giants have claimed that new 5G wireless networks that run on radio waves will transform high-speed internet access in America and make broadband deployment irrelevant. President Trump even announced a $20 billion grant program in 2019 to bring 5G to rural America. But here's the thing about 5G wireless: *it still needs wires*. Fiber-optic wires, in fact, which serve as a backbone to the system. So while it costs less than fiber to the home, the telecom industry's objections to building out capacity in low-density areas still apply to 5G. Plus, even with that fiber backbone, 5G is worse than wired internet in bad weather, or just because of obstacles in the physical terrain, which is bad news for folks in the forests and mountains of Tennessee. "You don't even need trees; one tree can be a barrier," Mitchell said. The smaller antennae that deliver 5G also have limited range. This is fine in populous cities like San Jose, which are using streetlight poles to house Wi-Fi transmitters for free public use. But in the expanse of rural America, you would need many more of them for true universal coverage, raising costs relative to urban deployment. Indeed, most 5G build-out to date is happening in large cities.

"We're a long way off from building out 5G to everybody's home," said J.Ed Marston. AT&T sort of admitted this in February 2019 by promoting its new 5G Evolution service—even slapping a "5G E" icon on its phones—when it was actually just a slightly upgraded version of the old 4G network. When analyst OpenSignal ran a speed test against Verizon and T-Mobile's 4G versions, it found that AT&T's 5G E was actually slower. More and more, 5G is coming to look like a bluff, a way to scare communities into thinking they'll waste money by investing in fiber. But waiting for private industry to ride to the rescue and connect the country has proven a fantasy since the earliest beginnings of the internet.

Somewhat protected from the scourge of community broadband, Big Telecom is swelling up. Sprint and T-Mobile, the third- and fourth-largest cell phone companies, merged to consolidate the sector further. They had to divest some assets to Dish Network to maintain a fourth carrier, but that just created a weaker version of Sprint. State attorneys general have sued to block the deal.

AT&T's $85.4 billion purchase of Time Warner brought together one of America's largest telecom companies with a suite of valuable program-ming to distribute on its networks. Though sold as a consumer-friendly team-up, the new AT&T wasted no time raising prices for its services and blacking out its channels on competitors. AT&T's stated goal was to com-pete with tech platforms in a war for your attention by using personal data to dominate advertising on internet-connected televisions, mobile phones, wired devices, and its own streaming video services. The AT&T play was itself a bid to keep up with Comcast, which purchased NBCUniversal and is now implementing the same array of full-spectrum ad barrages. It's nothing less than a surveillance tax on every man, woman, and child, an endless repetition of using your every waking thought to bombard you with corporate pitches.

None of this helps people like Carolyn Horowitz connect to the internet. Rural Americans have become collateral damage in a war for control of the broadband wires. Carolyn and some of her neighbors have formed a community group, called Citizens Underserved by Technology, to fight for better outcomes. They've even met with Tennessee's lieutenant governor. But she's skeptical that it will ultimately do much good.

"You've got people in rural areas screwed over left and right by corporate socialism," said Carolyn, who describes herself as a libertarian. "My degree is in economics. As Adam Smith pointed out, inequality is a really big problem. It causes revolution."

When delegates to the United Nations–affiliated World Health Assembly gathered in Geneva, Switzerland, in the spring of 2018, they didn't expect to be openly threatened. The Ecuadorian delegation had planned to introduce and swiftly pass an innocuous resolution supporting breastfeeding as the healthiest option for nourishing infants, which governments around the world should "protect, promote, and support." The international community had long encouraged breastfeeding, based on the latest science. It was the equivalent of a resolution in Congress naming a post office or supporting the American flag.

But then the U.S. delegation got involved.

It wanted "protect, promote, and support" removed, along with killing a section urging limitations on marketing alternative products that potentially harmed children. The United States warned Ecuador that it would face trade sanctions and withdrawal of military aid if it introduced the pro-breastfeeding resolution at all. A feel-good UN statement without practical impact wasn't worth the trouble, so Ecuador dropped out. So did a dozen other countries, fearing retaliation. Finally the Russian delegation took over, and even then deliberations on the measure took two days. The resolution passed, but not before the United States killed the language committing the World Health Organization to assisting countries with improving infant nutrition, among other tweaks.

You can assume that the U.S. delegation didn't wake up one morning and decide to blackmail the world over a meaningless UN resolution for sport. The delegates were operating on behalf of the $70 billion, deeply concentrated global baby formula industry, which seeks to eliminate any threat to its marketing machine. Two companies, Abbott Laboratories (Similac) and Reckitt Benckiser (Enfamil), control around 70 percent of the global baby formula sector, with Nestlé picking up another 10 percent. Reckitt Benckiser is a British household goods manufacturer best known for Lysol cleaners; it bought Mead Johnson, maker of Enfamil, in 2017. In the United States, the three companies control around 95 percent of the market.

Baby formula consists of little more than dehydrated cow's milk and vitamins (and lots of sugar), yet it somehow costs $150 a month to feed it to an American baby. Formula manufacturers ran a price-fixing ring in the 1990s, and baby formula prices remain elevated enough today that there's a rather incredible black market, with thieves ripping off stores and warehouses, or gathering excess boxes from women on government programs, and illicitly selling the formula on Craigslist.

But the developed world, with its relative sophistication around breast-feeding, wasn't baby formula monopolists' main concern. They were more preoccupied with their lock on emerging markets, which dates back to the 1970s. According to a 1974 paper called "The Baby Killer," Nestlé, at the time a bigger player in formula, convinced young mothers in Africa, Latin America, and Asia that their product was a modern, safe, and indispensable option that improved child development. They played off dreams of the Western world's efficiency and progress to sell sugary milk when mother's milk would do far better. Hospitals in the Third World were given samples of formula to hook families. The success of this strategy has been credibly linked to millions of unnecessary malnutrition deaths, as poor women in developing countries couldn't afford the full cost of formula and diluted it with water to stretch the supply. Today, the British medical journal The Lancet estimates that 800,000 child deaths per year could be prevented if all mothers switched to breastfeeding.

A UN resolution declaring formula inferior to breastfeeding would carry some weight globally. The United States, home to the largest formula company, was all too happy to bully the world into preventing that outcome. The political power resulted directly from the industry's extreme and concentrated economic power. Such substitution of the interests of public health and security for the interests of a private monopolist is commonplace in international trade and diplomacy disputes. In geopolitics, the corporate wish list often sits at the top. And monopoly power serves to direct these initiatives, even at the expense of child nutrition and health, as in the baby formula case.

The New York Times, which broke the story of the chaotic negotiations, wouldn't say directly that the baby formula industry played a role. But we don't have to accept such a naive conclusion. After all, we aren't infants.

CHAPTER 5

Monopolies Are Why Teamsters Stormed a Podium to Tell One Another About Their Dead Friends and Relatives

Travis Bornstein first learned about it in the car. He was driving his eighteen-year-old son Tyler to an evening course at a local college near Uniontown, Ohio. Tyler was supposed to be in class already, but Travis had spied his car in a friend's driveway. "I went up and got him, went into town, and he was just out of it," Travis told me. His son was groggy, not really responding to questions, just staring blankly.

Travis decided to pull off onto the side of the road. "What's wrong with you?" he asked Tyler. His son turned to face him. "He said, 'Dad, I'm using heroin,'" Travis said. "I was the first person he told."

Despite the looks of things, Tyler wasn't high at that moment. He was in withdrawal from not getting a fix in a few days. It was a sickness, a slow chewing up of Tyler's body as it craved that next dose. To the observer it might look like a young person on drugs; actually, it was a young person in need of them.

Travis Bornstein couldn't process the information. Tyler was an athlete, adept at virtually any sport. He made two holes-in-one before the age of sixteen and become an all-county golfer. His senior year he switched sports and won the senior Iron Man award in football, which approaches a religion in this part of northeast Ohio. At Walsh University in Canton, Ohio, he walked onto the golf team and wound up with a scholarship. He decided he wanted to get into bodybuilding, and at the age of twenty-two became a runner-up Junior Mr. Ohio. "How's a kid like that get addicted to heroin?" Travis asked.

The seeds of the addiction were planted in high school. Through playing sports, Tyler broke his right arm four times and had two surgeries on his right elbow. The first came at age eleven and passed without incident. After the second, at age eighteen, Tyler's doctor prescribed him a painkiller. "I didn't know what an opiate was," Travis recalled. "The doctor didn't say 'You're getting an opiate,' none of that. I'm not a smart guy, but if the doctor said he was giving my son the equivalent of heroin, I might have said something."

For five years Tyler repeatedly got clean and then relapsed, moving from prescription opioids to heroin like hundreds of thousands of others. He never quite managed more than a year of sobriety. It would be six months on the wagon, then a setback, then back into treatment. All the while he excelled at golf and bodybuilding, compartmentalizing the addiction into a dark corner. The Bornstein family never shared their son's struggles with anyone, not even the closest of friends. Travis, an ex-Marine, was embarrassed about not being able to help his son out of the darkness.

Finally the Bornsteins moved Tyler to a sober living facility in Florida, attempting to free him from the temptations of home. It didn't work; Tyler relapsed down there, escaping to the streets and walking around homeless for five weeks. Travis and his wife, Shelly, found their son and brought him back to Uniontown. But this time the recovery lasted only a few months. In September 2014, Tyler relapsed while living with his girlfriend. He tried to get help at a state-funded facility but was put on a waiting list. Soon after, Tyler went with a friend to shoot up, and he overdosed. Instead of calling 911, the friend dumped him in a vacant lot in Akron and ran away. A resident found the body later that day. Tyler was twenty-three.

It's a sickeningly familiar story to countless families who have struggled through the worst drug epidemic in modern history. Someone dies at the hands of opioids every nineteen minutes in America, with a total of well over two hundred thousand deaths since the introduction of OxyContin, the first widely used prescription opioid painkiller, in 1996. The experience turned Travis Bornstein and his family into activists, working to help others and hold accountable those who contributed to his son's death in that field. It took him to his union, the Teamsters, where to his surprise he found many of his brothers and sisters in similar pain, confused and embarrassed but ready to fight. But to determine what to do about it, Travis and his colleagues had to understand the entire transaction, scrutinizing every corporate entity responsible for getting opioids into a patient's hands.

Monopolies at every stage of the supply chain placed their bottom lines ahead of the health of the recipients of those drugs. They manufactured and marketed addictive substances that cut a trail of death through society. They looked the other way as millions of pills were shipped into small towns, ripping them apart. They sold accessories for self-destruction, knew what they were selling, and kept doing it. Opioid companies and their enablers "created the epidemic and profited from it through a web of illegal deceit," reads a complaint from the Massachusetts attorney general in 2019. "A small group of executives led the deception and pocketed millions of dollars."

That's what our entire pharmaceutical system looks like today. It finds weak points in the system, islands of dependency, and milks patients for maximum value. It uses patients as props to sell products, and ruins the careers of doctors who have alternative treatment ideas. It takes a cut at the expense of independent pharmacies, putting what is for many communities the only manifestation of the health care system out of business.

It didn't have to evolve that way. Public money creates life-altering medications for society's benefit. No irreversible forces get you from there to a concentrated industry with one of the highest profit margins in global business. And we don't have to endure concentrated shippers, concentrated distributors, and concentrated middlemen in between. These are policy choices. And they have resulted in millions of families like Travis Bornstein's, scarred and angry and damaged for life.

The pharmaceutical industry is a special type of monopoly, one granted specifically by the government. While there are dozens of drug companies, each one gets exclusive access to a particular micromarket by patenting treatments for specific ailments or illnesses. Often only one drug treats a disease, and the peculiarities of drug reimbursement, where health plans can choose to cover just a single drug treatment, furthers the monopoly.

Industrialized countries around the world place significant price controls on prescription drugs, a function of single-payer systems that buy in bulk and a general belief in access to affordable medications. The United States is the exception. Allegedly to spur innovation, we grant private companies exclusive patent rights to prescription drugs for twenty years, with no restrictions on what they can charge. With the glaring exception of the Veterans Administration, all negotiations on price are carried out in private. Even Medicare is barred from direct bargaining for lower drug prices, thanks to a 2003 law that explicitly authorized private-sector middlemen to handle negotiations. Other countries provide patent protection, but the combination of monopoly without price controls creates the uniquely American situation.

If you're a drug company that wants to save lives—who am I kidding, if you're a drug company that wants to enjoy profit margins that are two to five times as large as those found in the rest of the Fortune 500 (pharmaceuticals are the most profitable sector in the U.S. economy), you take advantage of the system. You offload research and development spending onto the National Institutes of Health and other publicly funded scientific enterprises while collecting enormous publicly funded tax breaks for your own R&D. Every one of the 210 new medicines approved by the Food and Drug Administration (FDA) between 2010 and 2016 had its origins in government research, and drug companies can access that basic science and apply it to their drug development. You will hope for that to continue. You further lower your tax burden by moving your patents into tax havens, or merging with a foreign company to put your on-paper headquarters in a low-tax site overseas. Then when your wonder drug is approved, you can start marketing it by bribing doctors and hospitals, or even patients.

Dawn Neiderhauser's daughter Jordan was born with a rare metabolic disorder; her body cannot break down fatty acids into glucose, and the buildup can cause heart and liver problems. Her version of the disease, known commonly as VLCAD (very-long-chain acyl-CoA dehydrogenase deficiency, if you must know), can be managed decently with diet and vitamins and by avoiding overexertion. That was the assessment of Dr. Richard Kelley, who diagnosed Jordan during his twenty-five-year stint at the Johns Hopkins University School of Medicine. Kelley based his diagnoses of VLCAD and related disorders on the level of defects in the gene and the underlying enzyme activity in the patient. "Doctors learn to treat from reading a cookbook without really understanding metabolism," said Dr. Kelley. "I was trained in a different era. It allowed me to see aspects of these diseases other people weren't seeing."

Drug companies aren't interested in doctors calling for different treatments depending on the patient. And they're certainly not interested in doctors prescribing vitamins when pharmaceuticals could be used. A company can try to persuade the doctor to dispense its product, or persuade the patient to demand it.

Dawn told me about a national family support group for fatty acid disorders that issued newsletters twice annually. The newsletters can still be found online. The support group had a corporate sponsor named Sigma-Tau Pharmaceuticals. Newsletters featured numerous references to Ken Mehrling, Sigma-Tau's director of marketing and sales; one from December 1991 thanks Mehrling and Sigma-Tau "for offering to cover all the expenses for this newsletter."

Sigma-Tau made an enzyme supplement called Carnitor, which Dr. Charles Roe, a preeminent researcher in the field, pioneered as a treatment for mitigating hypoglycemia when patients with fatty acid disorders fell ill. Dr. Roe happened to treat the child of Deb and Dan Gould, the founders of the support group. He was listed in the newsletters as a "medical advisor," and his curriculum vitae from his most recent job at Baylor University lists two consultancies with Sigma-Tau, one of them unpaid. "They funded a lot of his research," said Dr. Kelley.

Soon Carnitor became the standard treatment for all patients with VLCAD disorders. "People are easily swayed by constant exposure to something," said Dr. Kelley. "Every meeting has Sigma-Tau sponsoring all this research. Everyone jumps on board." Dr. Kelley even prescribed Carnitor for Jordan Neiderhauser briefly, but she developed leg muscle pain. He took her off the drug, and the leg pain went away. When Dawn informed other parents about her daughter's experience with Carnitor, they lashed out. Dr. Roe in particular defended its continued use. "I kind of became a problem in the support group," Dawn said. "It became this battle." Only later did she put together all the financial interests attempting to convince patients to use a potentially harmful drug.

An even stranger development happened years later. When the internet grew in prominence, the support group morphed into a website and finally a Facebook group. There, Dawn learned about new clinical trials for a drug called triheptanoin, or C7 oil. Several VLCAD families put their children in the trials and were touting the drug to the support group. Ultragenyx, a large drug company, held the patent; it had not yet obtained FDA approval.

In spring 2016, a fellow support group mom asked Dawn to join what was called a "focus group" for families of disorder sufferers. It would take place during an all-expenses-paid two-day retreat at a high-class resort in Scottsdale, Arizona. The mom presented herself as a "patient ambassador" working for a group called Snow Companies, really a PR firm that works for dozens of pharmaceutical manufacturers, including Ultragenyx. Snow recruits and trains patient ambassadors to advocate for widespread adoption of their clients' drugs. This is quite common: some drug companies hire Instagram influencers to hawk their products.

Dawn called Dr. Kelley and told him about triheptanoin and the focus group. "There are cases where triheptanoin improves the patient," Dr. Kelley told me. "Some tolerate it and some can't, and it causes problems. One child in France was given it and nearly died." Again, companies like Ultragenyx didn't want to hear about how their drug may not be right for everyone. The economics of so-called orphan drugs, which are intended to treat diseases that affect very few people, demands a universal embrace of one treatment to justify the R&D expense.

Dawn decided to attend the focus group. "It was a small group—we could fit into a conference room," she said. Representatives from Snow Companies and Ultragenyx were on hand, along with a medical expert from Boston Children's Hospital who was employed directly by Ultragenyx. Dr. Kelley had joined Boston Children's a year earlier, and so when Dawn greeted the expert, "I said, 'Do you know Dr. Kelley?' And she got a stone-cold look on her face."

After an opening-night dinner, participants sat through a daylong session where they were asked to tell their family's stories of living with the disorder. Dawn got emotional, even crying when she discussed Jordan's illness. In the first half of the day, Ultragenyx never got mentioned. By the second half, Dawn got the sense she was in an infomercial for triheptanoin, with presentations from the doctors who ran the clinical trials. It was presented as a miracle drug that would improve cardiac function in patients. But what if the patients didn't have abnormal cardiac function to begin with?

"I blew my cover the last night, [when] I was sitting next to someone from Snow," Dawn said. "I said to her that this was fodder for the marketing department. I relived those six days in the hospital when they didn't know what Jordan had. I said, 'You're using that pain to sell drugs.' She said, 'No, we want to understand the patient's experience.' But they have nothing to do with the patient. They are hired by the drug company to get people loyal to it."

As for Dr. Kelley, he was gradually edged out at Boston Children's. After he was hired, an associate chief of his department told him he couldn't see patients; the administrator didn't want him filling the beds. As he became more outspoken about the need to modify treatments for metabolic disorders based on the individual patient's profile, he became more alienated from the profession. "There's a lack of interest among doctors of finding out about this," he said. Dr. Kelley set up his own practice in Pennsylvania, mostly for managing existing patients. He wants to initiate research, but the drug companies have scooped up all the patients; doctors without a sponsor cannot compete. Ultragenyx is hopeful that its clinical trials will get them FDA approval for triheptanoin.

"I've had drug companies threaten me," Dr. Kelley said. "They've tried to buy me off. They will play hardball."

These tactics are part of a mad grab to earn monopoly profits as long as companies can hang on to the patent. Maximizing profits even goes into the most basic engineering. If you have glaucoma, the reason liquid from your eye drops constantly rolls down your cheeks is that companies deliberately make the drop larger than the human eye can hold. Every milliliter that falls out of your eye represents a tiny profit, and it adds up.

But even more brainpower and effort goes into ensuring that the patent clock does not run out after twenty years. "When you have government protection there are all these rents associated, so you try to extend it," said Dean Baker, an economist who focuses on government-granted monopolies. Evergreening—also known by the appalling corporate PR term "lifecycle management"—involves slightly changing the chemical makeup of a drug without improving the medication, to earn new patents and restart the exclusivity period. The 1968 National Institutes of Health patent program paved the way for this abuse, which is widespread. Celgene has twenty-seven patents for its multiple myeloma drug Revlimid; one patent refers to the coating on the pill. Another company, Allergan, even tried to sell some of its patents to a Native American tribe so that it could claim sovereign immunity from patent laws. That scheme proved unsuccessful, but if you layer the patents right, you can extend exclusivity for decades. Patents also drive health decisions; in 2015 Pfizer researchers discovered that its rheumatoid arthritis drug Enbrel showed promising results for treating Alzheimer's, but it never made the research public and declined a clinical trial because Enbrel was about to fall off patent.

The government requires that manufacturers of drugs that are considered potentially dangerous develop a Risk Evaluation and Mitigation Strategy (REMS) for each of those drugs. Generic manufacturers seeking to compete with an established drug have to use that same protocol, forcing them to negotiate with a monopolist that can just refuse to allow them in. Generic drug companies also need access to samples of patented drugs so they can run comparison tests; monopolists routinely restrict this access, making it impossible for a generic to prove equivalency and complete a clinical trial. Monopolists also engineer "citizen" petitions urging the FDA to delay approval of generic drugs. And when generics do eventually get approved for use, manufacturers of the patented drugs bribe hospitals with rebates to keep prescribing their drugs in preference to cheaper alternatives.

And then there's pay-for-delay, a process whereby a monopolist simply bribes a would-be competitor to stay out of the market. It's corruption in its purest form, and patients bear the cost, paying billions of dollars for the name-brand drug instead of what would otherwise be lower drug prices. Though the price-fixing is so obvious that even the Federal Trade Commission has strongly condemned it, the practice continues. As Dean Baker put it, "They're attempting to innovate around the protection."

Schemes to acquire and hold patents can result in a situation like that of insulin, a one-hundred-year-old diabetes drug whose patent was sold in the 1920s for $1 to promote affordable access to all sufferers, but which pharmaceutical companies eventually co-opted by promising to expand supplies. When we had worthwhile antitrust enforcement in America, regulators kept insulin producers honest by imposing fines for anticompetitive behavior. In the absence of enforcement, insulin manufacturers in the 1980s began to alter the drug repeatedly to keep it on patent. Sanofi, one of three major producers, has an insulin called Lantus with seventy-four patent applications that could extend its monopoly by thirty-seven years. Insulin has risen from $25 a vial in 1996 to $275 today; the wholesale price has tripled in the past decade. As a biologic drug made from human genetic material, insulin enjoys additional patent protections, and biosimilars are complicated to produce, slowing generic entry. When generics attempt to enter the market, companies like Sanofi sue them for patent infringement.

In human terms, this is a tragedy for 30 million diabetes patients in the United States, many of whom cannot afford price spikes. One in four patients report that they've rationed their own insulin because of the cost. Proper insulin doses are critical, and reducing intake can lead to death by ketoacidosis. In 2017 Alec Raeshawn Smith was found dead in his apartment, which was littered with empty insulin vials that had been tampered with in order to extract every last drop; he had not been able to afford to refill his prescription.

Over the years we've seen insulin-style price gouging replicated through-out the pharmaceutical sector. Gilead Sciences set the price for its hepatitis C drug Sovaldi at $84,000 for a full treatment. The company's CEO considered it "a very good value," with the only problem being that hundreds of thousands of patients needed Sovaldi and couldn't afford it. Out-of-pocket costs for drugs used to treat multiple sclerosis patients jumped twenty-fold in twelve years. Novartis released a drug in May 2019 to treat a muscle-wasting disease; with a list price of $2.125 million, it is the most expensive drug in history. Even as both political parties condemned the high cost of prescription drugs and advanced all sorts of policy proposals to fix it, pharma companies raised prices on 3,400 drugs in the first half of 2019, with an average increase of five times the rate of inflation.

The price of the EpiPen, which provides quick-acting emergency treatment for allergies, jumped 450 percent in seven years, despite no changes in the formula. Two vials of the proper dosage of epinephrine and manual syringes would cost only $20, and some put the cost of the dosage in each EpiPen at as little as $1; in 2016, a two-pack cost $608. Heather Bresch, the CEO of EpiPen manufacturer Mylan, is the daughter of U.S. senator Joe Manchin; the price increases coincide with Mylan purchasing the rights to EpiPen and Bresch taking over the company. Mylan controls 87 percent of the U.S. market for the drug. When a rival, Auvi-Q, reached the United States, Mylan paid out rebates to health plans and middlemen under the condition that Mylan would get exclusive reimbursement rights, knocking Auvi-Q out.

Valeant, a darling of Wall Street and hedge funds for years, used its control over orphan drugs to implement price increases for those drugs that averaged 66 percent annually. Companies get enormous tax breaks for creating orphan drugs, but Valeant's strategy was to piggyback off other companies' R&D through relentless debt-fueled acquisitions of already-developed medications, thereafter hiking the prices. Valeant also had a secret specialty pharmacy known as Philidor, which changed patient prescriptions to Valeant products instead of generics. Employees of Valeant quietly worked at Philidor under aliases like Peter Parker, the alter ego of Spider-Man.

Notorious "pharma bro" Martin Shkreli of Turing Pharmaceuticals also had an acquisition-to-spike strategy, purchasing a drug called Daraprim, which treats a parasitic infection, and raising the price from $13.50 per tablet to $750 overnight. Shkreli, brash and pompous, eventually went to jail for an unrelated securities fraud; there are some offenders even our system cannot wave through. But he served as a convenient target for public anger about drug prices, while companies guilty of similar abuses safely slotted in behind him, free from personal scorn. Corporate giant AbbVie, in a meeting with an investment bank in 2017, declared that the "the intensity of the drug pricing debates and political risks is waning," due to Trump administration inattention and political gridlock. The release of pressure that resulted from Shkreli's comeuppance likely played a role. (The fact that AbbVie obtained hundreds of patents and struck pay-for-delay deals on their signature drug, Humira, probably also put their minds at ease.)

By the way, the drug Shkreli bought, Daraprim, still cost $750 a pill as of 2019. EpiPen prices haven't dropped much either. Sticky pricing is a common feature with prescription drugs, all the more so when companies refuse to compete. A wide-ranging investigation in 2018 found that some of the biggest generic drug manufacturers in the world conspired to inflate prices of more than a hundred drugs, some by as much as 1,000 percent. According to the complaint, the companies agreed to a "fair share" deal where each would get to control pieces of certain markets. They called the market the "sandbox," and expected everyone to play nice within it.

Meanwhile, monopolist drugmakers have another strategy to reap all the profits from the system while bearing none of the costs: takeovers. In 2019 AbbVie, the company relieved at the lessening of demands to reform drug prices, bought Allergan, which attempted to sell patents to Native American tribes. The impetus for AbbVie was to scoop up patent-protected bestseller Botox, just as Humira fell off patent. Disgraced Sovaldi producer Gilead bought rival Kite Pharmaceuticals in 2017, also searching for blockbusters. Bristol-Myers Squibb paid $74 billion for Celgene, the company with that lucrative thicket of Revlimid patents. Pfizer combined its off-patent drug business with EpiPen maker Mylan. Drugmakers have consumer health divisions as well; GlaxoSmithKline and Pfizer just merged those operations to create the largest over-the-counter health product manufacturer in the world. Aquafresh, Flonase, Nicorette, Polident, Sensodyne, Tums, Advil, Caltrate, Centrum, ChapStick, Emergen-C, and Robitussin now all come from the same company.

An amazing study out of Yale, titled "Killer Acquisitions," puts another spin on the takeover strategy. It found an empirical basis for the theory that pharmaceutical companies buy competitors developing drugs that might one day compete with the acquiring companies' products. Once the acquirer buys the rival, the new innovations typically fade away. New drug projects are nearly twice as likely to fail to advance to a higher stage of development if they are acquired during the early phase. The researchers found at least forty-five killer acquisitions per year.

For example, Questcor Pharmaceuticals, which had a monopoly on certain hormone drugs, bought the rights to develop a competing drug, Synacthen, in 2013, and killed it. The Federal Trade Commission managed to fine Questcor $100 million over this, and forced the licensing of Synacthen to a competitor, West Therapeutic Development. However, since the license went through in July 2017, FDA approvals for the drug have not been completed. So Questcor has cemented its lucrative monopoly for seven years and counting, while paying a mere pittance for its anti-competitive practices. More recently, Roche purchased Spark Therapeutics, a gene therapy company. This was in part a way for Roche to pick up a valuable drug after development: Luxturna, a medication for blindness that costs $425,000 per eye. But Spark had also been testing a one-dose hemophilia A treatment that showed 97 percent success in reducing bleeding in patients. Roche already has one hemophilia A drug in its portfolio called Hemlibra, which requires a dosage every four weeks. What happens next is presumably clear: the one-dose drug, what some might call the cure, will get placed on a shelf, while the treatment Roche gets to collect on once a month thrives.

As ever, monopoly drugs create brittle supply chains. If you live in the United States, your EpiPen comes from a single Pfizer manufacturing facility in St. Louis; problems at the plant in 2018 created dangerous shortages. Supplies of an antianxiety medication called buspirone suddenly dried up in 2019, creating chaos for sufferers who need consistent dosages to maintain chemical balance. For buspirone and other generics, suppliers have driven prices so low that manufacturers exit the market. But shortages also create opportunities for price hikes that go well beyond the expected supply-and-demand curve, like a 1,107 percent increase in May 2018 for a

muscle relaxant called methocarbamol. Valsartan, a blood pressure medication that saw supply disruptions, went from $30 a bottle to $155.

And if everything just mentioned were all that was wrong with pharmaceutical monopolies, we'd be in pretty good shape.

After Tyler Bornstein died of a heroin overdose in 2014, his father, Travis,
was distraught. "You can't prepare to lose a child," he told me. "I felt like I
failed as a father." Travis kept the pain bottled up, despite knowing opioid
deaths were hitting epidemic levels; Tyler was the third young man to die
in the Uniontown area that year. All of them had sisters, and it took those
young women to lead the community out of silence.

The three siblings worked with a guidance counselor to tell their stories
publicly. "I was embarrassed that my daughter had more guts than her
dad," Travis said. He decided to emerge from the shell he'd constructed
around himself, discussing his experience at the local high school. The
family created a Facebook page, and it led them to found a nonprofit organization called Breaking Barriers: Hope Is Alive. It involves talks given
around the country, support groups, and a long-term goal of creating a
relapse prevention and wellness center, the first in Ohio. They wanted to
put the center, which they called Tyler's Redemption Place, in the vacant
lot where his body was dumped in 2014. "The traditional treatment is
thirty, sixty, ninety days," Travis said. "It takes a year for your brain to
heal off opiates. Tyler could never get a year. Somebody could come out
of a thirty-day treatment, come to our place in an outpatient setting, and
get the support and counseling that they need." The center would prioritize addressing the physical trauma that leads people to addiction, Travis explained. "You can't get out of addiction without addressing the root
cause. We have to treat the whole person, mind, body, and spirit."

This vision required money, and Travis turned to the people who'd
stood with him throughout his adult life. Travis declined a college football
scholarship to join the Marine Corps, and after his six years of service, he
became a dockworker, a union job, joining Teamsters Local 24 in Akron.
He was elected as a full-time business representative of the local at age
twenty-nine, and became president at thirty-two, a job he's kept for over
twenty years.

Travis wrote Teamsters general president James P. Hoffa, outlining his
story and asking for fifteen minutes at the 2016 annual convention in Las

Vegas. "I said as union leaders, we're community leaders, and there's nothing bigger impacting our community than this epidemic," Travis said. Hoffa agreed.

Members gave Travis a standing ovation before he got a word of the speech out. "You guys are gonna make me start blushing if you clap every time," he told the crowd. He related the story of Tyler's life, stressing that he'd been smart and kind and had worked hard. And he related the story of his death, the final moments in that vacant lot. "I'm learning to forgive myself and I'm not embarrassed of my son," he said. "He is a hero to have accomplished so much with such a gut-wrenching disease."

Travis ran through the astounding statistics of the opioid crisis: a drug overdose death in America every nineteen minutes, 80 percent of heroin users beginning first with opioid use, the United States home to 4 percent of the world's population but 80 percent of opioid consumption. "It's in every workplace, craft, or division that our union represents," he said, asking members for their assistance in getting the treatment center funded. "If you partner with us, I do know how to stand up and fight like hell until the mission's accomplished. To my son in heaven, now we fight for you!"

What happened next was unprecedented. For the next ninety minutes, Teamster members started coming to the microphone, making pledges of support. Some would name their own family members who died from opioid use: a nephew, a cousin, a mother or father. Others spoke of their own addictions. Travis's speech brought forth a hidden, simmering pain shared by many within the Teamster family. By the end, over $1 million was raised for Breaking Barriers. "It was a humbling experience," Travis told me. "They brought us back onstage. It was everything we could do to not sit there and cry."

But the Teamsters wanted to do more. It turned out that the general secretary-treasurer of the union, Ken Hall, came from West Virginia, which was overrun with opioid addiction. He wanted to use the union's power to hold accountable those responsible for the epidemic. The problem was that there were so many targets.

Physicians had to write the prescriptions for opioid medications, and many prescribed them illegally in exchange for money or even sex. Kickbacks for prescriptions were commonplace; even small-ball corruption like meals for doctors led to increased prescriptions of opioids. A 2017 study from Boston Medical Center found that one in twelve doctors in

America (and one in five doctors in family practice) received money from opioid companies, totaling over $46 million in payments from just 2013 to 2015. According to the study, for every three additional payments in a metropolitan area, overdose deaths increased by 18 percent. In 2010, a new version of the tentpole opioid medication OxyContin was produced that made it harder to abuse. About one-third of doctors dramatically lowered the number of OxyContin prescriptions they wrote, shifting to prescribing other opioids. The lure of more money from addictive products overrode the imperative to dispense safer drugs.

The other party in that transaction sits in drug company boardrooms, and mainly one of them: Purdue Pharma, makers of OxyContin. The timed-release opioid was approved for use in 1996, and Purdue sold it to doctors as a safe pain management treatment, though it was actually more powerful than morphine. In the late 1990s, Purdue lobbied the Joint Commission, an accrediting agency for hospitals, urging that pain be considered a "fifth vital sign" and treated aggressively. The company transformed pain relief into a human right, and despite little clinical evidence of its effectiveness in treating long-term, chronic pain, opioid prescriptions quadrupled from 1999 to 2014. As early as 2001 OxyContin was the most-prescribed pain medication in America, responsible for more than half of the brand-name opioid trade. According to a lawsuit by New York counties, company executives knew early on about the "widespread abuse" of the drug—the pills were easy to crush and snort for a quick-acting high—but they continued to market it persistently; in fact, they pushed doctors to prescribe higher dosages. A retrospective study released by the National Bureau of Economic Research in 2019 attributes "a substantial share of overdose deaths over the last two decades" to the introduction and marketing of OxyContin.

Two branches of the Sackler family built a fortune as high as $14 billion from Purdue's success. They ran a family business, filling more than half of the board seats and all the important executive slots. They bolstered their name by spraying cash into some of the world's most important museums, including the Louvre in Paris, the Tate Modern in London, and the Met in New York City, along with Harvard, Cambridge, and other prestigious universities. Everyone in the pharmaceutical supply chain got a taste as well: doctor junkets and speaking engagements, academic grants, pharmacist refunds, wholesaler rebates, and patient coupons (the classic drug pusher tactic—offer a freebie to get the target hooked). To keep the scheme alive, lawsuits brought by parents of dead patients were settled quietly with the help of top-notch lawyers like future attorney general Eric Holder. Purdue and the Sacklers were history's wealthiest drug kingpins, building an empire deadlier than Pablo Escobar's.

Authorities slapped a $634 million fine on Purdue in 2007 for misleading the public about OxyContin's addiction risks, and the company released a safer version in 2010. But it was too late; in fact, the main consequence of the 2010 reformulation was that patients sought other painkillers, or a cheaper fix like heroin. Even at the end, the Sacklers brainstormed how to move into addiction treatment services, in a brazen attempt to profit from the very pain they caused. In 2019, Purdue filed for bankruptcy as part of a deal to settle over 2,600 lawsuits, and that didn't even eradicate their legal troubles. The Sacklers were singled out as villains, with their museum donations rejected and events protested.

Insys Therapeutics, maker of the even more potent opioid Subsys (fentanyl), followed Purdue's playbook of encouraging higher dosages and pursuing doctors. It promised doctors appearances on lucrative speaker programs to encourage sales, and misled health plans to get them to approve reimbursement. A former Insys vice president pleaded guilty to bribing doctors, five other top executives (including founder John Kapoor) were convicted in court, and the company filed for bankruptcy in the face of a nine-figure federal fine. Throughout the epidemic, generic opioid manufacturers rushed out products to capitalize on it, including two Ireland-registered companies, Mallinckrodt and Endo, and Teva Pharmaceuticals, a top investor of which is a guy named Warren Buffett.

For the past couple of years, rumors have grown about a global settlement with opioid companies, bolstered by the successful 2019 lawsuit against Johnson & Johnson, responsible for only a tiny share of the opioid market, that ordered the company to pay $572 million to the state of Oklahoma. The opioid lawsuits are the twenty-first-century equivalent of the legal fight against Big Tobacco. Even the same lawyer, Mike Moore, has involved himself in recruiting states to sue opioid manufacturers. But several other industries, all of them highly concentrated, play a role in the opioid epidemic.

Patients get their drugs through retail pharmacies, and in 2017 the top six pharmacy outlets controlled 64 percent of the prescription revenues.

Two of those are strictly mail-order pharmacies, so if you are paying for a prescription in person, you're probably getting it from CVS, Walmart, Walgreens, or Rite Aid. The latter two tried to merge in 2017, and even our desiccated antitrust agencies rose up in opposition. But Walgreens bought half of Rite Aid's stores anyway, making Rite Aid a weak fourth option to the Big Three.

CVS in particular is interesting, as in 2018 it purchased large health insurer Aetna, and it already owned a pharmacy benefit manager (PBM), Caremark. Pharmacy benefit managers, the quiet middleman in the drug supply chain, negotiate with drug companies on behalf of insurance companies and health plans, and give reimbursements to pharmacies. CVS, by itself, represents three of the four players in that set of transactions.

When you have one company that reimburses pharmacists and also competes with them directly, the potential for mischief is pretty obvious. When CVS bought Caremark in 2007, Caremark got to see all the information in CVS's other PBM deals, data it could use to underprice rivals. It could also steer its giant patient network toward CVS drugstores, promising lower co-pays or exclusive access to particular drugs. Prescription revenue from Caremark plans nearly tripled from 2007 to 2014.

But even outside of that unique situation, PBMs are hazardous to the system's health. Created in the late 1960s to help with claims processing, PBMs presented themselves as able to negotiate across the system and reduce costs. In actuality, PBMs began to control the marketplace, dictating what drugs patients can get and how much everyone gets paid. Only PBMs have perfect information about the distribution of funds to health plans, drug companies, and pharmacists—a crazy circumstance, if you think about it.

"PBMs reimburse generic drugs based on MACs," or maximum allowable cost, said Rob Frankil, an independent pharmacist in Sellersville, Pennsylvania. The PBM sets the MAC for every drug. But the actual number is hidden to the pharmacist until the point of sale; the contract every pharmacy signs just says "MAC." Unlike practically every retailer, Frankil has no idea how much money he'll make, if any, until the moment of the sale. "I get a prescription, type in data, click send, in a second or two comes back, and I'm told getting a dollar or two," he said. After subtracting the patient's co-pay, Frankil sees whether he will actually turn a profit on the sale or not; it's like a pull of a slot machine. The MAC changes with the price of the drug, but sometimes the lists aren't updated, leaving pharmacists to sell prescriptions at significant losses. Frankil could decline to fill the prescription after the fact, but that'd hardly inspire repeat business. "What do I do?" Frankil asks. "Fill the prescription and lose money, or don't fill it and lose customers? These decisions happen every single day."

PBMs also profit through spread pricing, a better name for which would be "stealing money." They charge the health plan more than they pay the pharmacy in reimbursement, and take the balance for themselves. They take rebates from drug manufacturers and pocket them without passing them on to health plans and their patients. They encourage higher list prices because then their rebates rise, which can harm patients with out-of-pocket costs, as the list price determines the co-pay. They get kickbacks from drug companies to steer patients into higher-cost products. They even charge pharmacies additional "direct and indirect remuneration" fees months after a sale based on performance ratings, such as dinging those with patients who go off their medications. PBMs use these ratings to claw back as much as 50 percent of the value of a single prescription. Through these maneuvers, PBMs skim as much as one in five dollars out of every prescription drug purchase, harming pharmacies, health plans, and patients alike. In particular, they squeeze any pharmacy that isn't aligned with a corporate giant, dislocating a critical link between health professionals and patients, particularly in rural areas, where the pharmacist often is the health system.

Having read this far in the book, you might have guessed that PBMs are highly concentrated. Three firms—CVS, Express Scripts, and Optum Rx—control over 75 percent of the market. That allows them to give pharmacies take-it-or-leave-it contracts. All now have a health insurer partner after a flurry of recent mergers (CVS/Aetna, Express Scripts/Cigna, Optum/UnitedHealth), and all have their own mail-order pharmacies, which they aggressively steer patients toward. Byron Hanson, a tech worker in Seattle in his twenties, takes medication to control epilepsy. When CVS and Aetna merged, his PBM changed. "I don't know if this was just tricky wording on their part or way they were presenting it, but were pushing us to go mail-order instead of going through the pharmacy," Hanson said. Rep. Doug Collins, a Republican from Georgia, alleged to me that PBMs solicit customers for the mail-order pharmacy while they're filling prescriptions in stores. Not only does the lack of human contact increase bureaucracy and weaken patient compliance with taking medications, but frequent autoshipping before pills run out leads to them piling up and creating massive amounts of waste.

As a key part of the supply chain, PBMs were involved in the opioid epidemic. PBMs control the formularies, lists of drugs that they choose to reimburse. Despite knowing the public health risks of OxyContin, most PBMs kept it on formularies. In fact, an investigation by Stat News found that Purdue Pharma paid off PBMs with rebates to keep OxyContin on their formulary with low co-pays, over the howls of a state employee health plan in West Virginia. PBMs didn't even require prior authorization from the health plan to dispense the drug. It took until 2017 for CVS to limit dosages on some opioid prescriptions.

Congress has shut down some PBM schemes, though the companies have shifted profits elsewhere. Drug manufacturers spurred many of the changes, as they find PBMs a convenient target to deflect attention from their own culpability in high drug prices. PBMs do the same by pointing to the drug companies. It's a symbiotic and convenient battle between two large monopolistic industries that in many ways need each other to survive. But Travis Bornstein and the Teamsters found one more monopoly that played a signature role in getting opioids into the hands of addicts—the distributors that ship the drugs in the first place.

Wholesale drug distributors McKesson, Cardinal Health, and AmerisourceBergen collectively deliver about 90 percent of all medications in the United States. In a sign of the lucrative nature of moving around pharmaceuticals, all three companies made the top sixteen in the most recent Fortune 500 list. McKesson, not a household name, is the nation's seventh-largest company by revenue. In 2016, AmerisourceBergen, itself the product of a 2001 merger between the two companies in the smashed-together name, generated $7.9 million per employee, the highest ratio in the S&P 500 index; Cardinal and McKesson were both in the top twelve.

The Teamsters happened to have pension money in the stocks of all three of these distributors, including $30 million worth of McKesson. In many cases, Teamsters shipped the pharmaceuticals and manned the warehouses from which the opioids emerged, on behalf of these companies. "They're the top three, they control the market share," said Travis Bornstein. "They say, 'We don't prescribe, we're just a distributor.' But a small pharmacy in nowhere Ohio is getting millions of pills. They're chasing the dollars. It was profit over people, no doubt in my mind."

A notorious example occurred in Kermit, West Virginia, a town of just 392 residents, where distributors shipped 9 million opioid pills to a single Sav-Rite pharmacy over two years. McKesson alone shipped 10,000 pills a day on average to the Sav-Rite in a ten-month stretch. Over a decade, Williamson, a hamlet of 2,900 in Mingo County, West Virginia, got 20.8 million pills. Overall, the numbers are astonishing: 780 million opioid pills just to West Virginia between 2007 and 2012, enough for 235 pills for every resident in the state. Nationwide the number is 76 billion pills from 2006 to 2012. Some of the highest opioid death tolls in America occurred in West Virginia, an epidemic that distributors kept fueling with more agents of destruction. Meanwhile, the Big Three companies enjoyed $17 billion in profits over that period.

Other attempts to hold distributors accountable had petered out. Distributors are required to report suspicious orders of unusual size or frequency, and the sheer volume of opioids shipped without such red flags violated the law. Many of those pills ended up on the streets. When pharmacists or doctors are indicted for writing illegal prescriptions and distributors are made aware of it, they should raise an alert. And when suspicious orders are reported, the distributors should stop shipping. But the Big Three didn't follow the rules, which had the side benefit of keeping the money flowing. And they appear to have known the risks. A New York complaint in 2019 alleged that McKesson kept shipping to pharmacies in the state that they knew were filling illegal prescriptions, six years after learning of it. Documents in a long-running case in Cleveland quote McKesson executives struggling with profiting off misery. "I feel that I am going down a river without a paddle and fighting the rapids," said one regulatory affairs director.

The Drug Enforcement Administration (DEA) put nine field divisions on the case, and by 2014 it had hard evidence that McKesson in particular ignored suspicious orders and failed to withhold deliveries. DEA agents were ready to pursue giant fines and criminal charges. But the Justice Department never filed anything, and DEA agents were pressured to be nicer to their distributor targets. The whole thing ended with an inadequate settlement with McKesson in early 2017, the second within a decade, for $150 million. That year McKesson CEO John Hammergren took home a pay package of $98 million by himself, part of $781 million in compensation since he took over as chief executive in 2001. Afterward, Congress passed a law taking the teeth out of drug enforcement efforts, allowing even shipments flagged as suspicious to make it to the streets.

Travis Bornstein and the Teamsters were determined not to let the distributors off easy. In letters to the boards of directors and public pleas, they demanded reforms to business practices and clawbacks in runaway pay for the Big Three CEOs. And they started attending shareholder meetings, first at AmerisourceBergen, using their voice as investors to call for change. On July 26, 2017, Travis joined members in Dallas for McKesson's annual shareholder meeting, and was given time to speak. "I shared our story. I think the biggest impression that I wanted to make to each of them is that these are real people, this is real life. You're contributing to destroying our communities. Imagine this being your kid, imagine this being your grandson."

That day, shareholders voted down McKesson's executive pay package, one of only four rejections at public companies that year. But the vote was only advisory. McKesson also agreed to split the position of chair and CEO, though only after Hammergren's tenure ended. McKesson agreed to have a board committee study company operations and CEO compensation. Unsurprisingly, the board cleared itself of wrongdoing, though it did recommend strengthening compliance and oversight. And despite Hammergren calling criticism of McKesson "nonsense," the board cut his pay by 10 percent the following year.

These small achievements failed to satisfy Travis, though he remained undeterred. "The reforms we proposed were voted down, but we brought the attention to the cause," he said. "It takes some time, but eventually when you start holding people accountable to the little things, it helps the bigger things get in line."

In tandem with the Teamsters' push, distributors were added as defendants in the array of lawsuits against opioid companies. Arguably the legal case against the distributors was better than the one against the manufacturers themselves. Proving that drugmakers knew about the addictiveness of their products was difficult, but waving through millions of pills to individual pharmacies obviously violated statutes requiring distributors to highlight suspicious orders. New Mexico, New York, Vermont, West Virginia, and many more states accused the distributors of unlawful sales, arguing that those sales had led to a sea of prescription pills being diverted onto the black market. California threatened to revoke AmerisouceBergen's license to ship within the state. The Justice Department got involved again too, though several disappointments there didn't presage success. But something did feel different.

In May 2018, a congressional panel asked distributors if they felt responsible for the opioid epidemic; the Big Three representatives said no, but the board chair of Miami-Luken, a smaller distributor, said yes. A year later the Justice Department criminally charged Rochester Drug Cooperative (RDC), the nation's sixth-largest shipper, for conspiring to traffic drugs and defrauding the federal government. Even the former chief executive and head of compliance was charged, and RDC spokesperson Jeff Eller admitted in a public statement, "We made mistakes, and RDC understands that these mistakes, directed by former management, have serious consequences," he said in a public statement. Former Miami-Luken executives were criminally indicted in Ohio, too.

There's not a little irony that only tiny competitors to the Big Three wound up facing accountability. Meanwhile, executives at companies like AmerisourceBergen write letters to the *New York Times* shrugging off responsibility for hundreds of thousands of deaths. The executives at big companies with vast resources for legal counsel don't have to worry about prison cells. If giants dominate an industry, governments can't stop the misconduct. It becomes systemic, built into the business model. Maybe the small cases are tests to check the law enforcers' theories before they move on to bigger fish. Or maybe some monopolies sit above the law.

In one sense, the crackdown on distributors, opioid manufacturers, or other monopolies in the supply chain is now too late. Addicts have moved on to heroin and fentanyl. It's a crisis induced by powerful narcotics, but the ultimate pushers responsible wear business suits and don't get their hands dirty by walking to the street corner.

"Any money coming out of these lawsuits all needs to go to treatment," Travis Bornstein told me. "They helped create the problem, they should help solve the problem." He's still raising funds to open Tyler's Redemption Place, his facility to help addicts rebuild their lives. He'll take it wherever he can get it. "I work with a lot of nonprofits, they say they're not going to take any money from a drug company. I have no problem taking their money. If anybody should be paying for this, it should be them."

It's difficult to theorize whether our current economy inexorably trends toward monopoly. There are so many business-specific variables and intervening factors. But we have two natural experiments in the sector I would call Big Sin.

People have smoked marijuana for thousands of years, and virtually that entire time, small independent growers and dealers have operated under the legal radar. But with legalization efforts under way globally, the sector has professionalized. In that sense, the cannabis economy is a new animal. And there appeared to be a tipping point in 2018, when venture capital in pot-related businesses spiked to nearly $1 billion and companies spent $15 billion on an array of mergers. The world's largest product maker, Curaleaf, grew through acquisition of numerous brands. The world's largest recreational distributor, MedMen, scooped up medical marijuana company PharmaCann. It was like a starter gun went off and the entire industry rushed toward one another to couple up. Call it pot speed dating, or weed dating, or something.

The frenzy has been most pronounced among Big Sin's establishment: the alcohol and tobacco industries. The parent company of Corona and Modelo, Constellation Brands, made a $4 billion investment in Canopy Growth, the largest cannabis producer in Canada. Beer maker MolsonCoors also joined forces with a marijuana company out of Quebec. Anheuser-Busch InBev (AB InBev), the largest beer brewer in the world, has a deal with cannabis giant Tilray. And Altria, the maker of Marlboros, took a 45 percent stake in another Canadian grower, Cronos, which itself just bulked up by swallowing CBD "beauty brand" Lord Jones (which makes lotions and oils, along with edibles).

Altria had already navigated a tobacco market in the United States that over time was winnowed down from seven major companies to two (the other is Reynolds American). Together they control 80 percent of all tobacco sales. Consolidation has made the tobacco business viable despite fewer smokers, as the duopoly can raise prices without losing market share. The number of cigarettes sold in America fell by 37 percent from 2001 to 2016, but revenue went up 32 percent, as the price of an average pack jumped from $3.73 to $6.42.

Altria's other strategy has been to become a full-service vice factory, offering a variety of mind- and body-altering substances. It owns a 10 percent stake in AB InBev and a profitable collection of wine estates known as Ste.

Michelle. It bought into the cannabis market with Cronos. And Altria completed its sweep of Big Sin with a 35 percent stake in Juul, another example
of an industry trending to monopoly from a standing start.

Fourteen years ago, e-cigarettes couldn't be found in America. Four years
ago, Juul didn't exist. But the Altria deal in late 2018 valued the company
at $38 billion, a market capitalization rivaling that of Target, Delta Air-
lines, and Ford. In just a few years, Juul captured close to three-quarters
of the e-cigarette market, obliterating rivals that themselves were attached
to established tobacco companies. Vaping is now often known as "juuling."

How did this nascent industry whittle down to just Juul? Though e-cigarette
makers sold themselves as public health saviors that could convert smokers,
Juul's most explosive growth occurred among previously nonsmoking teenagers. By one measure, a generation of falling nicotine use among twelfth-
graders has been wiped out by the rise of Juul.

Juul's products and especially its marketing was designed to appeal to
teenagers. Kids could easily conceal the slick devices, which resemble USB
drives; take quick odorless puffs at school or home; and enjoy dessert-like
mango, crème brûlée, and cucumber flavors. Almost half of Juul's Twitter
followers were not yet eighteen, the legal age for purchasing e-cigs. Social
media feeds, which habitually featured beautiful young people enjoying a
vape, expanded virally through fan accounts that spread the Juul message.
The #doitforjuul Instagram hashtag is a favorite. Juul even gave marketing
presentations in schools and held free "sampling events" with popular young
bands.

It was an exciting new delivery of a concentrated addictive drug—a single
pod has as much nicotine as an entire pack of cigarettes—and it hit its target.
Schools are struggling to deal with what they consider to be an epidemic.
"The dramatic spike of youth [vaping] . . . was driven in part at the very least
if not largely by Juul," said former FDA commissioner Scott Gottlieb on his
way out the door in 2019.

It was all going great until over a thousand people were sickened and dozens died from a mysterious vaping-related illness in the fall of 2019. Though
e-cigarettes had previously been associated with seizures, potential risk of
heart disease, and scarring of the lungs, the new cluster of illnesses appeared
to be related to vaping THC products. Nevertheless, when California issues an
edict telling everyone to "stop vaping right now," it's bad for business. Large
retailers like Walmart stopped stocking e-cigarettes, TV networks stopped

showing ads, and cities and states banned sales. Juul, already under federal civil and criminal investigation, dumped the flavored pods themselves and saw its CEO step down.

His replacement, K. C. Crosthwaite, was formerly an Altria executive. And that encapsulates Juul's survival plan. After the deal with Altria, an amazing article in the Wall Street Journal *bluntly suggested that Altria's 35 percent stake gives Juul "a benefit that would have been unthinkable from a cigarette company in the past: an easier path to Washington's approval." Altria CEO Howard Willard bragged in a conference call that the company would collaborate with Juul on an FDA application required of all e-cigarette makers before 2021 to remain on the market. The company hired a bipartisan all-star team of lobbyists, from former Massachusetts attorney general Martha Coakley to Trump administration top advisor Johnny DeStefano. Willard assured investors that "we have years of experience" navigating the FDA.*

Altria's stock has been battered by the Juul mess, and a planned merger with Philip Morris had to be shelved. But paradoxically, the crackdown on vaping could wipe out Juul's retail competition at mom-and-pop vape shops, leaving them as the only distributor able to withstand the blow. Put another way, the limitless resources and lobbying heft of an established merchant of death could rescue an upstart nicotine addiction device under federal attack. Monopoly could save Juul, as an escape hatch for an old Big Sin power to buy in on the next Big Sin wave.

And the fact that an industry built from scratch was whittled down to one dominant player so quickly, which an incumbent giant then bought into, suggests that our Second Gilded Age is a monopoly-creation machine.

CHAPTER 6

Monopolies Among Banks Are Why There Are Monopolies Among Every Other Economic Sector

In 1976, a bearded, blond, volleyball-playing California hippie named Michael Funk had a vision of selling produce that wasn't sprayed with contaminants or pesticides, that people could trust as coming unspoiled from the ground to their table. Organic food was just starting to blossom, but most Americans couldn't find it. Funk sought to change that. He bought a Volkswagen minibus and started roaming the Sierra Nevada foothills, offering fruits and vegetables out of the back of the van. The business, which Funk would name Mountain People's Warehouse, took off, growing throughout the West Coast. Funk kept to his crunchy roots despite the success. "Michael was the first CEO of a public company I ever saw in a ponytail, faded jeans and purple Converse high-tops," said one admirer in a 2012 retrospective.

On the other side of the continent, Norman Cloutier opened a tiny storefront in Providence, Rhode Island, called Cornucopia Natural Foods, with the same mission of selling healthy products. Cloutier converted the shop into an organic food distributor, supplying retailers throughout the East. He acquired competitors, including Rainbow Natural Foods of Denver. Before long, there were two giant distributors in the natural food distribution market: Cornucopia and Mountain People's Warehouse.

In 1996, they joined forces as United Natural Foods, Inc. (UNFI), so they could "operate more efficiently," according to the corporate hagiography. It became the first nationwide distributor of natural food products. Over the next two decades, UNFI would operate even more efficiently by poaching nineteen other organic food distributors and suppliers, including Stow Mills, Albert's Organics, Blooming Prairie, Roots 'N Fruits Cooperative, B. K. Sethi Distribution, Pacific Organic Produce, and Tony's Fine Foods. It now distributes meat and produce, nuts and seeds, dairy and deli products, baked goods, seafood, vitamins and supplements, specialty foods, ethnic foods from Asia and the Caribbean—pretty much everything you'd need to stock a grocery store. By 2018, UNFI had 43,000 business customers, including organic king Whole Foods, and $6 billion in quarterly sales.

But merely being one of the largest publicly traded grocery wholesalers in the United States and Canada wasn't enough. On July 26, 2018, this serial acquirer announced its biggest takeover yet: a $2.9 billion bid for Supervalu, another distribution giant. UNFI believed the acquisition would reduce shipping expenses, expand its customer base, and increase sales in new markets, especially for meat and produce. In reality, it seemed like a response to Amazon buying Whole Foods and other consolidations in the grocery industry. Monopolized buyers push the sellers to join up as well; that's concentration creep in action. But whatever the reason, this was the most significant decision in UNFI's history.

To assist in the particulars, UNFI sought the services of the biggest and most experienced mergers and acquisitions (known to the industry as M&A) firm in the world: Goldman Sachs. It wasn't a big surprise. Stephan J. Feldgoise, Goldman's head of M&A for the Americas, had a personal relationship with UNFI's new CEO, Steve Spinner (Funk stepped down as CEO in 2008 but still serves on the UNFI board). Back when Spinner worked at other food distribution companies, he worked with Feldgoise on other deals. "They were getting someone they trusted," a UNFI official with knowledge of the proceedings said to me.

Goldman's participation would go horribly wrong, however, as a nasty lawsuit from UNFI indicates. Merger activity has been in UNFI's bones for twenty years, but on the Supervalu deal it would run into a fundamental problem with the consolidation trend: how bank and legal advisors have come to treat monopolization as an opportunity to maximize deal flow and fee revenue. M&A bankers and lawyers get paid to advise companies on mergers, and often finance the deals they encourage companies to make. Though banks are hired to provide objective advice and reasonable financing, fees are typically contingent on the deal going through. After the Dodd-Frank Act hindered speculative trading to a degree, in 2018 investment banks earned $21 billion in fees from M&A deals, down slightly from $22.8 billion in 2016. The 2016 number accounted for close to one-third of all investment bank revenue that year. Just one big deal, like the Bayer-Monsanto tie-up announced in 2016, could be worth as much as $690 million in fees for the eight banks involved in it.

This all creates artificial pressures for concentration and conflicts of interest, as UNFI found out the hard way. And it puts critical decisions regarding the structure of the economy in the hands of a handful of self-interested financial institutions. The power relationship tilts to the consultants and bankers, even with the most experienced clients. Whether businesses thrive or even survive after a merger and whether the country is best served by consolidation throughout the economy are of no consequence to an M&A specialist who's just gotten paid. And not only do companies have few alternatives for M&A expertise, but mergers typically include a financial windfall for CEOs and top executives, a kickback to facilitate monopoly.

In a very real sense, we can answer why America lives in an age of monopoly today with just two words: Wall Street.

At the heart of Wall Street's interest in monopoly is its own monopolized industry. The modern financial system is a series of closed fiefdoms that has enriched a small class of elites while wreaking havoc upon the global economy. Anything that channels or manages or touches money has become concentrated. The system's tight coupling—where financial participants are not only linked together but dependent upon each other—was a primary driver of the 2008 financial crisis.

Post-Depression banking laws were intended to segregate the system to prevent tight coupling. The most well known was the Glass-Steagall Act, the successful firewall between commercial and investment banks. Separating banking functions allowed the system to withstand failures in any one corner, and prevented investment gamblers from using ordinary depositors' money in the Wall Street casino. It was the bedrock of a New Deal framework that held for fifty years.

When Citicorp merged with Travelers Insurance and its investment bank subsidiary Salomon Smith Barney in 1998, it was a dare to policymakers, leading them to remove the most important Glass-Steagall restrictions and allow investment and commercial banks to combine. But the firewall had been decaying since the 1960s. Everybody was in on it, from John F. Kennedy's comptroller of the currency, James Saxon, to functionaries of the Carter and Reagan years and on up to the Clinton administration, which delegated all changes in financial regulation to Treasury Secretary Robert Rubin, the former co-chair of Goldman Sachs. "Any financial services modernization effort would be a Treasury, rather than a Presidential, initiative," read a White House memo in 1997.

The bank lobby longed to create one-stop "supermarket" banks that could utilize depositor funds to finance trading, and they spent decades chipping away at Glass-Steagall so they could do it. They created certificates of deposit, money market funds, and "cash management accounts" that allowed brokerage customers to write checks—all of it blessed by the regulators. They found a reliable ally in Alan Greenspan, the longtime Federal Reserve chair who sought to deregulate any and all financial rules. Greenspan added exemptions allowing commercial banks to earn 5 percent of their gross revenue from trading at first, then 10 percent, and eventually 25 percent. By the end, the leading two dozen banks all had securities operations, and the Fed, the FDIC, and administrations of both parties spoke with a single voice, contented with that outcome. The Gramm-Leach-Bliley Act of 1999 only formalized the firewall's repeal. Glass-Steagall was dead before it was killed.

Within less than a decade of the firewall being removed, the worst financial crisis in nearly a century ensued. Lots of people, most of them either Bill Clinton or members of his administration, are invested in a narrative where the two events had nothing to do with one another. In reality, the repeal of Glass-Steagall did accelerate and magnify the financial crisis, as part of a continuum of financial deregulation. Citigroup, whose merger created the first "supermarket"-style bank, wound up the sickest, most overextended entity after the housing bubble collapse, with over $130 billion in assets needing write-downs from 2007 through 2009. The merger created a complex, difficult-to-manage firm where the philosophies of commercial and investment bankers were in open competition, and the investment bankers won. That strong risk appetite became common, while more prudent commercial bankers "became the B side of the record, nobody listened to them," as Robert Hockett, a law professor at Cornell and a financial reform advocate, put it to me. The dynamic fits with the possibly apocryphal quote "All you need for a financial crisis are excess optimism and Citibank."

Within years of joining with Travelers and Salomon Smith Barney, Citi had engaged in illegal transactions with Enron and WorldCom, presented dishonest research to investors to encourage them to buy their clients' stock, manipulated foreign bonds, and produced so much mischief out of a Japanese private banking unit that the bank shut it down. CitiFinancial was engaged in predatory subprime lending by 2000, after the purchase of corrupt non-bank lender Associates First Capital. Like other investment banks, Citi packaged the steady stream of subprime loans from non-bank originators into mortgage-backed securities and created derivatives based on the securities' value. At the top of the bubble, Citi doubled its subprime lending exposure between 2005 and 2007. Richard Parsons, former board member and chairman of Citigroup, admitted in 2012, "To some extent what we saw in the 2007–2008 crash was the result of the throwing off of Glass-Steagall."

Clintonite apologists focus on non-bank mortgage originators, who swindled home buyers with crappy loans that preyed particularly on people of color. But the originators wouldn't have existed without the big banks; that's who funded their businesses. Banks needed those mortgages as raw material for mortgage-backed securities, and they demanded specific types of high-risk loans in exchange for that funding. The banks all lent to each other too, while issuing the mortgage bonds and derivatives that blew up and drove the crisis. The system was desperately interconnected, everyone chasing the same risk and all dependent on each other's bad ideas, building up leverage that eventually gave out. And it wouldn't have been possible under a Glass-Steagall firewall regime.

When the rot cascaded through the system and the giants were days from collapsing—an email from a September 2008 weekend indicated that Morgan Stanley would be unable to open that Monday, and if it didn't, then Goldman Sachs would be "toast"—the government rounded up trillions of dollars to make sure they were nursed back to health. In fact, they were strengthened. Goldman and Morgan Stanley converted into bank holding companies that could tap Federal Reserve lending windows for cheap borrowing. JPMorgan Chase, Bank of America, and Wells Fargo were offered up failed and failing lenders to increase their portfolios, and bailout money to absorb them. The biggest banks emerged from the crisis bigger. Regulators were under duress to bless these shotgun weddings because of the collapse of the system; now they have an even more bloated system to monitor.

That's what "too big to fail" is all about: the conviction that megabanks are so critical to the economy's functioning that they will always be protected from ruin. This expectation, that monopolies in finance cannot be run out of business, enables the buildup of risk that inevitably leads to a boom-bust cycle. That's true throughout the financial system: investors are happy to lend into a too-big-to-fail bank if they know they will eventually get paid back, regardless of the risk.

As of June 2019, the six biggest banks—JPMorgan Chase, Bank of America, Citigroup, Wells Fargo, Goldman Sachs, and Morgan Stanley—control over $10.5 trillion in financial assets. These banks also happen to be serial transnational criminal enterprises, paying $182 billion in (inadequate) penalties for rap sheets of incomparable length. Few of the violations even relate to the financial crisis's run-up and aftermath, though those were significant. Incidents of debt collection fraud, market rigging, money laundering, misrepresentations to clients, kickback schemes, and unlawful securities sales all occurred *after* the crisis.

Some megabank offenses involved direct collusion, as seen in the pension fund lawsuit against six banks for conspiring to corner the $1.7 trillion stock lending market, which facilitates short selling. The banks jointly controlled a firm called EquiLend to block other platforms for stock lending to emerge, maintaining excessive fees. A similar antitrust suit accused the biggest banks of dominating the credit default swap market by shutting out competitors. None of this has provoked so much as a knee scrape for the bank giants, who correctly deem themselves unassailable. Profits have soared to new heights, leading to windfall salary increases for chief executives, though not ordinary bank employees.

Not only are consumers, workers, and investors threatened by megabanks; so is the rest of the world. "A common source of financial instability is everybody piling into the same asset, whether it's the subprime mortgage or the junk bond," said Robert Hockett. "That's much more likely to happen with larger institutions. There's more groupthink within institutions of that kind."

At the lower end, consolidation and a dearth of new bank charters have narrowed options. In 1984 there were 14,400 commercial banks; today there are around 4,600. The Federal Reserve didn't reject a single bank merger application between 2006 and 2017. Bank mergers have quickened under the relaxed Trump regime, especially after a 2018 deregulatory law that encouraged community banks to team up by loosening the asset threshold for tighter regulation. Mergers in Virginia, Ohio, Mississippi, and Wisconsin started even before the 2018 bill officially passed. Analysts have been screaming for community banks to merge, particularly before the 2020 elections, after which a new president might change regulations. "Merge now, if you're going to do it," said top stock analyst Mike Mayo in May 2019.

SunTrust and BB&T answered that plea, uniting to create the nation's sixth-largest commercial bank, with $442 billion in assets. Black farmers opposed the deal because of the bank's concentration in the Mid-South and the expectation that branches would be closed after the merger, something that would particularly impact minority-owned and rural small businesses. But it didn't matter. The merged bank was renamed Truist, because when you think banks, you think truth.

Challengers to the banking industry throne have been collectively described as financial technology firms, or fintech. These tech-based upstarts yearn to upend the big bad banking system through automated investing platforms, peer-to-peer lending services, and faster ways to transfer money. Of course, financial titans have preempted the market shift, amid hundreds of fintech acquisitions in the past few years. BlackRock picked up robo-investor FutureAdvisor; JPMorgan snapped up payments startup WePay; Goldman Sachs has a peer-to-peer lender. In addition, while peer-to-peer lending is supposed to connect borrowers to individuals with excess money, the peer on the other side of the loan is often a private equity fund, asset manager, or investment bank, all of whom have plowed money into these sites. Even banks that want to use new fintech apps find that the back-end suppliers have consolidated, with three core providers forcing burdensome contracts and poor quality on the industry.

Bank consolidation is only one piece of the integrated puzzle. Credit rating agencies have been concentrated for decades, with the three leaders—Moody's, Standard and Poor's, and Fitch—controlling around 95 percent of the market. Rating agencies are paid by the issuers whose securities they analyze; if they make it easier for a client to sell questionable securities by rating them highly, that client will likely return with future business. During the housing bubble, this led to AAA stamps of approval for abominable subprime mortgage bonds; investors had nowhere else to go for good information. In 2010, the Financial Crisis Inquiry Commission asked Warren Buffett, a major Moody's investor who also holds over $100 billion in financial services stocks, what he knew about the company's management. Buffett said he knew absolutely nothing, and that the major reason to buy Moody's was "pricing power," by which he meant a monopoly. Congress passed an amendment in the Dodd-Frank financial reform to change the issuer-pays model, and the Securities and Exchange Commission simply ignored it.

Experian, TransUnion, and Equifax are the Big Three credit reporting bureaus, responsible for 90 percent of all lender decisions. Despite committing millions of errors and doing little to fix them, despite allowing the largest data breach in American history, nothing has dislodged this triopoly from its perch. Stock exchanges, once nonprofit overseers, have become private corporations, exploiting exclusive dominion over market data to sell faster feeds of exchange data to maximize profits. Twelve of the thirteen major equity exchanges are owned by just three companies. A few firms control much of the $4 trillion municipal bond market. Two retail brokerages control 60 percent of customer assets, after Charles Schwab bought TD Ameritrade. There are four main auditors that double-check public company accounting, and they have not been dismantled by overlapping scandals, including an incredible one at KPMG in which partners obtained confidential information from the auditing regulator about upcoming annual inspections and then revised audit work after the fact in response. Staffers at KPMG even cheated on internal ethics and integrity tests, sharing answers and manipulating the testing system to ensure passage. Despite *cheating on ethics tests*, KPMG remains firmly ensconced in the Big Four.

The trend toward index fund investing has bestowed tremendous power on asset managers Vanguard, BlackRock, and State Street, who together manage 81 percent of index funds and are on track to control nearly half of all shareholder votes at large publicly traded companies. This has driven a phenomenon called common ownership, where the top stockholders in Apple are the same as the top stockholders in Microsoft. Harvard Law School's John Coates calls it the "Problem of Twelve": the idea that in the near future twelve individuals will own and hold power over most U.S. companies, "the greatest concentration of economic control in our lifetimes." As we saw in Chapter 1, on airlines, some research suggests that institutional investors encourage market leaders to not compete against one another. Others have correlated common ownership with lower wages and even lower economic growth. Investors like it fine, of course, as long as stock dividends and other forms of enrichment keep flowing. But John

Bogle, the late founder of Vanguard, sounded the alarm before his death that his index fund invention had become "too successful for its own good."

When giant investors control most stocks, they tend to conflate consolidation with maximizing returns. An April 2017 Bloomberg article entitled "Verizon Subscriber Losses Highlight Need for M&A Exploration" exemplifies this trend. The largest wireless carrier in the United States lost 307,000 subscribers in the previous quarter, and this story—purportedly a news article—argued that, to compensate, Verizon needed not to increase quality or create a more affordable product but instead to snatch up whatever companies it could find. You also see this mentality in a more recent *Wall Street Journal* piece, "Auto Consolidation Is Vital but Needs a Crisis," which pines for a deep slowdown in car purchases so that companies can find themselves desperate enough to team up. It's not foreordained that investors favor monopoly; long-term durable growth could be pinned to all kinds of business models. But governments have presented no risk to breaking up the monopoly party, so the Warren Buffetts of the world seek it out.

So the investors are concentrated, the research is concentrated, the data holders are concentrated, the banks are concentrated, the disruptors are concentrated, the connections between all these layers are concentrated, and the industry chatter trends toward demanding more concentration. And that's before you get to a key sector of the financial industry, a group of men and women with the mission of concentrating the rest of corporate America.

It was the biggest merger anyone in the beer industry had ever seen. In 2015, AB InBev, itself a private-equity-directed mash-up of Anheuser-Busch and Belgian/Brazilian brewer InBev, announced a $106 billion acquisition of SABMiller, the result of South African Breweries' purchase of Miller Brewing in 2002. These were the two largest beer makers in the world before the deal, and although the combined firm would divest the Miller brand to Molson Coors, it would still control about 30 percent of the global beer market. In the United States that number would be around 41 percent, and if you added Molson Coors, it would be about two-thirds. After this merger, if you wanted a beer in America, you'd probably get it from one of two companies.

Over five hundred different brands would come under the aegis of AB

InBev, including all the Budweiser, Busch, and Michelob variants, Rolling Rock, Natural Light, Stella Artois, Bass, Becks, Boddington's, St. Pauli Girl, and close to a dozen so-called independent craft beers it had picked up since 2011. Drinkers don't necessarily know about the craft beers, because AB InBev does its best to hide its ownership on the labels. (Incidentally, the remaining craft brewers have all begun to merge with each other to keep up.)

The announcement article in the *New York Times* was rather perfunctory, considering the impenetrable duopoly that was about to be created. The author supplied vague thoughts about what markets the new company could access and what regulators might demand. And all the way down the page, in the thirty-fourth paragraph, came this boilerplate:

> Lazard, Deutsche Bank, Barclays, BNP Paribas, Bank of America Merrill Lynch and Standard Bank and the law firms Freshfields Bruckhaus Deringer; Cravath, Swaine & Moore; and Clifford Chance advised Anheuser-Busch InBev.
>
> SABMiller was advised by Robey Warshaw, JPMorgan Chase, Morgan Stanley and Goldman Sachs and the law firms Linklaters, Hogan Lovells and Cleary Gottlieb Steen & Hamilton. Molson Coors was advised by UBS and the law firms Kirkland & Ellis and Cleary Gottlieb.

Eleven banks and eight law firms advised this single merger. What exactly did all of them do? After five banks counseled AB InBev on the economic and financial implications of taking in its chief rival, did it really need the sixth? Are there not enough lawyers available at Linklaters and Hogan Lovells, two of the largest, triggering the need for SABMiller to bring in a third?

The short answer is that concentration has become big business for those working in mergers and acquisitions. Self-appointed merger experts have been granted the power to set the direction of the economy, despite a host of conflicts of interest. The zeal to profit from monopoly has led to a desire, even if unconscious, to promote it.

M&A established itself in the mid-1960s. Around 4,400 companies were sucked up just in 1968, many into conglomerates organized by the major banks. Conglomerates weren't really monopolies but corporate robots composed of unrelated, ill-fitting business lines. It was an end run around antitrust laws, and it created a new subindustry of advisors, legal consultants, and accountants, who learned from each deal and imparted that wisdom to new customers.

Flash forward to the 2010s and the current merger wave, an unbroken wall of water since the 1980s. There were 11,470 U.S. deals in 2016, and another 13,024 in 2017; that was a new record in terms of number, though when assessed by the value of deals, the high-water mark was 2015. The Trump tax cuts fattened corporate wallets starting in 2018, leading to more records. In the first half of 2018, $2.5 trillion in deals were announced globally, exceeding the 2015 pace and shattering all previous six-month totals. A whopping $120 billion of that figure came in just one day in May. The 2018 deal cycle ended up the third-largest on record. And though analysts expected a slower 2019, that January yielded the biggest M&A bonanza since 2000.

All this requires advisors, because under the conventions of our modern system everything's better with a consultant. M&A services include assessing options for deals, analyzing the regulatory, legal, and accounting logistics around them, and in some cases even bringing deals to companies. Some advisors help negotiate terms between the merging participants. Some specifically work for the board, so it can appeal to an ostensibly neutral source when approving a transaction. And if the deal ultimately requires the purchasing company to unearth financing, it's helpful to have a bank around.

In the AB InBev/SABMiller deal, jurisdictional expertise probably played a role. With the two firms selling around the world, navigating international M&A rules required farming out bits and pieces of the analysis to different banks or legal shops. "In my firm, we have a lot of clients with mergers initiating overseas," said Erik Tikkanen, an M&A lawyer. "Sometimes we're brought on for the U.S. side of the due diligence."

Other current and former M&A officials describe the business as very relationship-driven. Lazard has been the lead outside advisor on every Google deal over the past decade, a tie-up arranged by former Clinton aide Vernon Jordan. One Goldman Sachs banker who worked closely with Amazon moved his family from Los Angeles to Seattle just to be closer to Amazon headquarters. Executives stick with advisors they've trusted through past deals, and given the continuum of mergers and acquisitions, advisors tend to expand their portfolios. General Electric, in the midst of decades of restructuring, paid out $6 billion in M&A fees since 2000 to nearly every major investment bank in America. In the case of JPMorgan Chase, the $500 million haul paid off a relationship that had begun in 1892, when J. P. Morgan himself helped create GE through a merger.

Because M&A is a relationship business, bank strategies for growing the business often involve securing a high-profile name. Rahm Emanuel signed with Centerview Partners in June 2019, joining fellow Clinton veteran and Centerview advisor Robert Rubin. The boutique bank focuses almost entirely on M&A, handling marquee deals like CVS/Aetna and Disney/Fox. Centerview's specialty is pharmaceutical mergers; one pharma megadeal, the tie-up between Celgene and Bristol-Myers Squibb, is expected to yield $1 billion in bank M&A revenue. I say "expected to yield" because there's a code of silence around what banks actually make from M&A. "When you do a merger, you have to disclose everything but the bank or lawyer fee," said Rob Jackson, a commissioner on the Securities and Exchange Commission from 2018 to 2020 who worked as an M&A banker out of college. "It's one of the reasons I'm big on disclosure—the world is not informed."

Despite the boutique Centerview model, the biggest M&A banks are usually the biggest banks, period. Though transparency is lacking, there's a convenient way of tracking the leaders, known in the industry as the league tables, which pit banks against one another based on deal flow and estimated fee revenue. In the first half of 2019, the league table leaders were, in descending order, Goldman Sachs, JPMorgan Chase, Morgan Stanley, Citigroup, Bank of America, and Deutsche Bank. JPMorgan's work on the 2019 pharmaceutical merger between Allergan and AbbVie yielded the bank $123 million, the largest fee ever disclosed.

It's almost human nature that when you arrange competitors in a list, they become supercompetitive about reaching the top. It becomes embedded in the self-worth of M&A bankers, who see their position in life as linked to that number on the league table chart. Almost incredibly, to industry professionals and observers the league tables matter not just as an indicator of profits but as a measuring stick against rivals. "You go to the websites of the institutions, and it's not at all uncommon for them to list big deals that they had something to do with," said Robert Hockett. "Once you have a system in place to keep score, there's a built-in bias to favor the deals. There's no list of deals you successfully tanked."

And so you see stories pop up from time to time about how Goldman Sachs plans to win smaller deals, or how Bank of America wants to regain market share on M&A. The desire to win the league tables also leads banks to pile into deals where they aren't the lead advisor, just to capture a piece of the action. JPMorgan Chase, for example, will not lend money into a deal unless it is included as an advisor, which keeps the bank aloft in the league tables. Sometimes bankers show up to one meeting just to get included. These aren't passive strategies; banks are actively hunting for business to rise through the ranks. There's a ton of money on the table and an artificial contest being waged over snatching that money.

Then there's a second factor: the success fee. "Their fees are contingent on the merger happening," Jackson said. Typically the success fee is calculated as a percentage of the value of the merged company after the deal. This allegedly aligns the interests of the bankers and the companies involved, but it also enlarges the incentives to close deals—and to open other deals with the hopes of closing them. Another factor is that M&A has historically been a stepping-stone position to higher-level jobs at investment banks. Junior M&A bankers striving for something more want to cash in those success fees and grow the business: that's how a stepping-stone works.

Factor number four is the belief that dealmaking leads to better returns for shareholders. An entire segment of activist investors argues the opposite, but industry reports, like a late 2018 one from Willis Towers Watson, bombard decision makers with evidence that M&A is a successful growth strategy. Banks like a flush stock market, in part because it provides more money for deals. In addition, most of the investment banks that dominate M&A used to be structured as private partnerships, but over the years many of them went public. That bakes in an investor-driven incentive to grow, and with M&A a larger profit center, growth must be found in that business line. Advice can become conflicted when the future positioning of the bank within the capital markets takes precedence over cautioning against a merger that may not work out.

The final and perhaps most important factor concerns how these deals are structured. The golden parachute, where a corporate executive gets a large payout when there's a "change in control" of leadership, was actually invented to enable M&A. As junk bond financing became ubiquitous in the 1980s and even prestigious firms became targets of hostile takeover bids, nervous executives had large payouts written into their contracts to protect themselves if they were fired. Golden parachutes were insurance policies so that executives wouldn't fight consolidation, which monopoly-seeking investors appreciated. And they worked: according to a 2012 study, companies with golden parachutes in place for executives are 43 percent more likely to receive a takeover bid or be acquired by other firms.

This concept has now become standardized. In the AT&T/Time Warner merger, the outgoing CEO, Time Warner's Jeff Bewkes, took home $400 million. The CVS/Aetna deal was worth around $500 million to Aetna CEO Mark Bertolini. When Viacom and CBS merged in 2019, Viacom CEO Bob Bakish, who was staying on to run the company, received $31 million, and CBS's CEO, Joe Ianniello, got $70 million to be Bakish's number two, because of a clause in his contract entitling him to a bigger payout after a merger if he wasn't made CEO. To most observers, that would be seen as a bribe to facilitate the deal.

These days M&A acts as a corporate money hose, spraying executives and shareholders with excess dollars. In historical terms, more shares are retired through M&A than through stock buybacks, the signature example progressives use when they rant about shareholders and executives extracting the productive value out of companies. The merger extracts more efficiently, and eight- and nine-figure payouts to individual CEOs are disturbingly common. Wall Street arranges these deals and must bear some of the blame. They effectively offer a kickback of other people's money to guarantee their own fees.

Put all these factors together, and you have an industrywide drive for more monopoly. Sure, you can argue precisely whether it's CEOs who drive acquisitions, or shareholders, or the banks. The point is that every incentive within the structure points to finding and making deals. There are payoffs, prestige, and the promise of better times for all participants. Everyone is promised a cut. And the more deals that close, the more money that flows. In this sense, the planning of our economic architecture has been transferred from democratic institutions into the hands of bankers and executives, both working in concert, knowing that they personally benefit from consolidation.

This can create massive blind spots. The Monsanto/Bayer deal produced $700 million in fees for Morgan Stanley, Goldman Sachs, Credit Suisse,

HSBC, and JPMorgan, and more for the law firms. Yet no advisor managed to raise concern about the thousands of lawsuits from cancer victims who blame Monsanto's Roundup weedkiller for their illnesses. Multiple verdicts have granted hundreds of millions of dollars to victims, causing Bayer stock to plummet and executives to scramble to fix the public relations nightmare. A normal advisory process would have highlighted this headline risk, but getting the deal done seemed to matter more.

Because the economy has become so financialized, another by-product of concentration shares similarities to what happens when banks themselves merge into oligopoly. A recent flurry of deals in the health care sector has put half of all investment-grade corporate bonds in that space in the hands of ten companies. A downward trend in health care will concentrate risk at those ten and pull down the rest of their portfolios. A bubble can be defined as too much money chasing too few assets. Consolidated debt builds just this instability into our economic system. Monopoly and volatility, even financial crisis, fit together.

But the least-understood factor of endowing an industry dedicated to monopoly is how it creates an ecosystem of experts who must be respected and listened to. A power transfer to the consultant class inevitably leads to those consultants taking advantage.

UNFI picked Goldman Sachs, the market leader in M&A, to advise its Supervalu merger because of prior relationships with Goldman bankers, but also because of the conventional wisdom that an important deal requires an important bank in your corner. UNFI had been acquiring rivals for twenty years; only when the deal size rose was Goldman summoned.

UNFI explains in its legal complaint that Goldman wore multiple hats for the merger. It was UNFI's lead advisor, and it immediately recommended that UNFI up its offer to Supervalu to $32.50 per share, to ensure beating a rival bid. Goldman also became the lead arranger for the financing UNFI would ultimately need to buy Supervalu, a sum that increased with the larger bid. Stephan Feldgoise was the point of contact for both the advising *and* the arranging, and the conflicts here are obvious: to maximize Goldman's financing fees, Feldgoise could (and did) advise UNFI to sweeten the pot to complete the deal. But Feldgoise assured CEO Steve Spinner and his team that his dual role would create efficiencies, and given the existing trust, Spinner bought it. "Steve had no reason to think the world's preeminent investment bank would act badly," a UNFI official told me.

The deal required UNFI to take out a $2.15 billion loan. Goldman agreed to fund 45 percent of it and bring in two other big banks for the remainder: Bank of America (45 percent) and U.S. Bank (10 percent). The loan would net Goldman $14.5 million in interest, plus a $5.375 million bonus as the lead arranger of the financing, and another $9.4 million in advisory fees (this factored in a $2 million discount that Feldgoise offered UNFI if it upped its offer for Supervalu).

Goldman and the other banks had the option of syndicating the loan, which means finding other investors to put up the money. The banks had fifteen business days from the initial marketing date to syndicate. UNFI could veto any investors; after all, they would be holding UNFI's debt. On opening day, September 24, 2018, Goldman brought Spinner and UNFI's chief financial officer, Mike Zechmeister, to the posh Four Seasons hotel in New York City, where they presented a sixty-seven-page analysis of the deal to potential investors. A second meeting involving the same team was held later at the Park Hyatt. Both Goldman bankers and UNFI executives sweet-talked investors throughout the period.

But before the fifteen business days ended on October 15, Feldgoise contacted UNFI leadership with a problem. The broader stock market had dropped close to 10 percent during the marketing period, including in the grocery distribution sector. The combined UNFI/Supervalu company also received lower credit ratings from analysts than expected. With investors already licking their wounds, it was kind of the wrong time to syndicate a loan. Feldgoise asked UNFI to make "concessions" to entice more investors into the loan. In particular, he wanted UNFI to increase the interest rate significantly.

None of this was part of any document UNFI signed. There was no "in case of stock drop, break glass" clause, especially for the world's leading investment bank. "Goldman Sachs is supposed to have a little pulse on the markets," said the UNFI official. "Things always get volatile in a sector when a deal gets announced. I thought it was a shitty excuse."

Spinner and the management team said no to the concessions. Feldgoise responded that Goldman would now have to go into "full risk mitigation mode." On October 12, the Friday before the end of the marketing period, Goldman invoked "flex provisions" allowable under the agreement if the loan wasn't fully syndicated. This increased the interest rate by 1.5 percent, adding $183.2 million in interest to UNFI's loan. It also charged UNFI an "upfront fee" worth another $9 million. And Goldman asked for even more. Feldgoise stated that failure to increase the interest rate another 0.5 percent would "scare off" potential investors. The whole market would know that UNFI's syndicated loan was in trouble, and shareholders could revolt.

To UNFI, which was already out $192.2 million, it felt like a shakedown. Goldman conveyed it as an offer UNFI couldn't refuse, based on what seemed like a bogus rationale. A lesser company might have been pushed around. But UNFI again rejected the additional 0.5 percent interest rate increase. On October 18, Feldgoise called up Spinner personally, telling him "things would get ugly" if UNFI didn't agree to the concession. Spinner didn't budge.

Late that night, Goldman sent UNFI a "funds flow" detailing the final status of the loan. The funds flow was different from one submitted the day before. It now showed that Goldman intended to withhold $40.5 million from the loan value, while maintaining the same level of fees. There was only one business day before the close; if UNFI delayed it to work out this new charge, it would look to investors like the deal was suddenly shaky, and the stock might plummet. You could imagine Goldman saying, "Nice merger you've got there. It'd be a shame if something happened to it."

Spinner demanded a phone call. Feldgoise stated that Goldman was forced to initiate a second marketing period to complete the syndication. Because that second marketing period wouldn't have fifteen business days before closing, Feldgoise said, Goldman was entitled under the contract to $40.5 million in fees.

It was preposterous. UNFI's commitment letter clearly stated that there was only one marketing period. Goldman had never brought up a second marketing period until one business day before closing. It never did a new kickoff event or anything indicating it was renewing a search for investors. All materials set the end date for marketing the loan at October 15. Goldman claimed that Supervalu's third-quarter financial statement, issued at the end of the marketing period, necessitated the reset. That was the first time such a claim had been made, and Goldman never updated marketing materials with Supervalu's new information anyway.

Feldgoise had another ask. The weekend before the October 22 closing date, he suggested that UNFI add Supervalu as a co-borrower on the loan. This seemed somewhat pointless: UNFI and Supervalu would be the same company, so why would naming Supervalu as a co-borrower make a difference? UNFI asked Goldman to explain, and Goldman assured the company it was a pro forma change with a "muted impact." It was just important to some "select accounts" Goldman was trying to get into the loan. Spinner and his team talked it over, and shortly before the closing date they agreed to that change.

At closing, UNFI alleges that Goldman tried to grab even more money. It withheld $9.4 million in advisory fees from the loan, and added the $2 million fee it had previously vowed to discount UNFI. While UNFI objected to this, it had to go through with the closing, or else it would risk legal action from Supervalu. "It's very gangster, isn't it? Gangsters often change the terms of the deal after it's made," opined Robert Hockett, the Cornell Law professor.

Two days after the close, Bloomberg ran a story entitled "Goldman Strikes Unusual Concession in Struggling $2 Billion Deal." That the media would term the deal "struggling" based on little more than Goldman's manufactured sobbing is notable. But the story was really about how Goldman had found new investors willing to take the UNFI loan: "hedge funds that had been betting against the target company." The hedge funds, who happened to be Goldman clients, held some of the $470 million in credit default swaps on Supervalu's debt, which would pay off if Supervalu failed to pay back its creditors in a timely fashion. If UNFI completed the merger by paying off all Supervalu claims, Supervalu's debt would no longer exist, and the credit default swaps would be extinguished. That's bad news for the hedge fund guys. But if Supervalu remained a co-borrower on the main loan, those credit default swaps would remain alive.

Feldgoise's co-borrowing ask to UNFI made sense now. Those hedge fund investors would have a potential incentive to push the merged company into default to collect on the credit default swaps. And they could do so deliberately, through schemes designed to assert technical defaults just so CDS holders can profit. One of the hedge funds that pioneered this type of debt activism, Anchorage Capital, was one of the investors let into the UNFI loan. It was like Goldman brought a herd of sharks into a swimming pool.

In aggregate there was more money in the loan betting on UNFI to succeed (over $2 billion) than there was out there hoping that UNFI would fail ($470 million). But in an ideal world, none of a company's lenders would have any incentive for a default. And UNFI had no idea about the situation at all until reading about it in Bloomberg. Even though UNFI had veto power over any investor, Goldman Sachs never provided a final list in the syndicate, only identifying prospective lenders. Goldman simply neglected to mention that primary holders of the new UNFI's debt were hedge funds that would profit from its failure. According to UNFI's allegations, Goldman also never mentioned that the Goldman market-making desk helped *create* Supervalu credit default swaps. By virtue of its integrated business lines, Goldman's market-making desk could inform its lending division about the hedge funds' predicament, and the lenders could subsequently persuade UNFI to make the co-borrowing change.

Within a day, the value of the Supervalu credit default swaps tripled, increasing by $70 million. It was a huge windfall for the hedge funds, and a source of anxiety for UNFI. UNFI alleged later in a nearly $500 million lawsuit against Goldman Sachs that this amounted to market manipulation. As the complaint states: "The fact that Goldman Sachs was willing to manipulate the CDS market to benefit some of its customers while severely harming others, and all to the severe detriment of its client, UNFI, is clear evidence that Goldman Sachs had abandoned its duties to UNFI in a brazen effort to preserve and enhance its profits on the transaction."

Incredibly, UNFI alleged, Goldman was also trading UNFI stock the entire time, capitalizing on knowing when concessions would be accepted and how that would impact the market. "We expected our extremely well-paid transaction advisors to provide ethical counsel and unbiased support around this landmark acquisition," Spinner would later say in a statement, "not leverage their positions to pursue larger profits for themselves and other clients at our expense and ongoing damage."

Goldman Sachs responded to the charges with a curt statement: "These claims are entirely without merit. We intend to vigorously defend ourselves toward these allegations."

The episode was an extreme example of Goldman Sachs's ability to push its M&A clients around. Controlling both advisory services and financing, Goldman could use its various business lines strategically to maximize profits. One indicator of Goldman's motives can be seen in this fact: once it got the hedge funds into the UNFI loan, it didn't need to *also* raise the interest rate to entice investors. Goldman did so simply because it could squeeze more cash out of UNFI, which isn't some sap but a decades-old company with a history of mergers and acquisitions. "For the partners on the deal, it's their scorecard, their profit on the deal, their incentive structure," said the UNFI official.

The most valuable thing an M&A banker can do is to advise a client not to make a deal. Historically, that's how M&A giants earned their reputations. But the modern M&A landscape has too many incentives not only to encourage dealmaking but also to use the power and influence of the advisor's position to squeeze clients for more profits. As banks consolidate with more business lines under one roof, threatening financial stability, they have more opportunity to pull extra cash out of merging companies, with CEO payments used to keep the extortion quiet. Corporate America is being reshaped by shortsighted financiers who persuade and even bully while they monopolize the business world. They've convinced the world to listen to them, and they use this leverage for their own devices.

The UNFI case remains tied up in state court in New York.

I'm down to one addiction these days: fulfilling my daily step count. (There could be worse vices.) So when my wife and I reached the Hampton Inn near the George Washington Bridge in Teaneck, New Jersey, a couple of Christmases ago, I told her I had to get my steps in before the day ended. As usual, she rolled her eyes. With the hotel room a little too small to pace back and forth, I decided to take my urban hike into the hallway.

I'd walked a few hundred steps, focused mostly on my phone, when I noticed an almost imperceptible transition. The rug reached an endpoint, followed by a small anteroom of paneled tile; then the rug picked back up again. But the pattern had changed, from horizontal black and white stripes against a beige background to vertical and diagonal black and white stripes against a beige background. The walls had a light brown cross-hatched wallpaper on them now, too, as opposed to the eggshell-white walls previously. Why would the hotel change its look in the middle of a floor?

Actually, that wasn't it. I had stepped into a different hotel. A Homewood Suites, to be precise.

The building in Teaneck was a combination Hampton Inn and Homewood Suites. I had assumed that meant the two hotels were adjacent and separated by a wall, like a town house. But no, there was just a little tile-floor demilitarized zone, with a separate hotel on either side. In fact, right at the crossing was a little sign that read "You are now entering the Hampton Inn."

Hampton Inn and Homewood Suites, as you might have guessed, have the same corporate parent: Hilton Hotels. Also under its corporate umbrella are Hilton, Hilton Garden Inn, Signia Hilton, Hilton Grand Vacations, and Conrad, an upscale brand named after the late founder. Not to mention Canopy, Doubletree, Embassy Suites, Home2 Suites, Tru, the "microhotel" Motto, and luxury hotel groups LXR, Curio Collection, Tapestry Collection, and Waldorf-Astoria Collection. Seventeen brands, 5,500 properties, six continents, one company.

In 1999 Hilton bought Doubletree, and in a separate deal it bought Hampton Inn, Embassy Suites, and Homewood Suites, which were all at one point part of Holiday Inn's empire. The rest are homegrown, or born out of other one-off purchases.

I cannot be fully certain, because I did not knock on someone's door to inspect a room, but outside of the slight change to the wallpaper and floor pattern, there certainly didn't seem to be anything different between the Homewood Suites and Hampton Inn co-hotel space in Teaneck. You could reach your room from either the Homewood or Hampton Inn side; one night the area around the Hampton Inn elevator was crowded, so we took the other hotel's, without incident. The Hampton Inn offered a buffet breakfast, and I see no reason why a guest at the Homewood wouldn't have been able to walk over and get some—we weren't asked for a room key to enter the buffet area, and we didn't have Hampton Inn name tags.

Hilton is currently the world's second-largest hotel chain by number of rooms, behind Marriott, which in 2016 purchased Starwood, combining with the Sheraton, Westin, W, and St. Regis brands. At the time of the Starwood merger, Marriott's CEO told the Associated Press, "We've got an ability to offer just that much more choice."

When Marriott integrated its rewards program with Starwood, angry frequent travelers complained that they couldn't access their accounts, that hotel points had disappeared, and that their elite status was downgraded. Hackers didn't have any technical difficulties stealing four years' worth of data on 500 million Starwood Marriott customers. It was a textbook example of how monopolies neglect legacy IT systems, frustrating consumers and creating an open target for criminals simultaneously. Marriott and Hilton have also been sued for tacking on hidden "resort fees" to every hotel stay, some for amenities that guests don't even use.

So collecting dozens of brands under the auspices of the same company, with the same executives at the top dictating how those brands operate, gives "more choice" to the customer. But the choices include watching your guest reward points vanish; paying for bottled water you never drank; and having your name, address, phone number, passport number, and date of birth plastered on the dark web.

And in Hilton's case, it includes the choice of a hallway rug with horizontal stripes or a rug with vertical ones.

That kind of choice.

CHAPTER 7

Monopolies Are Why America Can't Build or Run a Single Weapons System Without Assistance from China

Murray Sanderson—whose name I have changed at his request—used to go to the meetings every quarter, at a hotel ballroom in downtown Cleveland. Each division head from his parent company, TransDigm, would get up and tout their recent successes, their year-over-year earnings growth, what have you. And then came the roundtable. "We would discuss what pushback we were getting from the government for price increases," Sanderson told me. "And whoever was most successful would go over what tactics they employed to combat the pushback."

The tactics were honed over the years, even distilled into a PowerPoint presentation often shown at the meetings, entitled "Understanding How the Government Buys." The sessions were intended to teach sales staff the TransDigm way, to drill into everyone's heads the company's prime directive, which essentially involved ripping off the Defense Department.

TransDigm makes aircraft and weapons parts—well, it doesn't make them so much as it corners the market, and gives the government only one way to obtain them. The parts aren't big enough to stand out on a spreadsheet of something like the F-35, which will set you back $100 million per jet. That's TransDigm's strategy: to fly, as it were, below the radar, and use the insights gleaned over years of procurement and legal close reading to maximize profits.

Sales personnel were taught to avoid long-term contracts with the Pentagon, enabling annual price spikes. They were taught to lower the order size to avoid an audit, knowing that seventeen small contracts would never garner the attention of one big one. If they had to, they could route the sale through different subsidiaries around the world, splitting up a large contract into smaller parts. They were taught to seek exemptions to rules that required disclosure of information about total costs, so the government could assess whether the purchase price was reasonable. In fact, they were told to avoid supplying cost information no matter what, to make up any excuse, to follow the letter of the law but do nothing to make the procurement officer's job easier. And if they were audited, they were told to use whatever could be justified as a cost to make the profit margin look relatively normal.

"The purchasing agent was at a disadvantage," Sanderson said. "At TransDigm, each division, they get people in those jobs that are killers. They're going to know the percentage they must sell to get their bonus. To the Defense Department, let's be honest, that person is not incentivized financially like a TransDigm person is. They're just filling buckets." So sticking these contracting officials with a bad deal that produced an outrageous profit? "It was child's play."

Sanderson was eventually let go from the company, after refusing to produce forecasts showing growth numbers he considered legally unattainable. "The chiefs didn't want to listen to what the Indians had to say to them," he said.

TransDigm got away with its pricing games for a long time, until a freshman member of Congress named Ro Khanna (D-CA) started to pay attention. But TransDigm is just one defense contractor with one set of parts in a system that has become increasingly concentrated, in ways large and small. There are a handful of giants building the tools for battle, and there are sole-source parts makers burrowing their way into the system, quietly but persistently taking their cut, buoyed by monopolization. The contractors spray work across practically every congressional district, giving every politician a stake in constructing more means of death, biasing the foreign policy of the United States toward more deployments, more bombings, more war.

At the same time, defense contractors outsource as much as other large industries. The United States has hollowed out its defense industrial base, ceding the guts of these systems to other countries, mostly China. Production capability and technological know-how has moved offshore, encouraged by Wall Street financiers seeking low labor costs. It's hard to find a stateside facility to cast the steel for a submarine or to manufacture internal parts for fighter jets. Dozens of vital components, from chemicals to metals to batteries to circuit boards, have single providers located in a country that has increasingly become an economic adversary. If that ever shifts into a military context, China would have the same advantage that the Union did against the Confederacy in the Civil War: it makes all the stuff.

The only real innovation left in the U.S. defense industry comes from financial roll-ups like TransDigm, scheming to acquire market control and swindle the taxpayer. Threats to national security from outsourcing military production have taken a backseat to figuring out how to outsmart the procurement officer. Strategy sessions for assembling the most innovative systems for troops to use in combat or, God forbid, how to use diplomacy to de-escalate conflict were replaced with strategy sessions for maximizing exploitation. Defense contractor gouging of the government has been a dedicated American tradition for at least a century. Today it's the only thing the industry has the capacity to pull off.

In 1919, a year after the end of World War I, the House Select Committee on Expenditures in the War Department held a series of hearings on profiteering and cost overruns among businesses supplying the Western Front. "War is a racket," wrote Major General Smedley Butler in his 1935 book of the same name, recounting how the war produced "at least 21,000 new millionaires and billionaires" through profiteering, and reordered the economic structure of the country. Butler, recounting what countries he invaded on behalf of what industries, called himself "a high-class muscle man for big business, for Wall Street, and for the bankers."

During the Depression, the Senate Munitions Committee, led by Republican Gerald Nye of North Dakota, further investigated whether contractors had precipitated America's entry into the Great War. Nye, who advocated nationalizing all military production, lamented, "War and preparation for war is not a matter of national honor and national defense, but a matter of profit for the few." By the end, Congress had passed three neutrality acts that kept the United States isolated from the initial fighting against Hitler in Europe.

In March 1941—before America entered World War II—Congress formed the Truman Committee, chaired by the haberdasher-turned-senator from Missouri whose leadership gained him such a solid reputation that he wound up on the 1944 Democratic ticket, and soon after as president. The committee saved between $10 billion and $15 billion rooting out fraud, waste, and abuse in military contracting. Truman uncovered major overruns in military housing construction, defective wire and cable sold to the army and navy, faulty engines requisitioned for army aircraft, and collusion among Army Air Force inspectors who overlooked malfunctioning equipment, a story line that would be employed in Arthur Miller's play *All My Sons*.

My point is that financial corruption in military production has a long history. And while Harry Truman had some success, the kinds of frauds he exposed kept recurring, both before and after his career. Dwight Eisenhower warned in his 1961 presidential farewell address of the creation of a "permanent armaments industry of vast proportions," rather than an improvised private-sector mobilization at first sight of war. But *both* structures enabled companies to reap profits from sending American boys toward foreign guns, and influence geopolitics to that end. The "misplaced power" Eisenhower feared didn't spring from nowhere.

Politicians did actually take heed of Eisenhower's warning. A year after his departure from office, Congress passed the Truth in Negotiations Act (TINA) to deal with a particular problem. Defense procurers kept down prices through competitive bidding for parts. But what about parts supplied by a single source? In those cases, TINA required that the supplier disclose a full analysis of the manufacturing costs. The Defense Logistics Agency, which handled procurement, would then allow a reasonable markup. So either market competition or informed purchasers would keep profiteering from spiraling out of control. The Defense Department could even take control of the special tooling of parts and license it to other contractors, making a sole-source part multisource.

None of this was foolproof, especially when Ronald Reagan initiated a large military buildup that provided greater opportunity for windfall profits. Reagan-era defense secretary Caspar Weinberger was forced to admit that his agency failed to increase competitive bidding during the buildup, particularly in the spare parts sector, a foreshadowing of TransDigm's business strategy. The cases of the $435 hammer and the $640 toilet seat are the stuff of legend; some say actual legend, because the prices were artifacts of an old Pentagon bookkeeping structure that spread overall research and development into the cost of everyday items. At the time, the Pentagon was mostly a source, rather than a beneficiary, of R&D. Products created out of the Defense Department were often spun off for commercial use: for example, the Defense Applied Research Projects Agency's concept for networked communications protocols eventually turned into the World Wide Web.

But whether the TINA contracting regime reined in procurement abuse or not, when the Berlin Wall came down, the defense budget fell with it. Even a few years before that, the Reagan buildup had peaked, in part because of the Gramm-Rudman-Hollings Balanced Budget Act, which put constraints on all spending. But after 1989, policymakers started to cash the Cold War dividend, even during the Pentagon leadership of defense secretary Dick Cheney, who was nobody's dove. According to figures from Gordon Adams, a professor emeritus at American University who worked in the Office of Management and Budget in Bill Clinton's first term, George H. W. Bush dropped the defense budget 26 percent in constant dollars over the course of his tenure, while Clinton in his first four years dropped it only 10 percent. "The statistical policy reality, this was the Bush-Cheney-Powell drawdown more than the Clinton drawdown," said Adams. R&D and procurement were slashed in particular, making military officials more reliant on the commercial marketplace, and with less expertise to demand the best equipment at the lowest prices.

That deflating balloon of military spending set the context for an event that came to be known as the "Last Supper." Defense secretary Les Aspin, his top deputy and eventual successor William Perry, and undersecretary for acquisition and technology John Deutch held a dinner meeting at the Pentagon with a dozen heads of the major defense contracting companies. "Part of it was a face slap," Adams said. "Perry was blunt: 'Some of you are going to live, and some will have to either die or merge. You have to figure it out among yourselves.'"

This amounted to a direct order to the permanent armaments industry. They were told to consolidate, because there just wasn't enough money to spread around to facilitate their existence. Perry put a number to it: he wanted half as many contractors within five years. And he got his wish, with $55 billion in mergers in that span. In 1994, Northrop purchased Grumman to make Northrop Grumman. Lockheed bought out twenty-two suppliers, taking over Loral, Unisys Defense, Ford Aerospace, and Martin Marietta, which partially provided the current name Lockheed Martin. Raytheon gobbled up the defense units of Texas Instruments, Chrysler, and Hughes Aircraft. Boeing took units of Rockwell International and McDonnell Douglas. General Dynamics absorbed Bath Iron Works and pieces of Lucent Technologies and Ceridian. (The consolidation has continued to this day: seventeen thousand firms exited the industry between 2001 and 2015, and in 2019 Raytheon bought United

Technologies to create the nation's second-largest aerospace and defense company, behind only Boeing.)

These five companies became America's leading prime integrators, in control of the vast majority of contracts for weapons and delivery systems. A 2006 research paper on aerospace consolidation by U.S. Air Force major Judy Davis found that between 1990 and 1998 the number of tactical-missile contracts dropped from thirteen to four, fixed-wing aircraft makers went from eight to three, and makers of expendable launch vehicles from six to two.

The expectation that military spending would continue its post–Cold War downward trajectory changed the moment planes hit the Twin Towers. In a flash, there were five giant mouths ready to feast on a new buildup, as troops shoved off to Afghanistan and Iraq. "They're now the behemoths that Eisenhower called the military-industrial complex," Adams said. "Too big to fail is what you get."

The prime integrators, of course, make out better when more people fight each other with guns and tanks. General Dynamics, Raytheon, Lockheed Martin, and Boeing have earned $30.1 billion off contracts from Saudi Arabia to prosecute the war in Yemen. Despite congressional efforts to cut off these sales, the Trump administration invoked an emergency provision to grease the arms shipments. Trump's rejection of the Intermediate-Range Nuclear Forces Treaty helped Raytheon earn over half a billion dollars in missile contracts; Lockheed and General Dynamics also have a trade in nuclear weapons. In investor calls, defense contractor CEOs have nonchalantly mused about how good war with Iran would be for business. Because military dollars flow to every state, reducing the budget, or the thirst for war, is a difficult task.

Below the top, the roster of manufacturers dedicated solely to defense has been narrowed significantly. "There's no such thing as a defense industrial base because over a long period of time, it has come to rely on civilian technology and commercial inputs to build equipment," Adams explained. Pieces of equipment that go into a plane, a periscope, or a battleship come mostly from a commercialized technology sector (with the minor exception of Raytheon, one of the few military contractors still producing technology). And since our commercial sectors trend toward monopoly, that translates into a lot of sole suppliers.

Jason Dickstein, president of the Washington Aviation Group, a legal consulting firm, explained that government regulators have issued 1.3 million different parts numbers for commercial aircraft to firms they grant design and production approval. "The majority of those parts have no competition," he said. Regulatory barriers to certifying equipment cement the parts monopoly in place. While military and commercial aircraft are different, the gatekeeper approval process largely proceeds the same way. And while companies often underbid the Big Five to get contracts for weapons systems parts, they make their money on the back end, in the aftermarket, when the government is at their mercy.

Just as the Defense Department got out of the research business, it also in many ways got out of the procurement business. The Federal Acquisition Streamlining Act and the Federal Acquisition Reform Act, both signed by Clinton, sought to simplify the process of procurement, reduce compliance costs, and make it more business-friendly. Contracts under certain thresholds could go through with the contractor disclosing only minimal information. Procurement officials didn't have to select the lowest bidder, and waivers to the Buy America Act meant that parts and weapons could be manufactured overseas. "The Clinton folks went to the defense industry and said, 'You are the seller, we are the buyer, how would you like us to buy from you?'" said Richard Loeb, a former procurement official and an adjunct professor at the University of Baltimore School of Law. "Imagine going to a car dealer and saying that."

Plus, the new laws gave defense firms a broader "commercial item" exemption. This meant that if the part was available in the commercial marketplace, the contractor didn't have to reveal what it cost to make it. The contracting official would have to consult price lists, historical pricing data, and other sources to determine a fair and reasonable price. But the assumption that this could be done was a fallacy, says Loeb: "There's no market price. Sometimes the market consists of either no actual sales or an infinitesimal number of sales." Even noncommercial items were dubbed commercial, in order to cut through the red tape; in the George W. Bush administration that was made stated policy. In 2004 Lockheed Martin listed its entire C-130J cargo plane as a commercial item. I don't remember seeing that in the J. Crew catalog.

Finally, with streamlined rules and less data to analyze, procurement officers were let go in large numbers. The institutional memory of the Defense Department was slowly ground down, while contractors grew in

power and knowledge. By the end of this wave, with procurement deregu-
lated, purchasing back at a high baseline, and more mergers proceeding
apace, Obama-era Pentagon officials began to sound the alarm about too
much industry consolidation. The givers of the warnings included, in a
remarkable bout of chutzpah, William Perry, the host of the Last Supper.
"Maybe we should be more explicit in saying we already have enough consolidation," Perry said, falsely assuming that the bell he rang in 1993 could
somehow be unrung.

Freedom from rules keeping supply chains in America led commercial
military producers to seek out cheap labor abroad. Contractor profits and
outsourcing soared, egged on by Wall Street analysts demanding higher
profit margins. Manufacturing of everything, from specialized high-grade
steel to small fasteners, has just left the country. The typical trajectory
today is that U.S. companies design, factories overseas build, and domestic
salespeople peddle to the government. This leads to decision making being
driven by financial considerations rather than by quality engineering.

It's one thing to offshore production of fast fashion or children's toys. But
when you send the defense industrial base abroad, national security can
undeniably be undermined. It's not like the military hasn't thought about
this, though they haven't done much to stop it. A remarkable interagency report assessing risks to national security in defense manufacturing,
released in September 2018, outlined how globalization has led to over-
reliance on single-source domestic products and foreign supply chains,
particularly through "competitor nations" like China, which subsidizes its
producers. Most worrying to the authors, lack of engineering capacity has
presented "the possibility of not being able to produce specialized components for the military at home."

The report listed dozens of items for which there is little or no domestic manufacturing. Howitzer barrels and mortar tubes are made on only
one diminished production line. The only silicon power switch maker lost
its supply of semiconductor switches and had to shut down. There's one
qualified source for chaff, and two for flares, though in 2018 both flare factories experienced explosions and shut down assembly temporarily. Since
2000, the shipbuilding industry has lost over twenty thousand establishments in the United States, and the navy routinely relies on sole-source
providers. The textile market has been so battered that there's no domes-

tic supplier for high-tenacity polyester fiber. The merger between L3 and Harris Technologies announced in 2018 made them the only U.S.-based supplier of military-grade night vision goggles, and the tube that makes them work comes solely from Germany.

A particular element of this is the loss of materials production. One company in China has cornered half the global production of lithium, the key element in advanced battery technology. China produces about half the world's printed circuit boards, a critical electronic component; 90 percent of that sector comes from Asia. China also supplies the military with specialty chemicals for missiles and munitions. "In many cases, there is no other source or drop-in replacement material," the report states.

China also enjoys near-total control of the market for rare earth metals, a group of seventeen chemical elements used in almost all communications, vehicle, and weapons technology. America pioneered the development of rare earth magnets for F-15 and F-16 fighter jets in the 1970s, a technology spun out to the commercial sector for use in electronics and cell phones. A company called Magnequench manufactured these magnets in Indiana until 2004, when the plant closed and shipped out to China. In fact, China bought the entire company, using as a front a hedge fund operated by Archibald Cox Jr., son of the famed Watergate prosecutor. Rare earths are among at least twenty minerals sourced exclusively in China, according to a 2017 Interior Department report. A technology invented in the United States is monopolized in China.

During Trump's trade wars, Chinese state-run newspapers implied that the country would ban exports of rare earths, causing technology prices to soar. President Xi Jinping toured a rare earths factory in 2019, heightening the threat. China did try to carry out a rare earths export ban against Japan in 2010, after patrol vessels arrested a Chinese fishing boat around disputed islands in the East China Sea that both countries claim as their own. There are conflicting assessments of how effective that ban was, and the incident alarmed the rest of the world enough to secure alternative sources in Japan (where years' worth of expensive excavation will be necessary), Australia, and the United States, which revived a once-mothballed rare earth mine and processing facilities. But domestic efforts are in the early stages and will have to surmount several environmental hurdles (processing rare earths is a dirty business). China is likely to maintain its virtual monopoly for some time, which means that unless the Defense

Department mandates domestic sources for rare earths, America cannot build a weapons system without cooperation from the Chinese.

The interagency study concludes that Chinese takeovers of vital military inputs could create "potentially dangerous interaction between Chinese economic aggression guided by its strategic industrial policies and vulnerabilities and gaps in America's manufacturing and defense industrial base." The possibility for counterfeits also looms large, as it does in any situation when manufacturing leaks beyond borders. We're seeing numerous examples of shoddy military equipment, from continuing problems with the F-35 fighter jet, including erroneous battery failure reports and cabin pressure spikes that cause searing ear and sinus pain for pilots, to the $13 billion aircraft carrier USS *Gerald R. Ford*, which was delivered without the elevators necessary to move bombs from below deck.

Alexander Hamilton, in his 1791 report on the subject of manufactures, recognized that the government should set aside funding to annually purchase "military weapons, of home manufacture," to bolster domestic industry but also, and more importantly, to maintain public security. "There appears to be an improvidence, in leaving these essential instruments of national defence to the casual speculations of individual adventure," Hamilton wrote. Two hundred years later, the United States stopped listening, handing over military manufacturing to speculators. Once the plants closed, the know-how left in America was purely extractive, using information advantages to sucker the government into a sweetheart deal. Sheet metal gave way to balance sheets.

It's a misnomer to call TransDigm a defense contractor or manufacturer. The Cleveland-based company, co-founded in 1993 by Doug Peacock and Nick Howley, is more like a private equity roll-up; in fact, it passed through three private equity firms before going public in 2006. Since its founding, TransDigm has borrowed money to buy around seventy companies that make aerospace parts, used in both military and civilian aircraft. It piggybacked on the demand for consolidation after the Last Supper to pick off bits of a fragmented aerospace parts sector and build a powerhouse.

TransDigm overtly tells investors that it seeks "private equity–like returns," intended to be higher than stock market yields, and certainly higher than an ordinary parts supplier. Investors love this, not only because of the outsized stock returns but also because TransDigm issues a "special dividend," hefty cash payments for everyone with a share of common stock, nearly every year. Though TransDigm's profits keep rising, the company's debt has tripled since 2012, with money siphoned out to executives and investors. In 2017, then-CEO Howley took home $61 million in compensation, sixth-highest in the United States that year.

TransDigm's acquisitions are extremely precise. Murray Sanderson spent his career at an aerospace firm that TransDigm scooped up. "TransDigm is extremely good at going through prospective company finances and contracts," Sanderson said. "It can spot where a company has sole-source content. If you have sole-source content, you have a license to raise the price, and not a lot of negative consequences. Like Warren Buffett figured, you build a moat around your business."

According to TransDigm's 2016 annual report, "About 80% of our sales come from products for which we believe we are the sole-source provider." Current executive chairman (and longtime CEO) Howley and current CEO Kevin Stein have publicly described their pricing strategy as "razor/razor blade." They sell parts to the original equipment manufacturer—for example, an aircraft maker like Boeing—at lower margins. That gets them into the plane as the sole-source part provider, and complex safety and production requirements make it very difficult to certify alternatives. TransDigm then makes its money in the aftermarket, selling spare parts to the purchasers of the airplane, like American or United or the U.S. military, which need consistent supplies. Prices for those parts get jacked up because the purchasers have nobody else to buy from.

For some reason, Howley and Stein see this as just a normal business strategy. But what they're describing is the textbook definition of market power. The "razor/razor blade" model, which shavers well understand, means that the razor is sold relatively cheaply, but the price of the razor blades, which fit only that particular razor, goes up and up. (By the way, the razor market is an oligopoly, with Schick, Procter & Gamble, and Unilever recently buying up startup competitors, but that's another story.) In this case, TransDigm buys companies who spent the money to develop products, ensures that purchasers come to rely on those products, and then squeezes out as much as it can get. That's the company's *justification*. Its alibi is monopoly.

Sanderson described to me the "TransDigm-ification" of his company after the acquisition. Anyone who wasn't willing to do things TransDigm's way was purged. Managers and directors were shown the door. "I was an engineer at the time," Sanderson said. "TransDigm cleaned out the sales department. I was the only person left who knew what was where, so I became a salesman." Mass firings were common, other former employees allege: the best way to raise profit margins is to cut head count and lower labor costs.

TransDigm-ification involved charging as much as possible in the after-market, particularly for military parts. Over 30 percent of TransDigm revenue comes from military sales. The aftermarket for commercial aircraft is bigger, because passenger planes fly much more than military jets. But the business sector is also more incentivized to buy from TransDigm at reasonable prices; they have entire teams striving for a reduction in costs or at least a flat rate, so they can show an on-paper benefit. "If they don't get that, they're fired," Sanderson said.

Especially after the Clinton-era procurement reforms, no such incentives existed on the military side. Contracting officers were told to work cooperatively with parts sellers. It created a jumbo-jet-sized loophole for companies like TransDigm to fly through. And we know TransDigm capitalized on it quickly, because the firm got dinged back in 2006 for overcharging the government.

"Given the constraints of a sole-source contracting environment, Defense Logistics Agency contracting officers were unable to effectively negotiate prices for spare parts procured from TransDigm subsidiaries," the Defense Department's inspector general wrote in an audit. Because of Clinton-era restrictions, procurement officers could not obtain cost data from TransDigm on small contracts and items deemed commercial. Looking at a sample of seventy-seven parts costing $14.8 million, the inspector general determined that TransDigm charged $5.3 million above what would be considered a reasonable profit margin.

Sanderson explained that after the 2006 audit, managers were sat down and told how to raise prices more subtly. "I would say the word to use is 'relentless,'" he said. "There was general contempt for the contracting officials with the Defense Logistics Agency." Sales managers were given a precise dollar figure as a target every year, and their bonuses depended on them hitting it. If it was harder to get other purchasers to agree to markups, you could always go back to the government to make it up. Sometimes sales staff played accounting games to hit numbers, particularly through a maneuver called "channel stuffing." The government had "massive depots for inventory," Sanderson explained. So if a salesperson needed to sell a hundred additional parts by the end of the month, they could just get the government to buy them, filling orders far into the future. "We could apply for a modification of the government contract and ship parts early," Sanderson said. "If it was September, we'd pull in an order from the following July and ship it in." This made it look like sales were growing, but it was just borrowing from the future.

The deceit on investor metrics paled in comparison to the deceit toward government contractors. "We didn't have a problem getting price increases to the government," Sanderson said. "The purchasing agent, they need to buy it or else they wouldn't be trying to buy it. The sky was really the limit. I had prices at a 30 percent margin, moved it to 80 when I got done. It was just brutal."

At quarterly sales meetings, executives pressured managers to goose prices. If the contracting officer wanted a long-term contract with extra volume, TransDigm taught its agents to refuse. "You'd say no, management doesn't like those because of inflation, energy costs, rare earth metals, Buy America regulations, whatever," Sanderson said. "You'd just make it up with some bit of credibility." Staying out of long-term deals allowed TransDigm to increase prices every year. It also minimized the size of individual orders. Under the new rules, any contract under $750,000 did not have to include cost information, which left procurement agents with no reference point for whether TransDigm's prices were too high.

Sales officials were also taught to come up with a commerciality justification, which was another way of evading cost information rules. Sanderson gave the example of a sensor. "The government was complaining about the jet engine component for the F-16, about the price. We found one for the A320 and the 737. They looked somewhat similar, they both had a little end and a big end, and a wire that feeds the power. We took a drawing of one and the other, showed them the list price. We didn't tell them that the A320 component had a superalloy that cost $5,000 a pound. We just showed them that it was commercially similar and our price is less." The government bought the sensors.

Sanderson gave me several examples like this: an engine thrust part, a starter valve. TransDigm would mislead the government into believing they were getting a fair deal, hiding the true information of how much the part cost and how much more the Pentagon was being charged. Anytime they were asked for more information, TransDigm sales staff would simply deny the request. "We were coached not to provide cost data," one former employee told staff on the House Oversight Committee in 2019. "We were going out of our way not to disclose costs to the government," said another. "Nick Howley and management gave a wink wink, nod nod that we want to avoid disclosing any cost data."

Monopoly means never having to upgrade your product; nobody's competing with you on quality. Like the plotline in *All My Sons*, defective parts seem to be part of the TransDigm story, as monopoly breeds complacency. An advanced air force surveillance drone, the MQ-9 Reaper, kept dropping out of the sky, and officials blamed a faulty starter-generator that a subsidiary of TransDigm manufactured. Twenty Reapers had to be destroyed or repaired in 2015 alone.

TransDigm never gave back excess profits after the 2006 audit; it said, "We believe that such a refund is not warranted." And though another inspector general's report in 2008 condemned overcharges from the exclusive distributor for one of TransDigm's subsidiaries, that didn't stop the strategy. And it probably would have continued indefinitely if it weren't for a freshman member of Congress looking to make a name for himself.

Ro Khanna was a former Commerce Department official who made two unsuccessful runs for Congress, in different districts, before succeeding in 2016. He represented the heart of Silicon Valley, and living in the shadow of Google and Facebook gave him an interest in monopoly power and its significant impact on the economy. A couple of months into Khanna's first term, in 2017, he had coffee at a Capitol Hill–area Starbucks with Matt Stoller, at the time a fellow at the Open Markets program at the New America Foundation. Stoller told him about research that was bubbling up about a defense contractor monopoly that had been gouging the government. Khanna, who had a seat on the House Armed Services Committee, wanted to know more.

The information originated with a financial news website called The Capitol Forum. With the understated title "Military Revenues at Risk from Promised Trump Administration Crackdown on Military Contract Costs," the story laid out the TransDigm business model of acquiring companies with borrowed cash, firing employees, and jacking up prices. Most notably, the story pointed out how selected parts would jump in price after TransDigm acquired the company. Before being acquired by TransDigm, Whippany Actuation Systems sold a motor rotor for $654.46. Afterward, it was $5,474.00. Before acquisition, a Harco cable assembly was $1,737.03; afterward, it was $7,863.60. The article explained that while commercial customers had begun to push back against these increases, the military had not. The Capitol Forum followed up on the TransDigm story vigorously. It analyzed thousands of TransDigm products, finding prices increasing more after an acquisition than before; it found that subsidiaries submitted incorrect information to federal databases to hide TransDigm's ownership; and it highlighted "channel stuffing," which, as we've seen, is the practice of pushing inventory on distributors and the military to hit sales goals. It reported on TransDigm's quarterly sales meetings as well.

A short-seller named Andrew Left, who runs Citron Research, added to the revelations about TransDigm in an article with the not-so-understated title "Could TransDigm Be the Valeant of the Aerospace Industry?" TransDigm's gross profit margins were four to ten times the rest of the industry's, Left explained, something that was wholly explained by price increases. Obviously, Left was making a short bet, hoping that government action would pound TransDigm's stock price. In this case, his intentions were aligned with the taxpayers' interest.

"I had expressed concerns of increasing the Defense Department budget by $54 billion when there was considerable waste and no sense of first tackling that," Khanna told me. TransDigm appeared to be a perfect target. So on March 21, 2017, he did what a member of Congress does in these situations: he wrote a letter. Specifically, he asked the Pentagon's inspector general to open another investigation into TransDigm, just as the office had done in 2006. "Reports suggest that TransDigm Group has been operating as a hidden monopolist," Khanna wrote, "engaging in a series of unreasonable price increases of products for which it is the only supplier . . . to enrich a few individual financiers who stand to benefit at the expense of our troops and weapons systems." Khanna even added The Capitol Forum chart of price spikes after TransDigm acquired a company.

The letter rebounded across Washington and Wall Street. TransDigm stock dropped more than 10 percent in two days. The business press highlighted the story; the *Huffington Post*'s Zach Carter called TransDigm "the Martin Shkreli of defense contracting." In a nation with a rich history of high-profile military profiteering investigations, the TransDigm story appeared to have legs.

But a month later, TransDigm's stock was right back where it had been before the letter. The investor class coveted those private-equity-style returns from TransDigm, and they circled the wagons to maintain them. TransDigm's chronic need to float debt hooked in the major banks. A single TransDigm debt offering in 2016 was handled by Morgan Stanley, Credit Suisse, Citi, UBS, Barclays, Crédit Agricole CIB, Goldman Sachs, HSBC, and Royal Bank of Canada. Analysts for Barclays and Royal Bank of Canada, two of these creditors, defended the company as a "top pick" that was a "victim of its own success." Banks also take fees when hedge funds trade the stock. The whole thing was a mutually reinforcing cycle: one business line profited from TransDigm, and another touted its stock.

Members of Congress, particularly from TransDigm's home state of Ohio, tried to get Khanna to take meetings with company executives, a common tactic in Washington to sweet-talk critics. Meanwhile, investors went after Khanna personally. A Twitter user with the handle "Aces and Faults" who used the headshot of Ted Weschler, one of Warren Buffett's top traders, conjured up a conspiracy theory that a short-seller behind the TransDigm information used to work for an investment fund that donated to Khanna. This whisper campaign lasted for weeks. "They floated a bogus story," Khanna told me. "Anytime you raise questions about the corporate sector or a defense contractor, they will try to throw mud as a way to intimidate." In an even more bizarre twist, someone impersonating a reporter from the business outlet *Barron's* contacted The Capitol Forum and Andrew Left, defending the company's practices. A friend of the impersonator told *Barron's*, "He feels that there are lies being told about TransDigm, and he was seeking to out them."

For a couple of months Khanna was on an island, the only member of Congress willing to speak out about TransDigm; nobody else wanted the backlash. Finally House Democrat Tim Ryan and Senate Democrat Elizabeth Warren, both of whom would later run for president, joined Khanna to ask for an investigation. Faced with the requests, the Defense Department's inspector general complied.

Perhaps unwittingly, Khanna had injected himself into a long-running debate over military procurement, spurred by a former Raytheon executive named Shay Assad. During the Obama administration, Assad became known as "the most hated man in the Pentagon"—at least by his adversaries—for using an obscure office called the Defense Pricing Agency, and a new position created especially for him, to take on monopolist weapons manufacturers. From 2011 to 2016, Assad slashed over $500 million in contracting costs through aggressive scrutiny of cost information. "We generally overpay for almost everything we pay," Assad told *Politico*. "I know, because I was on the other side of the table."

Top military contractors, angered that Assad was criticizing their record profits and forcing them to supply cost data that they were legally obligated to supply, mounted a full-spectrum assault on Assad, working with allies in Congress to wring out more exemptions. In summer 2017, they even got one through: a dramatic expansion of the contract threshold for mandatory cost data from $750,000 to $2 million, pitched as a way to "reduce administrative burdens" on private business. Congress also repeatedly blocked reforms Assad supported to the commercial item rule. Assad sparred openly with contractors, even telling CEOs at an industry conference that the days of windfall profits were over.

The TransDigm investigation gave Assad a chance to prove his point that contractors were using market power to profit at the Pentagon's expense. But even he couldn't have imagined the sweeping extent of the inspector general's findings. The report, released in February 2019, examined forty-seven parts, thirty-nine of them sole-source, in 113 contracts TransDigm made with the Defense Department between January 2015 and January 2017. It determined that TransDigm earned an "excess profit" of more than 15 percent above costs in forty-six of those forty-seven parts. These included markups as high as a whopping 4,451 percent. A three-inch non-vehicular clutch disk for the C-135 transport plane cost $32 to produce; TransDigm charged $1,443. Another small part, a "quick disconnect coupling half" for the T-38 Talon, cost $173 to produce; TransDigm charged $6,986. The overall contracts, totaling $26.3 million, yielded $16.1 million in excess profits.

The one case where TransDigm earned a reasonable profit was the only time, by virtue of the size of the contract, that it was obligated to provide cost data to the government. In fifteen other cases, contracting officers asked TransDigm for cost data, and TransDigm simply refused to comply. The report also noted that TransDigm claimed that thirty-two of the forty-seven items studied were available commercially, but the inspector general could verify commercial status for only four of them. Even Khanna's most explosive charge, that TransDigm created the illusion of multiple distributors for a product by hiding from the Pentagon that they owned the subsidiaries, was not dismissed out of hand. The inspector general did not fully address that charge "because it was referred to the Defense Criminal Investigative Service for action deemed appropriate."

Overall, officers had scant ability to determine whether they were overpaying for TransDigm parts. They did, however, urgently need spare parts to keep aircraft in the sky and maintain mission readiness. "It was very gratifying and vindicating," Khanna said of the findings. "I had the surreal experience of having Grover Norquist's brother, the comptroller of the Defense Department, agree with my efforts."

The $16.1 million in overcharges came from only a tiny sample; TransDigm had nearly five thousand contracts with the Pentagon from April 2012 to January 2017, worth $471 million. A slightly more thorough review obtained by Bloomberg found profit margins up to 9,400 percent on a half-inch drive pin, which cost $46 but for which TransDigm charged the government $4,361. Excess profits were found on ninety-eight out of one hundred parts.

The House Oversight Committee, under the direction of Democrats but with Republican cooperation, initiated an investigation. Committee staff interviewed former TransDigm employees, hearing of its "one-two punch: one, raising prices, and two, cutting costs." The former employees all told the familiar story of TransDigm coaching sales staff to resist providing cost data and structuring contracts to stay under thresholds to allow them to hide that data. Dealing with procurement officers was like "taking candy from a baby," one ex-employee said. TransDigm responded to the committee that they have "no written policy" about refusing to disclose costs, which nobody had really suggested. It was a nondenial denial.

The Oversight Committee hauled in TransDigm CEO Kevin Stein and executive chair Nick Howley for a hearing that was remarkable in its unanimous condemnation. Democratic socialists Alexandria Ocasio-Cortez and Rashida Tlaib, following the lead of the Defense Department, demanded that TransDigm return the $16.1 million in excess profits. Freedom Caucus leaders Jim Jordan and Mark Meadows made the same request. "We in Congress can almost agree on nothing," Khanna marveled. Kevin Fahey, the assistant secretary of defense for acquisition, called TransDigm's business model "disgraceful," its pricing practices "outrageous," and its profiteering "sickening." This from a Donald Trump appointee.

For their part, Stein and Howley denied there was anything untoward about TransDigm. Howley claimed he was never even at the quarterly sales meetings. When asked to return the windfall, Stein said, "We are still evaluating and we have not come to a conclusion." Both argued repeatedly that they complied with all rules and regulations, to which Democrat John Sarbanes of Maryland archly replied, "Which may be why we need to tighten them up." A Republican colleague, Bob Gibbs from Ohio, referenced the $4,361 drive pin. "As a farmer, there's no way I'm going to spend $4,300 for a half-inch drive pin," he chuckled. Mark DeSaulnier, a Democrat from California, summed it up: "As long as they have a monopoly, you're not going to get the best price."

After taking a bipartisan beating, TransDigm relented, sending a $16.1 million refund to the government. "We saved more money today for the American people than our Committee's entire budget for the year," gushed Oversight Committee chair Elijah Cummings of Maryland (who would pass away in October 2019). Given how rare it is to witness accountability in any context, the incident was an example of how perseverance and effective use of congressional authority can pay off. "My personal experience highlights the extraordinary authority Congress has if we exercise influence," Khanna said. "There's a reason that Congress was created in Article I of the Constitution."

But of course it was no more than a tithing for TransDigm, a minor payback of some profits on about 2 percent of its contracts since 2012. House lawmakers did seek a deeper investigation into TransDigm's pricing, which could create calls for more refunds. But TransDigm's stock increased 37.5 percent from January to June 2019; investors didn't think the profiteering exposure would harm the bottom line. And Murray Sanderson was certain that TransDigm wouldn't be fazed either. "TransDigm is going to hunker down," he said. "It will tell every operating division president and sales director that the storm will pass. They will play nice for a little while. And back to business as usual. The collective memories of politicians are short. In a few years it'll blow over. That's exactly what they said in 2006, and it was true. It took thirteen years before it came back to bite them."

Shay Assad, in a letter attached to the inspector general's report, wrote: "We need to look to other ways to address and combat the unconscionable greed exhibited by companies like TransDigm." But he wouldn't be the one to look at them. At the end of 2018, Assad was reassigned out of the Defense Pricing Agency, allegedly for racking up $500,000 in travel costs flying back and forth at least once a week from Boston, where he lived, to Washington. This was an arrangement negotiated under the Obama administration, and the travel came over a seven-year period; Assad saved $500 million, a thousand times the travel costs, on just three contracts in 2016 alone. His new post had no authority over contract negotiations. Assad retired instead of reporting to the demoted position; there was no longer any point. His replacement at the Defense Pricing Agency would be based out of Dayton, sure to incur the same travel costs.

Assad got blackballed right after he proposed that defense contractors get paid for performance of their systems rather than completion of production. That didn't sit well with defense contractors, or the then deputy defense secretary, Patrick Shanahan, who personally announced the rule would be rescinded, days after learning about it. Considering Shanahan spent his entire career at Boeing, his role as the hatchet man for anything constraining the profits of the Big Five contractors is fitting. Shanahan would later become acting defense secretary, replacing Gen. James Mattis, who decamped to the General Dynamics board. After allegations of a cover-up around domestic violence incidents between Shanahan's son and his ex-wife felled him, Mark Esper took over the Pentagon; he was a long-time Raytheon lobbyist. Every defense secretary in the Trump era has had a direct tie to one of the Big Five.

As for TransDigm, its setbacks have been minor and its profits abundant. The Justice Department did force a divestiture of one TransDigm acquisition, to break up a monopoly in airplane safety restraints. But it was allowed to purchase Esterline, the only maker of chaff and one of just two makers of flares in the United States. The buyouts keep coming, and the potential for market power alongside them. In announcing the acquisition, TransDigm CEO Kevin Stein told investors, "We just think that there's juice here . . . there's juice here that we can go get." Juice is derived from squeezing, as TransDigm presumably would do to the government.

Khanna and his fellow members of Congress have discussed changing procurement rules to give contracting officers more information and leverage in negotiations. Khanna even authored an amendment to the defense authorization bill requiring the turnover of cost information on all sole-source parts, and a Pentagon memo stated that procurement officials must require this for TransDigm contracts (until Khanna's amendment becomes law, TransDigm could still stonewall those requests). But experts have heard that all before. "Everyone says they will fix this system," said former defense budgeter Gordon Adams. "We waste in my judgment a fantastic amount of time trying to deliver on the promise that this system will be adequately cost-controlled. At some point I simply threw up my hands. I thought, 'I can't believe I am spending this much time to fix a system that's unfixable.' This is a problem you manage, not a problem you solve."

A study from the Government Accountability Office is assessing whether other companies have adopted TransDigm's strategies. Murray Sanderson is convinced that they have. "Every other aerospace company has watched their meteoric rise, and they're jealous of it," he said. Defense Department inspector general Glenn Fine pointed out at the TransDigm hearing that the situation reminded him of issues listed in audit reports going back twenty years, and not limited to one company.

"They are convinced that their business model is correct," said Sanderson about TransDigm. "You cannot tell these guys they're wrong." In fact, that's how Sanderson left the company. While a sales director, he was told to forecast a 14 percent year-over-year sales increase in the middle of the Great Recession. "I could not get there," he said. He was replaced by someone more amenable to corporate directives.

But after all that, Sanderson doesn't completely blame TransDigm for profiteering. "You must ask yourself the question, is it the fault of Trans-Digm for identifying a weakly managed customer and taking advantage, or the fault of the politicians for not caring?"

As recently as a couple of decades ago, traveling the countryside as I did for this book would mean running into a lot of Walmarts. And yes, I did. Walmart had 5,362 U.S. locations as of April 2019; they are as much a part of the American landscape as highway wildflowers. Walmart remains the nation's largest employer, and the world's largest company by consolidated revenue. A report from the Institute for Local Self-Reliance released in June 2019 noted that Walmart is responsible for half or more of all grocery sales in forty-three metropolitan areas and 160 smaller markets. If Walmart were a country, its economy would be bigger than Norway's and in the top twenty-five worldwide. Walmart defines monopoly in America.

But driving through the Midwest and the mid-South, I definitely noticed another cluster of stores, downscale from even Walmart, nestled into poorer and more remote burgs. They have names like Dollar General and Dollar Tree, and together they have nearly six times as many outlets as Walmart, over thirty thousand in all. There are about three thousand of these things just in Texas. In Marlinton, West Virginia, last summer, I saw a Dollar General next door to a Family Dollar. The shops are small, the pickings are slim, the prices are dirt cheap, and the owners are willing to place outlets where Walmart won't.

Three new dollar stores open in the United States every day, full of processed foods and off-brand necessities. The stores concentrate in low-income communities. And companies like Dollar General make sure they maximize subsidies and tax breaks from cities for the privilege of plopping a stockpile of cheap Chinese-made goods into hardscrabble towns.

Dollar stores result from monopoly, from the abandonment of large regions of winner-take-all America. The desperation of certain sections of small-town and poor urban America demands a lower-cost alternative to the price tags of even a Walmart, long known for its low prices. When you've stripped families to the bone, their only recourse is the dollar store. "The economy is continuing to create more of our core customer," said Dollar General chief executive Todd Vasos in 2017. Poverty is a growth market.

In a way, Walmart is being chased on a field they plowed. When Congress repealed fair trade laws in the 1970s and allowed discount stores to offer goods at lower prices, Sam Walton pounced, offering "prices to fit your budget" nationwide. Walmart grew a thousand-fold from 1971 to 1993, making Walton the richest man in America for a while. But Walmart's incessant corporate outsourcing and immiseration of workers gradually put even its low prices out of reach for many. The company would wake up to find discount chains outdiscounting them. When a Walmart Express microstore experiment fizzled in 2016, Dollar General bought up dozens of the storefronts.

Dollar stores also capitalized on Walmart's big-box strategy, which attracted customers across many cities and hollowed out Main Streets nationwide. That small-town real estate was primed for dollar stores to come in with smaller, more convenient, and cheaper outlets. A 2018 Institute for Local Self-Reliance report calls dollar stores "an invasive species advancing on a compromised ecosystem."

Just as Walmart did, dollar stores have forced thousands of independent businesses to close their doors. Few employers want to run a mom-and-pop business anymore. This transfers profits from local business owners who recirculate them through communities to corporate offices far away, and it also hits workers. On average, small grocery stores have three times as many employees as the cut-rate behemoths, by one account.

Walmart store managers command an upper-middle-class salary, while dollar store managers make $40,000 a year without overtime. Dollar stores also carry few fresh foods, exacerbating the tragedy of food deserts. And often the products are $1 because they're smaller; dollar stores take advantage of desperation to raise the per-unit price.

When Family Dollar, a chain that catered to inner-city communities, went up for sale, it sparked a bidding war among the two duopolists, with Dollar Tree, a serial acquirer of smaller companies, winning the fight. A few years later, activist hedge fund Starboard Value took a stake in Dollar Tree, demanding that Family Dollar be sold off and that Dollar Tree raise prices, which seems a little off-brand. The duopoly could move to monopoly, with Dollar General standing tall on the mountaintop.

But to stay there, Dollar General will have to fend off a backlash. The dollar store resistance, though outmanned and outgunned, has notched a couple of victories. In 2017, the Tulsa, Oklahoma, city council put a moratorium on new building permits for dollar stores, and changed zoning rules to permanently restrict clusters of the discount retailers and promote more access to fresh food. Mesquite, Texas, passed a similar zoning ordinance. "Formula" business restrictions on chain stores are in place from Jersey City, New Jersey, to Mendocino County, California. Buhler, Kansas, rejected a dollar store chain a couple of years back.

This resistance feels like a pea shooter aimed at Godzilla, however. I would lose count if I tried to track all the dollar stores I saw as I traveled across America. They're almost the parasites of monopoly, feasting on flesh grown over decades of hopelessness and neglect.

CHAPTER 8

Monopolies Are Why a Small Business Owner and His Girlfriend Had to Get Permission from Amazon to Live Together

Jeff Bezos is a poor man, to hear him tell it. He made the catastrophic mistake of letting outside businesses offer products for sale on his little e-commerce site, Amazon.com, and, well, they've just taken over. According to figures Bezos released in his 2019 annual shareholder letter, these entrepreneurial geniuses went from 3 percent of gross sales on Amazon in 1999 to 58 percent in 2018. "To put it bluntly: Third-party sellers are kicking our first-party butt," said Bezos with shocking candor. "Badly."

It was a line I've repeated to several third-party sellers, mostly to snickers. For some reason, they didn't quite accept the claim that Bezos's empire, the most valuable public company in the world, was also the best friend small businesses ever had. Take Harry Copeland, or "Crazy Harry," as he calls himself.

Crazy Harry runs Harry's Famous Flowers in Orlando, Florida, a forty-employee retail and wholesale flower business. It's a nice shop full of bouquets, corsages, wedding displays, even a collection of succulents planted in a miniature 1965 Ford Mustang. Amazon reached out to Crazy Harry in late 2017 with an offer to sell on its marketplace, promising great success. He was unfamiliar with doing sales on the internet, but saw the world changing around him and thought he'd give it a go.

"We went live in November," Crazy Harry said. "I made three transactions, one on Valentine's Day and one on Christmas." The closest delivery was thirty-four miles away. By the time Crazy Harry paid his $39.99-per-month subscription fee for selling on Amazon and a 15 percent cut from all sales, his check came to $6.92. "The gas was $50," he said.

Crazy Harry told me he quickly found the source of the trouble: when he searched on Amazon for flowers in Orlando, his shop never came up. Without knowing the Harry's Famous Flowers name, customers couldn't find him. Fellow florists in the Orlando area had similar issues. He asked the representative who signed him up where his flower shop could be found on the website. Under groceries, she replied.

After he unleashed his frustrations ("I talk southern," Crazy Harry acknowledged), a second Amazon rep contacted him, promising to make things right, offering him a photo shoot for the store and a website exclusive. But the second rep never called back. Meanwhile, Crazy Harry's business revenue had shrunk by half since 2008, which equaled millions of dollars in gross sales. "The internet, and this is going to sound terrible, has killed us," he said. "It's killed brick-and-mortar businesses. I was in a Kroger, this guy walks up and says, 'I want to apologize, it's so easy to go on the internet.' I said, 'I did your wedding, I did flowers for your babies, and you're buying a box on the internet?'" Even Crazy Harry's own employees would receive Amazon packages at the shop every day. Eventually he closed his Amazon account, and in January 2019 he sold his shop after thirty-six years. "We turned it over to a new generation," he said.

There are at least 2.5 million third-party sellers on Amazon—close to 1 percent of the entire U.S. population—and many have stories like this. A few have managed to build successful businesses. But there's a certain precariousness to the entire enterprise, an underlying fear that the sellers harbor, because of the wildly uneven power discrepancy. Amazon is so big—it accounts for nearly half of all online sales, and in the 2018 Christmas shopping season that number rose to 81 percent—that anyone with aspirations of selling online has no choice but to sign up for its marketplace and abide by its rules. Amazon has disconnected this virtual mall from the normal regulatory and judicial structures, operating as its own private government, with its own private court of appeals. And it combines this rule-making authority with a ruthless streak, punishing its prodigious set of partners. After all, Jeff Bezos's original name for Amazon, which still forwards you to the site if you type it into your browser, was Relentless .com. Sellers are riding down the river with Amazon the way the frog ferries around the scorpion.

"There's so much at stake for these sellers," said Chris McCabe, a former Amazon employee who now consults at EcommerceChris.com. "They've left jobs, they're supporting themselves and their families. Amazon has woven through the economic fabric of the country and the world."

I could have taken this chapter in so many directions. Amazon, after all, sells products online, and runs a marketplace for millions of other sellers. It also runs brick-and-mortar bookstores. And cashless convenience stores. And stores that sell popular items from the website. And Whole Foods grocery stores. Another grocery store chain is on the way.

There are over 100 million Amazon Prime subscribers in the United States, roughly the population of Germany. Amazon knows that capturing customers in its Prime netting encourages them to buy more, to make the $119 annual fee worthwhile. "Our goal with Amazon Prime, make no mistake, is to make sure that if you are not a Prime member, you are being irresponsible," Bezos said in 2016. A few years ago Amazon created its own holiday, Prime Day, and the surge in demand for Prime Day discounts, followed by the drop afterward, had the power to skew the nation's retail sales figures.

Amazon is also a product manufacturer: Alexa controls two-thirds of the digital assistant market, and the Kindle represents 84 percent of all e-readers. And it's a cloud computing giant: Amazon Web Services is the source of much of the company's recent operating income, managing the data of an astonishing portion of the internet and the U.S. financial infrastructure. Amazon is a major television and film studio: it spends upward of $7 billion a year on programming, and it has three Oscars and a slew of Emmy Awards under its belt. It's the third-largest online advertiser by revenue, gaining fast on Facebook and Google. And it's a smart doorbell company called Ring. And a streaming video game company called Twitch. And also IMDb, the website where you can look up what movies George Clooney has been in.

Amazon is becoming a major shipping and logistics company. And a furniture seller. And a mattress seller. It's the nation's largest online fashion designer. It recently picked up an online pharmacy, expanded its medical supply business, and teamed with megabank JPMorgan Chase and Warren Buffett on a health care company. It's competing with JPMorgan at the same time, pushing Amazon Pay as a digital-based alternative to credit cards and lending to its small business marketplace partners.

When Amazon rolled out a limited service to have experts come to your house and set up your smart speakers, a version of Best Buy's Geek Squad, the stock price of Best Buy tanked. When it registered a trademark in 2017 for the phrase "We do the prep. You be the chef," meal kit delivery services like Blue Apron plunged. Some of these businesses prosper and some don't, but the specter of Amazon looms over America's corporate boardrooms. As Scott Galloway, NYU professor and Cassandra about the power of Big Tech, has put it, the three key inputs that move stock markets today are the underlying performance of the firm, the economic climate, and whether Amazon decides to go into the sector.

Oh, and its CEO owns the *Washington Post*.

A company this massive, even if benign and well intentioned, cannot help but instigate a massive transformation of American life. Amazon was not the only cause of the retail apocalypse; a shift to e-commerce was always going to hurt brick-and-mortar stores, and private equity looting must share the blame, as we'll discuss later. But its soaring scale and willingness to underprice everybody accelerated the decline. The past few years have seen dozens of companies evaporate; according to frequent Amazon critic Stacy Mitchell, in 2017 "more people lost jobs in general-merchandise stores than the total number of workers in the coal industry." An independent business survey conducted by Mitchell's organization in 2019 identified Amazon's market power as the number one threat to small retailers. Analysts at Swiss bank UBS matter-of-factly estimate that every percentage point that e-commerce takes from brick-and-mortar retail translates into eight thousand store closures. And right now e-commerce is only at 16 percent of all retail sales.

Dead malls dotting the American landscape not only trigger blight but also represent a severe loss in property tax revenue, constraining public service budgets. As foot traffic has dropped, delivery traffic has spiked. José Holguín-Veras, a logistics and urban freight expert at Rensselaer Polytechnic Institute, told me that in 2009 there was one daily internet-derived delivery for every twenty-five people. By 2017 this had tripled to one in eight, and in New York City it was closer to one in six. "The number of deliveries to households is now larger than the number of deliveries to commercial establishments," Holguín-Veras said. "In skyscrapers in New York City where 5,000 people live, it's 750 deliveries a day."

Stress on doormen aside, we did not design our cities for Amazon's rapid deliveries. Think of the difference between one trip to the grocery store for the week and five or ten trips from the warehouse to your house. That cannot help but trigger crippling congestion. Every extra delivery vehicle on the road spews more carbon into the atmosphere, a tragedy replicated across Amazon's business. In 2014 Amazon vowed to use only renewable sources for its energy-hogging data centers, but it quietly ended that initiative two years later, while making deals to supply technology for BP, Shell, and Halliburton. Amazon also reportedly destroys many returns, a waste of production resources.

The shift from offline to online shopping saps economic activity from local businesses, transferring it to corporate coffers in Seattle. Even Seattleites suffer if they don't work for Amazon. "Our employees struggle to live near our stores," said Robert Sindelar of Third Place Books, which has three locations in the Seattle area and has been battling Amazon, which sells 42 percent of all books in America, for years. "As the cost of living goes up, if I'm running a restaurant I can charge more for entrees. But the price is printed on our books." In 2018 city leaders in Seattle imposed a head tax on businesses to pay for desperately needed homeless services. Amazon threatened to abandon a downtown office tower if the head tax went into effect, and the city council slavishly repealed the tax. A few months later Amazon pulled out of the office tower anyway.

Areas lacking economic vibrancy would be thrilled to have Seattle's problems. Sure, to pull off one-day shipping and cloud computing expansions, Amazon must scatter warehouses and data centers across the country. But the company skillfully pits cities against one another and plucks tax subsidies for facilities it already needs to build, reeling in at least $2.7 billion as of August 2019. There's no evidence that corporate welfare brings jobs to communities rather than just offsetting losses elsewhere, so municipalities continue to fall behind.

At the same time, Amazon has become a key local government supplier. After Amazon won a nationwide procurement contract, over 1,500 cities and states can buy office items through the Amazon Business portal. And local police units have licensed Amazon's controversial facial recognition software for criminal investigations. Amazon is hard at work on federal procurement and data storage contracts too, and it spends more money lobbying for perks than any U.S. company. That's a big reason why it placed its second headquarters, after an absurd, game-show-style bidding war that gave the company access to valuable data on hundreds of cities' planning decisions, in a suburb of Washington, the seat of national power. Partnering with government inoculates Amazon from any hassle from government. "Amazon has used its lobbying arm to get special treatment," said

Steven Sterne of Keeney's Office Supply in Redmond, Washington, which battles Amazon for customers. "They've bullied localities to get unbeliev-able tax breaks. The rest of us pick that up."

And then there's the panopticon-like power of Alexa. When I was in Chattanooga studying its superfast internet service, there was an Alexa developer conference at the convention center, and I sat in on a lunch key-note by Amazon executive Paul Cutsinger. "Part of our thinking is how can we be like the Star Trek computer," he said, to my growing horror, as he outlined Alexa's role as Amazon's operating system. One device can now serve up music and podcasts, play games, order food and toiletries, set appointments, answer questions, run health and wellness programs, and raise the temperature in the shower (in my experience, the knob seems to work fine for that). Amazon has developed a $100 million Alexa Fund to support developers creating new "skills" for Alexa, which is really an investment in getting others to improve a device that Amazon owns and profits from.

Robert Epstein, who teaches at Harvard and has pioneered research into search engine manipulation, has done preliminary studies on Alexa. The device is constantly listening to users and even transmitting some of that sound back to Amazon staffers, who "refine" the machine's comprehen-sion. Alexa even transcribes what it hears after users say the wake word; Amazon has confirmed that the company retains records even if users try to delete them. (So do Facebook and Microsoft, through Skype; if you have a personal digital assistant, it's likely the company you bought it from can hear you.) The combination of raw data, machine learning, and the per-sonal touch of a helpful human voice can both understand human sub-jects and perfectly market to them, artificially narrowing their choices to whatever is most profitable for Amazon. "It looks like you can very easily impact the thinking and decision-making and purchases of people who are undecided," Epstein said. "That unfortunately gives a small number of companies tremendous power to influence people without them being aware that they're being influenced."

The spying happens not only on Alexa but also on the smart home devices it integrates with, and on the website where Amazon tracks search and purchase activity. There are Alexa features for the office and car, as well as the Ring video doorbell and in-home monitor, which also stores and transmits information. Amazon is working with property managers to get its devices into homes and apartments before anyone moves into them. The company's facial recognition technology could theoretically read a customer's expression and increase a product's price based on the reaction. Amazon is developing a mobile app that can read human emotions. "Devices all around us are watching everything we do, talking to each other, sharing data," Epstein said. "We're embedded in a surveillance network."

Amazon's ultimate goal is to become an indispensable digital partner navigating life, in the middle of every commercial transaction anyone makes, anywhere in the world. And that ambition relies on millions of workers and suppliers and partners, cogs in this incomparable machine, paid just enough to keep Amazon in gear but disempowered from seeking anything more.

The experience for workers inside Amazon's empire is, shall we say, unhealthy. Even the corporate headquarters seems dog-eat-dog, with office workers encouraged to work long hours and criticize one another's efforts. Crying at desks is routine. Meanwhile, Alexa devices and Kindles are made overseas, many of them at Foxconn, the Chinese supplier that once had to install nets beneath its windows to prevent suicides.

Airport-sized warehouses are supposed to substitute for all the retail store closures, but the jobs are famously unbearable. In a brutal application of Amazon's fealty to data, workers' every move is monitored. A quota of orders must be picked and packed, and poor performers can be fired, typically over email. Algorithms determine just how many workers are needed each day, creating a labor force of nervous temps who are pressured to take "voluntary time off" during their shifts. Seven employee lawsuits allege that workers were fired for the crime of being pregnant. In 2018 the National Council for Occupational Safety and Health named Amazon one of America's most unsafe employers. The daily monotony and burdens to perform push workers to despair and even death. And even these grunt jobs are insecure: Amazon had to reassure people in 2019 that it wouldn't turn over *all* warehouse jobs to robots anytime soon, although a week later it rolled out machines that box orders.

While less scrutinized than warehouse workers, Amazon's other jobs can be just as harrowing. Few delivery drivers work directly for Amazon. Some packages are farmed out to private shippers and the U.S. Postal

Service, which employ a low-wage nonunion workforce to haul the often backbreaking loads. Another chunk goes to Amazon Flex, an Uber-type gig service where drivers deliver in their own cars, using their own gas and parking money. It's less lucrative than advertised.

Thousands of delivery drivers wear Amazon uniforms, use Amazon equipment, work out of Amazon facilities, and are called by their employers "the face of Amazon.com," but are not classified as Amazon employees. That means they don't qualify for the guaranteed $15-an-hour minimum wage Bezos announced in 2018 to much fanfare. The nonemployee employees work for outside contractors called delivery service partners (DSPs). Amazon is so desperate to set up DSPs that it has offered warehouse employees $10,000 and three months' pay to start the businesses. The contractors get a flat rate to complete an enormous workload; the relative penury filters down to the workers. One DSP, TL Transportation, built two hours of overtime into drivers' base rate, an illegal activity under labor law. In sworn statements in a class-action suit, drivers testified that they routinely worked thirteen hours a day but got paid only the base rate. They also said they would have to urinate into bottles to keep on schedule.

Amazon also runs an "Amazon Air" fleet of cargo planes branded with the Amazon logo. These too are contracted out to freight carriers, who have too many packages to move around the country and not enough pilots to do it. "We've been critically short of crews," said Captain Daniel Wells, a pilot for Atlas Air, one of the contract carriers. "Everyone is scrambling to keep operations going." Atlas pays its pilots between 30 and 60 percent below the industry standard. The go-go schedule leaves little time for mechanics; planes go out with stickers indicating deferred maintenance. An Atlas Air flight carrying Amazon packages crashed in Texas in 2019, killing three crew members.

Atlas Air is that rare beast for anything related to Amazon: a union shop. Captain Wells is president of the local. But his pilots have been working under a contract forced upon them by a mediator in 2011. As a cargo transporter bound by the Railway Labor Act, the contract automatically renews, and workers cannot strike if it would interrupt the flow of commerce. "All we're asking to do is sit down and negotiate," said Wells. "Our company, they are relentlessly antiunion. They laugh at us, make fun of the fact that talks are going nowhere."

If Amazon was able to lock in such disadvantages for all its workers, maybe they'd let their workforce unionize. Instead they compel workers to watch union-busting videos, bring in union-busting consultants, teach managers antiunion tactics, and shut down workplaces before imminent union drives. And yet when you're as big as Amazon, with nearly 650,000 workers, you can dictate terms; the low-wage workforce will take what they can get. "I've got three kids to feed," Lisa Pendry told the *Washington Post* in 2017, outside an Amazon job fair for a warehouse in Baltimore. "It doesn't matter what it is anymore. I just need a job."

In this sense, Amazon's destruction of the models of our work creates the desperation it desires in a personnel pool. It builds reliance and inspires compliance. And it's the same way with third-party sellers, who functionally speaking are also workers, though disguised as entrepreneurs. Big Tech has constructed barriers to anyone with the dream of building a business on the internet. Amazon acquired online retailers Zappos and Quidsi just as they were gaining market share. In 2013 Facebook bought an Israeli data-security app that tracks phone usage, so it has an early warning of trending rivals and can scoop them up. CEO Tim Cook says Apple obtains a smaller company every couple of weeks, and for Google that number has been as high as one a week. In a forty-year stretch dating back to the dawn of the computer age, these four companies, along with Microsoft, made over eight hundred acquisitions. Seed funding has slowed in Silicon Valley, because what's the point?

It doesn't cost much to open and run an online store. This should be a great leveler for startup entrepreneurs. But if you want access to the audience where half of all online sales originate, you have to set up shop on Amazon. A generation of strivers with ingenuity and big dreams used to build computers in their parents' garages; now they stack rubber duckies and cleaning supplies in the same garages, hoping someone will click through and buy one. But there's a certain dependence to this independence, a pervasive loss of control, with the overlord perfectly willing to allow sellers to reach their goals, until one day they aren't.

Jeff Schick's parents were veterinarians, but he wanted to be a lawyer. His connection to the animal world inspired a business concept. He launched a website while in high school in Florida, selling horse tack. His supplier went out of business during the Great Recession, so the side hustle went on hold. In college at Cornell, Schick got the itch again. This time around, online businesses looking to succeed had to follow the eyeballs and register with Amazon. Schick got started in 2011, with a suite of pet care products through a manufacturer he knew. "It took off, kept growing, and is still doing well to this day," he said. "The beauty of selling on Amazon is that if you have the right policies and procedures in place, the companies kind of run themselves." The business paid Schick's way through law school, and he has consistently placed in Amazon's Million Dollar Sellers club, which less than 1 percent of all sellers can boast. (That's gross sales, not profits.)

At Penn Law, Schick, a strapping man with dark hair and enormous hands, gravitated to courses that involved what he saw as big issues on Amazon: corporate law, patents, intellectual property. He knew how the website operated, what the jargon was. The natural progression was to enter a field largely of his own creation: Amazon law.

Through his experience on the site, Schick has outlined a taxonomy of third-party Amazon sellers. There are the retail arbitrage people who find sales at discount stores, buy in bulk, and mark up prices for the marketplace. "I went to book sales, where you can get inventory cheap," said Cynthia Stine, a business consultant in Dallas who started selling on Amazon with her last $400, helping to support her family after the recession hit. Stine later graduated to household supplies and toys. "I was buying stuff at Big Lots, running through the doors with a barcode scanner," she said, referring to a device that allowed her to list products on Amazon as she bought them. "People thought I worked at the store." A couple in Arizona has made thousands of dollars reselling Trader Joe's Everything but the Bagel seasoning.

Retail arbitrage isn't exactly benefiting the world (did all this groundbreaking technical and logistical innovation really boil down to a digital flea market?), but it's a way for bargain hunters to earn a few dollars. It proved so viable that wholesale arbitrageurs took it to another level. Calculating technicians backed with research and connections find wholesalers willing to sell to them in bulk, which they mark up using pricing algorithms. This is Jeff Schick's business. Finally, you have a relatively smaller group: private-label sellers who have devised a new product and, instead of opening a store or licensing the product to other retailers, sell it directly on Amazon.

Like a landlord charging rent, Amazon charges entrepreneurs to set up shop. Every seller pays a monthly flat subscription rate, and there are referral fees for every sale (typically 15 percent, though they can range higher depending on the goods). Sellers also pay to use Fulfillment by Amazon, where Amazon handles customer service, storage, and shipping through its logistics network. Amazon's revenue from these fees grew to nearly $43 billion in 2018, equal to more than one out of every four dollars in third-party sales.

Outsourcing packing and shipping on every order has real advantages for sellers, but Amazon's profit margins on marketplace fees are high: around 20 percent, according to one Morgan Stanley estimate, as opposed to just a 5 percent profit margin on retail sales. And that doesn't include revenue from advertising, which many third-party sellers must invest in to get noticed (Amazon does offer special marketing support to sellers, as long as they agree to sell their brand to Amazon at any time for just $10,000). Last spring, Amazon abruptly stopped buying directly from thousands of smaller wholesalers, encouraging them to convert to third-party sellers. It's more attractive for Amazon to run the marketplace than to sell its own products. "If I want consumers to be loyal, I need more selection than anybody," said James Thomson, who helped build the Amazon marketplace, and now advises brands on their Amazon channels. "But I don't want the inventory risk. I need to get other people to hold inventory on my platform, and create a completely seamless experience whether buying from this or that seller or Amazon."

With so much money pouring in, you'd think Amazon would button up its marketplace, building something sellers can easily navigate and customers can easily trust. But several factors cut against that. First, Amazon takes its cut no matter who sells the goods. Second, sellers sign a mandatory arbitration agreement, locking them out of any court proceeding or class action if Amazon wrongs them. It's the largest employment-based arbitration agreement in America, consigning millions of small businesses to Amazon's private law. Finally, sellers don't have a good alternative venue for selling products online. This locks sellers into Amazon's world and gives Amazon no motivation to improve it. As a result, the marketplace runs the way a big city might if all the cops left. It's an experiment in digital Darwinism, where anything goes to muscle out the other guy.

Hazards for third-party sellers depend on the business model. Retail arbitrageurs often aren't authorized to resell goods, and brands can get Amazon to delist them. Wholesale arbitrageurs can get stuck with inventory if a brand decides to sell directly on Amazon and undercut them. Private-label sellers can get hurt in a million different ways: losing control of their listing, getting their search ads mislabeled, having their products labeled sex toys. "People are under attack," said Chris McCabe, a former Amazon employee who now consults with sellers. "They get their listings sabotaged."

Fake reviews are a particular scourge, one that has caught the Federal Trade Commission's attention. Because Amazon rewards higher review ratings with better site placement, entire websites have been formed to write phony reviews for cash. "I drop in on the seller Facebook groups, every day someone will say, 'This seller who looks like he's in China boosted reviews by 500 five-stars,'" McCabe said. "You'd think there'd be a tool that would stop that from happening." Reviews are also used as a form of sabotage to drop a rival's ratings. Sellers will pay for bad reviews, or buy a competing product and set it on fire, posting a photo of the smoldering mess. Or they'll flood a rival's listing with fraudulent five-star raves, framing the rival for paying for reviews, a big no-no for Amazon.

Then there's the patent trolling. "You have to be impressed with people's commitment," said Cynthia Stine, who consults with sellers as they try to survive on Amazon. "People will look around the platform, see a product doing well. They will file a design patent on it, get a patent or trademark. And they get on the platform and kick the brand owner off. That takes some balls." Other scammers won't go through such trouble, claiming patent infringement even if they don't own the patent. Jeff Schick told me about a case where the individual making the allegation claimed to be the inventor of the product. "But if you looked up the inventor, you saw his obituary on Google," Schick said.

In addition, knockoffs are everywhere: fake clothes, fake books, fake dietary supplements. The American Apparel and Footwear Association recommended in 2018 that Amazon get added to the government's "Notorious Markets" list for places where counterfeit goods proliferate. As with everything on Amazon, counterfeiting comes in many flavors. Sellers will spoof a rival's email account and then write to Amazon with frivolous infringement claims, which can get the rival suspended. Stine has two clients who have been suspended that way. "One was suspended for six months," Stine said. "Messages from Amazon were showing up in his account, saying 'Thank you for doing this,' and he's like, 'What? I never did that. What are you talking about?'"

Counterfeiters don't just prey upon the Louis Vuittons; they affect everyone. Jon Fawcett, an Ohioan who developed a popular stainless-steel phone charging cable, noticed a series of bad reviews after his brand Fuse Chicken had been selling on Amazon a few years. When he bought his own products, he received copycat cables; other returned fakes were packaged with a "ships from and sold by Amazon.com" label. He surmised that real and fake Fuse Chicken products were being intermixed at the Amazon warehouses. Amazingly, this is pretty common. "Let's say you're selling phone cables and I'm selling them," said C. J. Rosenbaum, an attorney who consults with and represents third-party sellers. "You're in Chicago, you ship to the Chicago warehouse because it's closer, and you're charging $2 a cable. I'm selling the same cable, I send to the New York warehouse. I'm selling for $1 a cable, I have the lower price, so I have the buy box. If the buyer is in Chicago, they fill the order with your cable and I get credit for the sale. If yours is counterfeit, they'll blame my account even though my inventory didn't fill the order."

An Amazon representative proposed to Fawcett that he lower his prices to match the knockoffs. He didn't take the advice, and managed to get around the arbitration agreement to file a lawsuit. But Amazon had precedent on its side: a 2015 federal court decision absolving it from responsibility in counterfeit cases, ruling that it's merely a go-between for a separate buyer and seller. A circuit court ruling in July 2019 may hold Amazon more accountable for counterfeits, but it was too late for Jon Fawcett; the Fuse Chicken case confidentially settled in April 2019.

The combination of commingling inventory and counterfeits puts every Amazon shopper at risk. A *Wall Street Journal* investigation in August 2019 identified 4,152 products "that have been declared unsafe by federal agencies, are deceptively labeled or are banned by federal regulators," nearly half of them shipped from Amazon warehouses. This included blankets known to have suffocated infants, motorcycle helmets that pop off upon crash impact, toys with elevated lead levels, and pesticides unregistered with the Environmental Protection Agency. No store shelf would house bogus products without opening up the store to a lawsuit. Amazon relies on shifting liability to third parties. As a result, a buyer simply cannot know if they're getting a genuine product or something dangerous. Flea markets, where "caveat emptor" is the watchword, don't have access to a billion consumers.

Amazon's halting efforts to clean up the site have only generated more opportunities for dirty tricks. Efforts to police reviews or protect patents led to black-hat sellers filing bogus complaints in a rival's name. Tools like Project Zero enable companies to instantly delist a seller's products; of course, fraudsters use that to delist their enemies after stealing their intellectual property. One seller was knocked off the site after a copyright infringement notice from a fake law firm.

Amazon seems to always be one step behind the latest scheme, and it's not eager to catch up. Weirdly for a company that has set up its own government, Amazon doesn't want to mediate disputes. Its role is entirely passive, thick with layers of bureaucracy, and without consistency or clarity. James Thomson told me this is calculated. "If they're proactive, they're creating liability," he said. "The lawyers have told us, 'Don't check anything, but if someone complains, check.'"

When I asked Cynthia Stine if the marketplace was truly the Wild West, she paused for a moment. "It's far worse than you can imagine," she finally said. "The first few years, maybe two or three times a year we would find someone messing with sellers. We now get those cases virtually every day. And these bad actors are big sellers. They're getting away with it." The marketplace, in other words, falls victim to Gresham's law, where dishonest sellers drive out honest ones who follow the rules. And Big Tech firms like Amazon invite this level of fraud, simply due to their vastness. They have made themselves totally unmanageable.

Nearly 85 percent of counterfeit goods originate in China or Hong Kong, according to the Organisation for Economic Co-operation and Development. Chinese companies are the fastest-growing cohort of new sellers on the site. Amazon recruits Chinese sellers, offers financing to them, and even ships directly from China. With Chinese sellers outside the reach of U.S. law, the only way Amazon can discipline them is by suspending accounts, which doesn't work when a seller illegally holds more than one. "A friend, he took a video of an office building in China, where there are two thousand employees managing three thousand Amazon accounts," said Jeff Schick. "That's one company making so much money off breaking the rules."

The suspension, Amazon's main disciplinary method, puts sellers in the phantom zone of the Amazon universe. They happen without warning, in middle-of-the-night emails curtly stating a violation of terms of service (the policy since changed to give thirty days' notice to sellers on suspensions, but it's so riddled with loopholes that Amazon can pretty much do whatever it wants). Sellers don't get a phone call; it's nearly impossible to talk to a human at Amazon. When a seller is suspended, Amazon not only deactivates that seller's product listings but also refuses to release funds from prior sales, which could total thousands of dollars. (This then becomes a vein of money Amazon can invest, like Warren Buffett's famous insurance float.) If the suspended seller's inventory is commingled with someone else's products, Amazon will continue to sell it without compensation. And if a suspended seller uses Fulfillment by Amazon, Amazon still holds the inventory and charges storage fees. Sellers must pay for a removal order to get their products back. With thin margins in retail, a few weeks off the site could lead to layoffs, bankruptcies, and foreclosures. Consultants told me about sellers crying to them on the phone, trapped and desperate.

The rule book sellers must follow is constantly updated. "Amazon doesn't necessarily trumpet from the rooftops when things change," said Chris McCabe. "You're supposed to check it and know." Amazon expects its sellers to be professional, to carry proper business and product licenses, to always maintain enough inventory, to deliver on time. But as the de facto judge in suspension cases, Amazon is hardly a bastion of professionalism.

Suspension announcements are maddeningly nonspecific, only listing broad categories of violation. A single user review expressing mild disapproval can trigger them. Entire businesses have been ruined by a dog destroying a toy too quickly, or an outfit not fitting the way the customer wanted. Sellers must become detectives to unravel what set off Amazon's sensors. It's the customer-is-always-right philosophy taken to painful extremes.

Even to the consultants, some suspensions can seem Kafkaesque. "I've had two suspensions in my history," Schick said. The first time, someone returned one of Jeff's products, a container of dog treats. Amazon handled Jeff's returns, and it has a default setting where it repackages returns and sends them to other customers. The shipper didn't see the open lid and sent the dog treats off. When the customer received them, they complained that the box was used. Though it was Amazon's fault, Schick got suspended.

The second suspension occurred while Schick was in law school and had to change his bank account. He did it in the law school computer lab, where IP addresses were randomly assigned. Amazon saw a bank account changed with a random IP address and suspended Schick's account for a week.

Paul Rafelson, a partner in the same law firm with Schick and founder of the Online Merchants Guild, a coalition of third-party sellers, told me perhaps the wildest suspension story, which also involved IP addresses. Through Facebook groups and meetups, sellers are often in close contact with one another, and human nature being what it is, some of them couple up. A client of Rafelson's met his girlfriend at one such event, and they moved in together. Within a day or so, their accounts got suspended. "They had the same IP address," Rafelson said. "They had to get Amazon's blessing to use two accounts in the same household. It's like you have to get permission from Amazon to get married."

The only real recourse for suspended sellers is the "Appeal Decision" button at the bottom of the announcement. That's where consultants come in, an ecosystem of lawyers, sellers, and ex-Amazonians helping break people out of Amazon jail. Stine has a twenty-five-person team; Schick has paralegals and assistants working cases. There are even Amazon-world versions of ambulance chasers, cut-rate advisors promising suspension lifts for a couple of hundred bucks. "There are chop-shop consultants, they produce canned content," said Chris McCabe. "The investigators throw them away."

Most consultants structure appeals as confessions. They include a plan of action explaining what the seller did wrong and how they'll comply in the future. Whether the seller actually *did* anything wrong is beside the point; disputing a suspension won't get you far with Amazon, which routinely takes the customer's side. Nor do Amazon's judges want to hear about fraud in the marketplace. Consultants mine seller accounts to find something to hang a confession on. They craft appeals that use Amazon's preferred language. "If you say, 'I'll try my best to help my customer,' they'll throw it out," said Schick. "You have to say it's Amazon's customer."

Even if the consultant does everything right and submits the appeal promptly, Amazon can go weeks before responding. "This Amazon court system is on par with North Korea in terms of fairness and transparency," Rafelson said. One problem is that the appeals team has been outsourced to low-wage countries, with an emphasis on volume. "They expect these guys to go through seventeen appeals an hour," said Stine. "So they have about three minutes. They fall behind and think, 'Oh crap, I have to get three done in the next five minutes.'" They'll send back what Stine calls "the punt," with a curt and vague response like "We need more information." It often asks for documents that were already attached to the appeal.

Sellers get only a few bites at the apple before the appeals process runs out. Continued nonresponse can lead to escalation, but where to escalate is anybody's guess. Sellers can contact seller support, but they cannot access case files and explain what went wrong. There are specialty groups at Amazon that deal with safety or quality, but appeals to them can fall into a black box. Amazon's legal department is another avenue, but they won't respond to anyone but lawyers. When Jeff Schick had his suspension problem, he even bought shares of Amazon stock and sent an email to investor relations. Sellers can take Amazon to arbitration, but that's where forced confessions can come back to bite them. "If sellers admit to doing something wrong, the chance of success in arbitration is zero," said consultant C. J. Rosenbaum.

A marketplace this vast and sellers this desperate cannot help but yield corruption. Amazon employees have allegedly unbanned accounts for a bribe, in addition to deleting bad reviews and releasing sales information. Every consultant has a story. "There's a suspension 'expert' who has a 100 percent success rate," said Jeff Schick. "If you want to be reinstated, you pay this guy $10,000. It looks to me like he wires money to a friend at Amazon who reinstates the account right away."

The final step is an email to Jeff Bezos. That's right—the livelihoods of thousands of businesses hinge on crafting a message to the richest person in the world. Bezos doesn't read the emails, of course; an executive seller team responds to them. But ever since Stine revealed to The Verge how she uses Jeff letters as a last resort, they haven't worked as well; what once took a couple of days for a response can now take weeks. Stine thinks it's a deliberate tactic to slow the flow of emails, but in the meantime sellers remain locked out. "All of us in the space have been scrambling to find other emails to be responsive," Stine said, describing an endless hunt for new people inside the company who might help free her clients. "I have a list of ten emails that I'm sending all the time."

Millions of small businesspeople, whom Amazon touts in glossy presentations about how it helps the little guy, find themselves at the mercy of an impossible process. Not only do they have to compete on price and quality, but they have to avoid sabotage and suspension purgatory. They're part of not a marketplace but a war zone, where nobody wears the same uniform. They must abide by the improvised, mercurial laws of a private company that is at once overwhelmed and strangely aloof.

Says Cynthia Stine: "People come to us and they want us to have the answer. With Amazon there is no for-sure answer. There's nobody to hold them accountable."

If sellers succeed at navigating the thicket of deception and confusion, they still may find that they have one bothersome competitor for the customer dollar: Amazon's own line of AmazonBasics house brands, which by spring 2019 grew to 138 product lines, some licensed from wholesalers and others manufactured for Amazon. There are generic batteries, notepads, velvet hangers, TV wall mounts, iPhone cables, and dog beds. There are also house brands that don't carry the Amazon name. For example, Amazon built a skin care line, Belei, based on the ingredients customers most frequently search for.

Defenders of the practice liken it to generic items sold in grocery stores. But Amazon has one enormous advantage over supermarket brands: knowledge. The company meticulously tracks every purchase on the site, which any businessperson will tell you gives them a decided advantage. In a few keystrokes, Amazon can figure out what's selling at what price, who's most likely to buy it, and who searched for it. Plus, as the website's controller, Amazon can give the house brand preferential treatment in searches, lower prices than competitors, and control of the buy box. It also offers freebies of its house brand products to frequent reviewers, goosing the mechanism that's crucial to sales. It even promotes its own products *within* third-party sellers' listings.

This self-dealing doesn't always happen; again, Amazon typically makes more money collecting rent on sellers. When Amazon adjusted its algorithm to favor the most profitable items, it was agnostic about which brands it boosted—whether its own products or those of third-party sellers. In a 2014 paper, Harvard researchers Feng Zhu and Qihong Liu found that Amazon was more likely to target successful niche products where it could take advantage of a built-in audience. "They don't seem to be interested in getting all of every customer's business; they want what they can do profitably," said Steven Sterne of Keeney's Office Supply. It's like an experienced angler keeping only the profitable fish and throwing the scrawny ones back.

But when it finds something to sell, Amazon spares no effort. Jeff Schick told me about one seller who had his products shipped directly to Amazon's warehouses from a manufacturer in China. Within weeks, that manufacturer was working directly for Amazon. "I wouldn't want Amazon to see my bill of lading; they'd know who makes my stuff," Schick said. He added that Amazon has visited sales shows for years, trying to persuade suppliers to break with third-party sellers and work with them.

Retail chain Williams-Sonoma accused Amazon in a December 2018 lawsuit of making "strikingly similar" versions of its products under the house brand Rivet and steering customers to its knockoffs. According to the lawsuit, Amazon used Google keyword search advertising for its furniture, with one ad reading "Williams & Sonoma at Amazon." Squatting on search advertising like this is commonplace for Amazon. Google reportedly gives Amazon higher search rankings than the brands it copies—an example of country club monopolism, where the oligopolists help each other out. Amazon sought to dismiss the charges, claiming it did nothing wrong, but a federal judge in California kept the case alive in May 2019, ruling that "the allegations raise the plausible inference that Amazon is not merely reselling Williams-Sonoma products but is instead cultivating the incorrect impression that these sales on Amazon.com are authorized by Williams-Sonoma."

Amazon also uses the vast unauthorized selling and counterfeiting inside the marketplace to entice big brands to sell directly to them, with the implied threat of a polluted marketplace for its goods unless they comply. Unauthorized sellers play a punitive function, pressuring brands to list with Amazon or lower their prices to compete with knockoffs. Some resign themselves to playing ball. Others have rebelled: Birkenstock quit the site in 2016, and its CEO has called Amazon an accomplice to widespread "modern-day piracy." Nike has also quit selling directly on Amazon.

Author Brad Stone explained the most notorious example of Amazon's power: the story of Quidsi, the startup behind Diapers.com. The site had developed a simple way for parents to schedule diaper purchases and other necessities. Amazon took notice. It sent an emissary to the Quidsi offices, making the founders an offer to buy the company, which was rebuffed.

After that, Amazon dropped its prices for diapers up to 30 percent. Every time Quidsi moved its prices, Amazon's would follow instantly. Sales at Diapers.com tanked. Quidsi executives decided to meet with Amazon in September 2010, and on the day of the meeting, Amazon announced a new service called Amazon Mom, with even bigger discounts. After calculating the wholesale and shipping costs, Quidsi estimated that Amazon was willing to lose as much as $100 million on diapers just to flush them out of business. A couple of months later Quidsi sold itself to Amazon. Incredibly, Amazon didn't even see the business through, shutting down Quidsi years later.

If you ask an Amazonian, this sharp-elbowed behavior is all done for the customer, to get them the most convenient and lowest-cost services possible. But Amazon's dominance hides a cold reality about its service: it's quietly been getting worse. Many products no longer arrive on time, even in Prime, where shipping is supposed to be guaranteed. It's so impossible to find human representatives that Amazon sells a book on its own website for how to reach customer service. Whole Foods shoppers signed up for online delivery get bizarre substitutions in their orders without warning. Even as two-day shipping is creaking, Amazon has announced a move to one-day shipping, which will strain systems further. Managing millions of outside sellers and drivers and pilots can be too much for any operation; it's what former Supreme Court justice and antimonopoly hero Louis Brandeis once called "the curse of bigness."

You can't even be assured that you're getting the lowest price on Amazon, a bedrock promise it makes to customers. Amazon changes prices multiple times per day, even tailoring them to individual shoppers. It has listed fake higher prices and crossed them out to mimic a discount; it has charged more for Kindles based on a buyer's location; it has steered people to higher-priced products where it makes a greater profit, rather than cheaper versions from outside sellers. Amazon's goal is personalized pricing, charging exactly what customers are willing and able to pay. Whole Foods has become a real-world laboratory for this behavioral engineering.

Amazon also forces sellers to raise prices on other outlets where they sell, by suppressing the opportunity for Amazon customers to find their products unless they do so. Amazon's own written policies explicitly threaten to discipline sellers who offer lower prices elsewhere, calling it "harming customer trust."

Of course, Amazon has played money games since its inception. For decades, it declined to charge sales tax in states where it had no physical presence, ensuring prices lower than offline competitors and building a business model on tax avoidance. It racked up so many annual losses early on that it can still apply them now and pay no federal taxes on billions in income. It has an entire stock of "can't realize a profit" products, or CRAP for short.

Sit on that for a minute. What company sells products that can't realize a profit? Maybe one that engages in predatory pricing, intentionally undercutting rivals to harvest market share and regaining those losses later. Amazon has been accused of this forever, and now it seems to have flipped the switch. It's driving the CRAP out of the marketplace, telling suppliers that Amazon will only advertise products on which it can generate a profit. It forces sellers to take discounts to get in the "Deal of the Day" promotion, or to raise spending on marketing. It's raising shipping and transportation fees for suppliers, and forcing them to reshape their packaging. It's converting those suppliers into third-party sellers, taking a cut from their sales. Amazon may capitalize on its dominance not by raising prices but by squeezing its partners, who have nowhere else to successfully launch an online business.

"They lured everyone onto the platform," said Shaoul Sussman, a law student at Fordham University who wrote an attention-grabbing paper suggesting that Amazon was employing this gambit. "They were subsidizing activity, but suppliers now have to incur costs." Entrepreneurship in an age of declining startups has devolved into setting up a stall at the virtual flea market and figuring out how to screw the guy in the next stall over, while hoping the boss doesn't crush you like a grape. But now the boss's strategy is to raise his profits while lowering everyone else's. The scorpion has trapped the frog; it was in his nature all along.

This used to be called the Walmart effect, and now it's Amazon's game. One company has organized the online marketplace, and millions must effectively pay taxes to engage in any trade there, enduring lower margins, smaller paychecks, and a tougher life. "They are killing the entrepreneurial spirit of this country," said the Online Merchants Guild's Paul Rafelson. "There was a time when the Union Pacific railroad would say, 'We need to look at your books to tell what we can charge you for freight.' Amazon is an e-commerce version of the Union Pacific."

Because it worked, Amazon's underpricing-to-monopoly strategy spawned imitators across the economy. Uber, WeWork, and Bird are all versions of Amazon: burning capital with underpriced services, hoping to drive out the competition and hook the public. None of them make money; they've all been revealed to be overly optimistic at best and outright fraud at worst. We have a MoviePass economy, which destroys honest companies trying to compete on value, and builds up a bunch of con men until their swindle is revealed. Amazon hasn't reached that point yet, and maybe it's become too big to fail. But its business model is littering the world around it with third-rate hacks.

Perhaps the biggest vindicator of Amazon's monopoly vision is this: after resisting tech stocks for decades, Warren Buffett bought Amazon stock for $860 million.

When people think about successful tech firms, they think Amazon, Apple, Google, and Facebook. But the most profitable tech company in America, and closing in on the most profitable in the world, is a company you've likely never heard of, which mostly sells one product for less than ten bucks a year.

Its name is VeriSign, and it gets your money when you register a website with the .com or .net suffix. There were 156.1 million such websites in existence as of June 2019. Website producers don't pay VeriSign directly: there's a middleman in the way. But suffice it to say that nearly all of VeriSign's profit comes from running .com and .net, secured through a monopoly contract from the nonprofit Internet Corporation for Assigned Names and Numbers (ICANN).

The 2006 agreement for .com allowed VeriSign to automatically renew the contract as long as it met certain performance metrics, making it a monopoly in perpetuity. When VeriSign got the go-ahead in 2018 to increase prices for .com, which had been frozen since 2012, its stock leaped 17 percent in a day. The reason is obvious. It costs no more money to manage website domains over time; in fact, it's cheaper on a per-domain basis once the computing infrastructure is set up. "If you're giving a near-monopoly in an industry where prices are falling, you would think you would have terms in the contract to lower the price," said progressive economist Dean Baker.

By one calculation, the agreement to raise prices on .com amounts to $1 billion in free money for VeriSign. As a result, in the first quarter of 2019, VeriSign's operating income as a percentage of revenues, a measure of profitability, hit 65.3 percent. Its $200 million in quarterly earnings is relatively modest, but a 65 percent profit margin is I'm-going-to-sue-you-for-price-gouging territory. Of course, no one will ever sue VeriSign for price gouging: website owners pay less than a dollar a month for its services. Get a lot of customers to pay a little bit extra and all of a sudden you're the most profitable company in the world.

That's probably why Warren Buffett owns nearly 13 million shares of VeriSign stock, which as of last summer was worth $2.3 billion. You've got to hand it to the guy—he's America's greatest monopoly spotter.

Would-be competitors to VeriSign have consistently offered to provide the same service for as low as $1 per year, but the contract has never been competitively bid. There was a chance for at least some competition in 2016. ICANN proposed a new domain name, .web, seen as a promising competitor to .com because of the web being synonymous with the internet.

Donuts, a competitor to VeriSign that owns .email, .church, .restaurant, and .plumbing, was among seven registries that vied for the rights to .web. Typically these contests would be resolved privately among the parties, but a relative upstart named Nu Dot Co LLC refused a private agreement, triggering a public auction. Jon Nevett, the co-founder of Donuts, called Nu Dot Co to ask them to reconsider; he was told "the decision goes beyond just us."

Nevett was immediately skeptical. The auction rules did not allow registries to change decision makers in midstream. "There was no transparency on who we were going up against," Nevett told me. Whether your adversary in an auction has limited resources or deep pockets changes the bidding strategy. Nevett demanded that ICANN investigate, but ICANN responded that it had "found no basis" for any violation by Nu Dot Co. Of course, ICANN was entitled to the proceeds of the auction, so it had strong incentives to move forward. In a last-ditch effort, Donuts filed a motion for a temporary restraining order to block the auction, but it failed.

The .web auction, with sealed bids and no transparency, was conducted on July 28, 2016. Nu Dot Co won with a record-shattering $135 million bid. Three days later, VeriSign issued a brief press release, announcing that it "provided funds for Nu Dot Co's bid." Already in control of .com and .net, VeriSign scooped up one of the only plausible alternatives, damaging rivals' attempts to challenge its dominance. "For it to go to the one entity in the industry with market power is problematic," Nevett said.

Donuts unsuccessfully sued to block the sale. The Justice Department opened an investigation into the auction and then quietly closed it without taking action. Another company filed for an independent review about the auction, which remains in limbo. But since the predominant theory is that VeriSign bought .web to bury it, delay isn't exactly a hindrance.

Concluded Nevett: "There's a long history of treating VeriSign a little differently. Saying 'I told you so' doesn't help."

Nevett seems to have learned from the experience, however. In November 2019 a just-created private equity firm named Ethos Capital announced a deal to buy the Public Interest Registry, which owns .org, the domain used by nonprofits. Price caps for .org had just been lifted by ICANN, meaning the new owners could charge whatever they want for it. The CEO of Public Interest Registry, a former nonprofit now absorbed into the private equity borg? Jon Nevett.

CHAPTER 9

Monopolies Are Why Hospitals Can Give Patients Prosthetic Limbs and Artificial Hearts but Not Salt and Water in a Bag

It didn't even register with Ben Boyer at first. Usually the nurse practitioner would set up an intravenous infusion for his wife, Xenia, start the cancer medication flowing, and walk away, leaving her sitting in the chair. But he wasn't leaving this time. "It took me a minute to go, 'What are you doing?'" Ben told me. "He was matter-of-fact about it; he said, 'It's the damnedest thing, we don't have any IV bags because there's a shortage.'"

The place Ben and Xenia heard this news, the Moores Cancer Center at UC San Diego Health in picturesque La Jolla, is one of the best treatment facilities in the United States. There were big-screen TVs everywhere, comfortable Barcalounger chairs, giant banks of glass windows offering a waterfront view, clean and gleaming equipment. It was the day after Christmas 2017, not a busy day on the floor. A skeleton crew tended to patients. Despite all that, Ben and Xenia were being told there weren't enough IV bags to go around.

Ben wasn't thinking too deeply about the situation, because he didn't say anything as the nurse practitioner took a syringe and hooked it up to a bag full of medication. It looked like he was going to approximate the function of a slow infusion manually.

"We were doing small talk. I had just seen *The Last Jedi*," Ben said. "And then I said, 'Wait, why don't you have any IV bags?'" That's when the nurse told him that all the IV bags for the hospital come from Puerto Rico. And because of Hurricane Maria, which had struck a few months before, there was a critical shortage.

An IV bag is simply a durable plastic shell filled with saline solution. It's used in countless procedures, from administering antibiotics to providing dehydrated patients with fluids. From the room in the hospital, Ben could look down the cliffs of La Jolla to the Pacific Ocean. He could see salt water all around him, except where he needed it. The surface of the earth is roughly three-quarters salt water, and yet there's a shortage of salt and water in a bag? Water, water, everywhere, but not a drop for a drip?

Ben watched in mild shock as the nurse squeezed the bladder of the bag and slowly guided the medicine through the syringe, which was attached through tubing to Xenia's arm. This is known as an IV push. Every five seconds, the nurse had to carefully depress the plunger, with machine-like precision, to dispense the proper amount of drug. It took about thirty minutes, with the nurse standing the whole time.

"I thought, 'This is insane, this is crazy, this is wild,'" Ben recalled. And the association with Puerto Rico made it doubly surreal. Ben's father was a health care professional in the navy who was stationed in Puerto Rico; Ben had spent years on the island growing up, and his sister had been born there. But though both parents worked in health care—his mom was a nurse—Ben didn't understand Puerto Rico's centrality to the U.S. health care system. It's been a haven for pharmaceutical manufacturing for decades, and Baxter International, which produces about half of the nation's IV solution, uses two facilities on the island for this purpose. Both of them were crippled during Hurricane Maria, leaving hospitals scrambling for months.

It was a classic consequence of concentration: supply chain disruptions magnify when one company makes too great a share of the product. But the even dirtier secret, the one that confuses this simple explanation, is that IV solution has been on the Food and Drug Administration's shortage list since 2013—*four years* before the hurricane knocked out Baxter's facilities in Puerto Rico. The Justice Department had already been investigating the matter. Once again—and I can't stress this enough—we're talking about salt, water, and a bag.

Stalwart capitalists snicker that shortages occur only in centrally planned communist countries. But here we have private-sector companies unable to match demand, with grave potential implications for public health. How did this happen? The complex, multifaceted answer can be found by trekking through the forest of monopolies that constitute America's health care system, not only among clinics and facilities, but everything required to deliver care. Competition has died, leading to absurd pricing, lower wages for medical workers, and substandard results.

We have a depressingly narrow debate about health care in America. Left behind by a developed world that guarantees coverage for every citizen, we fight about the benefits of single-payer or a tightly regulated private insurance market, while burn-it-down conservatives signal through their actions that access to medicine is a mere privilege for whoever can afford it. But we mostly remain silent about what matters in health care beyond whether the insurer is public or private. Our monopolized system is the chief reason why we pay more than anywhere in the world, with worse outcomes to boot. Our monopolized system has made GoFundMe pages one of the major insurance providers in America. Our monopolized system has turned errors at the hospital into the nation's third-leading cause of death. And our monopolized system was responsible for Ben Boyer shaking his head in disbelief as his wife was treated for cancer with a process last in widespread use around World War II. "That's the eye-opening thing," Ben said. "This is all being held together with fragile, gossamer-thin strands of business dealings."

In 2015, two proposed mergers were poised to transform the health insurance industry. Aetna announced a $34 billion deal with Humana, and Cigna laid out its own $48 billion combination with Anthem. With only UnitedHealth rivaling these firms in size and number of enrollees, the mergers would have left a Big Three among for-profit insurance companies. (The nonprofit Blue Cross Blue Shield Association is also a major factor in insurance markets, though Anthem is a subsidiary of it.) That frightened patients and advocates, who routinely lay blame for our dysfunctional health care system at the feet of insurers. History shows that when insurance companies merge, higher premiums result: prices jumped 7 percent after Aetna purchased Prudential's health insurance business in 1999, and soared 14 percent after UnitedHealth took over Sierra in 2008. Many recoiled at the thought of reduced choice, and of life-and-death decisions being concentrated in the hands of so few.

The insurance companies' logic, however, was compelling on a surface level. First, the Affordable Care Act (ACA, also known as Obamacare) capped insurer profits, with a percentage of premiums earmarked for actual treatment. Although this regulation could be gamed, the main variable to increasing earnings would be internal administrative costs. So insurers saw efficiencies of scale as a primary option. More important, insurers negotiate thousands of transactions every day with doctors, hospitals, and outpatient clinics, and need to maintain leverage over those negotiations to secure the best price.

Consolidated health care providers, by contrast, can dictate more favorable terms at the bargaining table. This isn't a guess; a gold-standard report in 2010 from then Massachusetts attorney general (and now Juul lobbyist) Martha Coakley, which looked at claims data from state hospitals, found that price variations had nothing to do with quality of care or the health of the patient population. Instead, prices were attributable "to market leverage as measured by the relative market position of the hospital or provider group compared with other hospitals or provider groups within a geographic region." In response to hospital networks swelling up, insurance companies felt the need to swell up themselves. Once again, it's concentration creep: in a two-sided market, merger activity on one side will inspire merger activity on the other. Call it a race to the top—or, for consumers, the bottom.

In health care, the public interacts with these two sides in very different ways. Hospitals and doctors heal you, provide you with medicine, fix your broken leg. Generally they inspire warm feelings among patients. But insurance companies tell you what you are on the hook for paying, and what treatment you're restricted from receiving. Generally they inspire outrage, often justifiably, for their greed or heartlessness. "It's really easy to hate the intermediary," said Leemore Dafny, professor at the Harvard Business School. "Individuals connect with their doctors and not their insurance companies."

The tragedy of Nataline Sarkisyan, a leukemia patient who died after being denied coverage by Cigna for a liver transplant, built momentum for the health insurance reforms in the Affordable Care Act. And anyone who has to shop for Obamacare coverage every year knows that local individual insurance markets are superconcentrated: according to data from the Kaiser Family Foundation, 42 percent of all counties have two choices or fewer. Accusations of anticompetitive behavior in these markets proliferate: in 2018, startup insurer Oscar accused Blue Cross and Blue Shield of Florida of signing brokers to exclusive Obamacare policy arrangements to lock out rivals.

So it was no surprise that the public, and their elected representatives, turned hard against this further proposed consolidation of the health insurance industry. Ultimately all four insurers abandoned their plans on the same day in early 2017, after Barack Obama's Justice Department had sued to block them a year earlier. Given the dangers to public health from a consolidated for-profit insurance industry that profits through denying care, that's probably a good thing.

Yet dangers also lurk on the other side of the transaction, with our caretakers and healers, whose efforts to gain advantage in payment negotiations have vital implications for patients. In this sense, the interaction between patients and caregivers has become a hindrance to rationalizing health care markets, because it hides the truth about who's causing the pain.

Health care providers began to consolidate in the late 1990s, the heyday of managed care. Firms capitalizing on the stock market boom spent that cash acquiring hospitals, clinics, and private practices to build an interlinked system. Though some expected the merger wave to peter out, it never did. Carnegie Mellon University's Martin Gaynor, a former director of the Bureau of Economics at the Federal Trade Commission, has identified 1,667 hospital mergers from 1998 to 2018, over 540 of them just since 2013. A good number of these were between hospitals in the same area, reducing choice in local markets.

Because everyone assumed Obamacare would increase hospital usage rates, markets judged them an attractive asset, spawning renewed merger efforts. (This didn't work out, incidentally, as admission rates have actually dropped since the law's passage.) Startup competition doesn't really exist, for several reasons. As part of the ACA bargain, the Obama White House extended a moratorium on physician-owned hospitals, at the request of the American Hospital Association. And most states carry "certificate of need" laws requiring regulatory clearance before a hospital can begin buying equipment. I can think of many good reasons for hospitals to be licensed, but practically speaking this has frozen the market, allowing large hospital systems to trade facilities like penny stocks.

By 2016, 90 percent of all metropolitan areas experienced high concentration in the hospital market, according to research published by Cal Berkeley's Brent Fulton. A majority of regions have one or two hospital networks that see most of the patients. Boston is dominated by Partners HealthCare; Pittsburgh by UPMC; San Francisco by Sutter Health. Some of these are nominally nonprofit networks, but studies have shown nonprofit status to be irrelevant in terms of whether hospitals impose market power. It certainly has no bearing on acquisition growth. In 2019 Catholic Health Initiatives and Dignity Health combined to form Common Spirit Health, with seven hundred locations in twenty-one states and 150,000 employees. It's the largest nonprofit health care provider in the country. A pair of Midwest nonprofit networks—Aurora Health and Advocate Health Care—teamed up in 2018.

Another player has joined this march to consolidation: private equity firms. Bain Capital and Kohlberg Kravis Roberts took Healthcare Corporation of America (HCA) private in 2006, the largest leveraged buyout of its time. The successful transaction signaled to a copycat industry that hospitals were a profitable play. Instead of cornering a regional market, private equity uses borrowed money to scoop up hospitals in different corners of the country, creating a diverse national network. Typically the firm will buy a "platform" hospital system, later adding smaller acquisitions that are below the threshold for an antitrust inquiry. Once you eat a hundred minnows, you're suddenly a big fish. "They're trying to nationally dominate the market," said Eileen Appelbaum, co-author of *Private Equity at Work*, who has studied the industry.

Appelbaum highlights Community Health Systems (CHS), a private equity roll-up that bought a series of rural hospitals in the 2000s and then a large chain, Health Management Associates, in 2014. "CHS was financially struggling, and it was allowed to buy another chain that was financially struggling," Appelbaum explained. "Guess what happened?" CHS, which had gone public, saw shares plummet, while closing and selling off hospitals and cutting unprofitable services. Steward Health Care, owned by private equity titan Cerberus, has gobbled up hospitals in ten states; a recent deal with IASIS Healthcare made it the nation's largest private for-profit hospital group. The debt for the cash borrowed to make these purchases gets thrown onto the hospitals, leaving them unable to invest in new equipment or technology or better care for patients.

The worst recent example of private equity's role in health care concerns Hahnemann University Hospital, a 171-year-old institution in Center City Philadelphia that primarily serves low-income patients of color. Private equity baron Joel Freedman bought the hospital in 2018, made no improvements for eighteen months, and then closed the facility with the intention of selling the real estate, which is in a "gateway location" for gentrification. "We have frequent patients that have cried, 'Where am I going to go?'" Lauren McHugh, a registered nurse at the hospital for seventeen years, told me at a rally to save Hahnemann. "This seems to have been [Freedman's] plan all along, to buy this place, let it fail, and shut it down." It could become another trend, and every hospital closed to turn a real estate profit consolidates the provider market further.

As hospitals enlarge, they have taken physicians in-house, in contrast to the tradition of private practices. In 2012 hospitals employed only 26 percent of all physicians; just three years later that number jumped to 38 percent. Physician practices not affiliated with hospitals are also combining; nearly two-thirds of specialist physician markets are highly concentrated, according to Fulton's research. This is a form of vertical consolidation, where the physician or surgeon who can refer a patient to a hospital for surgical or other treatment just goes to work for them. Not so mysteriously, referrals stay in the family, and doctors who don't comply are reprimanded.

Outpatient facilities are also highly concentrated. The most notorious of these are dialysis centers, about 70 percent of which are owned by two companies—Fresenius and DaVita. Dialysis treatments use machines as a substitute kidney to filter patient blood, a laborious process required up to three times a week. A kidney transplant, while more invasive, gives patients a chance at a normal life. But Fresenius and DaVita routinely play down the possibility of a transplant, even for those eligible, because committing patients to dialysis keeps them in their network.

Medicare, through a 1972 law, pays for all dialysis treatment regardless of age for the close to half a million people afflicted with failed kidneys. But because private insurance covers the first thirty months of a patient's treatment before turning it over to Medicare, Fresenius and DaVita charge four times as much to those insurers than the relatively low Medicare rates. In fact payments from insurers account for the dialysis companies' entire profit margin. And the companies funnel $250 million a year to a charity called the American Kidney Fund, which steers patients over to private insurance by offering to pay their premiums. This show of generosity is a smokescreen to goose corporate profits. Meanwhile, a 2010 study found that for-profit dialysis centers have higher mortality rates than their nonprofit counterparts. Critics have accused Fresenius and DaVita of untrained and undermanned staff and unsanitary conditions.

Did I mention that Warren Buffett is a big investor in DaVita, and he made $231 million in a day when the company sold off a division of outpatient surgical centers and physician groups to insurance company UnitedHealth?

Simple market economics suggests that concentration forces prices higher. One study found admission rates increased up to $2,000 in regions with fewer hospital options. Another found monopoly hospitals charged 12 percent more on average than those with three or more local competitors, while a single merger between hospitals near one another spiked prices 6 percent. Patients have reported quadrupling of rates at the same physician for the same treatment after a hospital network buys the office. A dominant hospital network in Solano County, California, boasted to investors of being able to "maintain very lucrative contracts without the competition." Even national networks like private-equity-owned hospital chains hold leverage in payment negotiations with insurance companies.

Sutter Health in northern California settled a lawsuit in the fall of 2019 over its all-or-nothing bargaining model with insurance companies: either every Sutter hospital goes into a patient network or none of them do. Because Sutter has gobbled up so many Bay Area rivals, this allows it to keep prices high, confident that no insurer can drop it from the network. Inpatient prices have been revealed to be 70 percent higher in northern California than in southern California, where hospital chains aren't as consolidated.

This flows down to the doctors; there are more medical professionals among the top 1 percent of income earners than there are bankers and lawyers, and they earn far more than colleagues in other countries, across every level of treatment. Part of this comes from deliberate, artificial doctor shortages driven by the cartel-like behavior of the American Medical Association, which limits the number of medical schools. It's another example of concentration creep: consolidated hospital networks lead to consolidation among doctors, who use accreditation to stand out amid shrinking options for their services.

Patients don't typically shop around to fix a broken leg, even if they had choices on where to get medical care. They are locked into the dominant provider, which usually doesn't post prices at all (a Trump administration proposal would force transparency, much to the consternation of hospital executives, who have threatened to sue). Beyond the premiums, deductibles, and co-pays, new charges can be sprung without warning. Surprise "out-of-network" billing occurs in close to one in five emergency room visits, as an anesthesiologist or assistant surgeon seeks separate pay at a higher rate, even though the patient had no opportunity to select anyone else. This has gotten so bad that even Congress considered doing something about it in 2019—until the two firms profiting most from surprise billing dropped a $28 million ad campaign.

But health provider monopolies harm patients even if you set aside price. Contrary to monopolist claims of efficiency and economies of scale, studies find that lack of competition leads to poorer outcomes. A 2018 report in *Health Services Research* found that when cardiologists concentrate local markets, patients had a 5 to 7 percent greater likelihood of heart attacks, as well as increases in emergency room visits, readmissions, and deaths. Older studies have found similar results for both Medicare beneficiaries and carriers of private insurance.

The plain fact that consolidation can put residents further away from the nearest hospital is a factor in health outcomes, particularly in sparsely populated areas. Many sick people can't get time off work or obtain child care enabling them to drive an hour each way to see a doctor. The gas alone is a tax on wellness. But hospital monopolists don't work to protect these lifelines for rural residents. America has lost over five hundred hospitals across the country in the past twenty years, and in rural areas there have been at least eighty-five closures since 2010, which amounts to one in every twenty rural hospitals. Patients are often left more than twenty miles away from any alternative for medical care. States that didn't expand Medicaid, and therefore lost the potential for new patients, have fared more poorly.

Hospitals are magnets for specialists, who pack up whenever one closes. Fewer than half of all rural counties have a practicing obstetric care specialist, meaning pregnant women in outlying areas must travel farther for deliveries. And this will get worse. A 2016 study from iVantage Health Analytics suggested that 673 other rural hospitals and facilities were at risk, impacting 11.7 million patients. Rural hospital closures lead to medical deserts, which have sprouted up across America. Lack of access to decent medical care devastates struggling communities; there are demonstrable effects on income and employment. And it widens the largest health outcome gap in the industrialized world.

Medical deserts and monopolized health care communities "raise the cost of employing labor and starves local economies," said Leemore Dafny. "It hurts the growth of small business. It's a huge drag on the economy." Dafny recalled a phone conversation she had with the CEO of Steel of West Virginia, right when two hospitals were merging in the company's hometown, Huntington. He feared that higher prices after the merger would threaten his business. "He called and said, 'Professor Dafny, all the politicians have these relationships with the hospital, the governor, the attorney general, nobody wants to oppose them. But it's choking the economy. It's choking me.'"

The workers in these hospitals, who have nowhere else to bargain for their services, often struggle. Eli Saslow's portrait in the *Washington Post* of a failing rural hospital in Fairfax, Oklahoma, showed workers coming in for eleven straight weeks without pay. And even when the hospitals aren't dying, concentrated networks have the power to depress wages. A 2019 study from UCLA and Northwestern found that wage growth for skilled hospital workers slowed down after mergers.

Consolidation leads to corporate outsourcing. EmCare, one of the leading emergency room outsourcing companies, which handle ER operations for hospitals, is largely responsible for the surprise out-of-network billing trend. TeamHealth, another ER contractor, uses the threat of out-of-network billing to negotiate higher in-network rates. Both have histories with the private equity industry. Another private-equity-owned subcontractor, Agilon Health, coordinates care for Medicaid patients and was found to have improperly denied or delayed coverage on a routine basis.

Hospital monopolies also try to prevent competition. Secret contract terms unearthed by the *Wall Street Journal* in 2018 show that hospitals lock insurers into exclusive deals, limit auditing of costs, and load on fees without patients' knowledge. Two recent antitrust lawsuits in California and North Carolina found that contracts prevented insurers from sending patients to cheaper hospitals, instead applying gag orders restricting them from giving patients any information. Hospitals have also blocked clinical data from leaving their networks.

Health data, in fact, is a massive global trading business, fed by a 2016 merger between IMS Health and Quintiles that created a $23 billion market leader. Now called IQVIA, it trades pieces of its half-billion-patient dossier to researchers and drug companies. Centralized data is perpetually a privacy risk. But in the health industry, where consolidation begets consolidation, it's hardly a surprise. There's also tons of cross-consolidation going on: hospitals launching a generic drug company, insurers jumping into hospice care, and Big Tech snapping up portions of the system.

You would think that, with all this market power, hospitals, physician groups, and outpatient clinics would have at least shaken down their suppliers by now and forced cheaper prices for medical devices, gauze pads, tongue depressors, and everything else they use. But you would be wrong.

The executive director of Physicians Against Drug Shortages is not a medical doctor. Phil Zweig still calls himself a journalist, after decades of investigative reporting for *American Banker*, the *Wall Street Journal*, and *Businessweek*. He broke the story in the early 1980s about Penn Square Bank, a small firm based out of a shopping center in Oklahoma City that made $2.5 billion in reckless loans to fraudulent oilmen at the peak of a production boom, passing the risk around to multiple banks. When it all went bust, Penn Square took the hit; regulators forced it to close in 1982. But its counterparties felt the pain too, including Continental Illinois, at the time the seventh-largest bank in America. The government had to step in and save Continental in 1984 with a $4.5 billion federal bailout, the largest in history to that point, which inspired Connecticut congressman Stewart McKinney to quip in a hearing that the government created a new class of financial institutions that were "too big to fail."

Zweig wrote a book about Penn Square in 1985, and he kept in touch with his contacts in Oklahoma City. One day in the late 1990s he met a former U.S. attorney for breakfast who had worked on the criminal case against Penn Square. "We were chatting about what he was up to and whether he had any cases," Zweig told me. "He starts telling me about this Texas company, Retractable Technologies."

Retractable was the brainchild of Thomas Shaw, an engineer from Little Elm, Texas, who in the late 1980s saw a news report about the surging incidence of HIV and hepatitis C infections among health care workers. They called the problem "needle stick": health care workers would accidentally prick themselves with used needles. Over 380,000 medical professionals experienced needle stick every year. Shaw was a mechanical engineer, and he saw it as a design challenge. "I had a couple friends I knew from childhood, they had contracted AIDS," Shaw said to me. "I knew I couldn't fix the biology side of it, but I could fix my part."

Shaw went to the nearest drugstore and bought a handful of syringes, spending years pulling them apart and testing different options until hitting upon a solution. Shaw's syringe, which he called VanishPoint, operated like a ballpoint pen. After the needle had been stuck into the patient, a ring would snap and retract the needle, allowing workers to safely pull it out. Shaw thought his invention had eliminated needle stick forever. Then he tried to sell it.

It turned out that one company, Becton Dickinson, sold the majority of all syringes in America. Moreover, it had practically locked in this dominance with hospitals through something called group purchasing organizations, or GPOs. Established in 1910 as co-op buying groups, these organizations sprang from the same impulse as hospitals merging to gain leverage over insurance companies. A similar dynamic could take hold with medical suppliers: a big hospital coalition could bargain down prices by securing volume discounts.

Hospitals outsourced supplier negotiations to GPO firms that specialized in the process. But the deals all had a curious clause: the vendors would pay the GPO's administrative costs as long as hospitals bought entirely from a narrow group of vendors. Many contracts included a "90-10" or "95-5" requirement. To use the syringe example, if a hospital purchased 1,000 syringes from Becton Dickinson in one year, it would have to buy at least 900 or 950 the next year. If not, it would lose the administrative discount and pay a penalty. The effect was to entrench the dominant supplier.

If you have a locked-in supplier, prices are likely to rise. A metal screw used in spinal surgery that costs $1 on eBay goes for as high as $800 in a GPO arrangement. And the GPO companies shared in this windfall, as they were paid by the suppliers. "If you're a major GPO facility, you get a check at the end of the year, a partial refund of the deliberate overcharge," Zweig said. The fees were typically a percentage of the product cost. So if that price ran higher, GPOs would get more in kickbacks; this created incentives toward inflation. Indeed, when economists ran tests on this, they found that supplies sold in a competitive market were between 10 and 15 percent cheaper than those sold through GPOs. Of course, many of these overpayments get kicked on from hospitals to patients.

You might ask why hospitals wouldn't use their clout to get fairer contract terms; the answer is that they also have a hand in the till. Checks go out to hospitals or sometimes the top administrator. Zweig would eventually find a contract between a GPO and a hospital describing these as "patronage dividend" payments. A now-defunct industry trade publication called *Healthcare Matters* bluntly stated in 2013 that it was "common knowledge" that GPOs gave "share-backs" to member hospitals, including hospital executives, who have "learned to rely on that share back as an integral part of their annual compensation." As Zweig explained, "The CEOs are the glue that keeps it together." So hospitals don't end up with cheaper supplies, as intended, but executives and middleman GPO companies are well fed. And entrepreneurs like Retractable's Thomas Shaw, who built a better syringe, couldn't get their products to market.

Shaw was unsuccessfully trying to get the Justice Department's antitrust division interested in investigating these contractual blockades. Zweig decided to write a story about it for *Businessweek* called "Locked out of the Hospital." Zweig caught up with Shaw a short time later, to see if his story helped. Shaw told him not much had changed, and offered him a chance to take a break from journalism and become Retractable's communications director. Zweig took it, staying in the position for several years.

Nothing really worked for Retractable. It got a $650,000 grant from the National Institutes of Health, lobbied Congress to pass the Needlestick Safety and Prevention Act, which required hospitals to reduce reliance on unsafe syringes, and successfully sued Becton Dickinson twice for anticompetitive behavior, winning $440 million in settlements and jury awards. Someone even made a movie about Retractable's struggles called *Puncture* (Zweig consulted on the movie). But Retractable got no further than saving itself from bankruptcy. It still couldn't penetrate the market, dwarfed by Becton Dickinson, which controls nearly two-thirds of all sales. In 2000, the Centers for Disease Control estimated 380,000 needle sticks at hospitals every year. Today, they estimate 385,000. "We went out to the market thinking we've done the technical part, and now we can make good on government's interest in making tech available," Shaw said. "I sit here today with zero hope that we will go into hospitals. Lower price and better technology doesn't matter."

The main consequence of the Retractable saga was to activate Phil Zweig. He agitated against GPOs, even forcing a series of congressional hearings in the early 2000s, which concluded that while GPOs were originally intended to save hospitals money, in practice they were doing the opposite. Zweig decided that the problem lay with a safe-harbor provision passed in 1987, making kickbacks between medical suppliers and GPO companies legal. Before then, hospitals paid the GPOs; afterward the funding came from the suppliers. Intended to save hospitals money, the safe harbor completely transformed incentives around purchase prices; in Zweig's estimation, it inflated costs by hundreds of billions of dollars.

While the fee to the GPOs was statutorily limited to 3 percent, Zweig found a bio from a major GPO executive with Novation, now known as Vizient, claiming that the company made $95 million a year on $1.3 billion in sales, which comes out to 7.3 percent. Often these additional charges take the form of "marketing" or "advance" payments, so GPOs could maintain the fiction of staying below that 3 percent number. The excess fees expose the GPO strategy of sticking up suppliers for access to exclusive buying groups. Zweig pulled one report from 1998 showing that Ben Venue Laboratories paid an amount equivalent to 56.25 percent of its overall sales of diltiazem, a blood pressure drug, to access the contract of major GPO Novation. "The more a vendor pays for a contract, the more market share it gets," he said.

This all grew worse in 1996, when the Justice Department and the Federal Trade Commission gave GPOs an effective antitrust exemption except in "extraordinary circumstances." This was also supposed to assist hospitals by increasing the size of the buying groups, but it only led to mass consolidation. Today, four companies—Vizient, Premier, Healthtrust, and Intalere—control the overwhelming majority of GPO purchasing, about $300 billion for five thousand different health systems. According to a 2018 report, 98 percent of all hospitals use a GPO, and the Big Four account for 90 percent of the market.

Zweig helped draft legislation to repeal the safe harbor, but the hospitals and GPOs teamed up to sink it—remember, hospitals were in on the kickback game as well. Then, during the Obama administration, Zweig noticed a story about an executive order instructing the Food and Drug Administration to prevent record drug shortages. Hundreds of drugs, mostly old, low-profit, generic medications like injectables that hospitals used routinely, were simply unavailable, causing hospitals and patients to scramble. The unavailable drugs treated bacterial infections, childhood leukemia, and numerous types of cancer; lack of access endangered the lives of countless patients. Even those with curable diseases had been forced into less effective alternative treatments, with uncertain results. (Obama's attention to drug shortages did reduce them for a time, but as of 2019 shortages sat near the peak before the executive order.)

Buried inside the article was a line that made Zweig's hair stand up: "Just five large hospital buying groups purchase nearly 90 percent of the needed medicines, and only seven companies manufacture the vast majority of supply." That was a reference to GPOs. (Since that 2011 story, the five GPO giants have shrunk to four.) "It took me five minutes to see the same anti-competitive contracting practices, the exorbitant pay-to-play fees, were creating the shortage," Zweig said.

Economists had come up with all sorts of conflicting explanations, but Zweig thought it was simple: if the GPOs were the only way to get drugs into the hospitals, then generic drug manufacturers would just shut down if they didn't win a sole-source contract from one of the Big Four. Because the margins were so low, manufacturers had consolidated to win through volume. Lack of competition can lead to shortages amid the slightest disruption. A Government Accountability Office report from 2014 backs this up; it maintained that quality problems and temporary manufacturing facility closures primarily caused drug shortages, but it added that the "operating structure of GPOs results in fewer manufacturers producing generic drugs and this, in turn, contributes to a more fragile supply chain for these drugs." The study did note that GPO executives disagreed with this assessment, as you'd expect.

Zweig started a Google alert for "drug shortages," and stories started rolling in from around the world; the problem was not limited to the United States. He attended a panel about drug shortages at a meeting of the American Society of Anesthesiologists. Officials from the FDA again meandered when discussing the causes, claiming that no single factor was responsible. "I was sitting next to this doctor. He jumps up and says, 'You're giving us nothing but BS,'" Zweig said. "He talks about the role of the GPOs. The woman from the FDA says, 'Well, economics may have something to do with it.'"

The doctor was named Joel Zivot, and in 2012 he and Zweig formed Physicians Against Drug Shortages, which is focused primarily on GPOs. It's a small organization that Zweig helps fund out of his own pocket. And while focusing on the known problem of drug shortages over the more obscure issue of hospitals being overcharged at least makes people take notice, it's been an uphill battle. "We've gotten a lot of resistance from even medical societies, because the purchasing groups have bought them off," Zweig said. "I'm talking literally here."

The industry does seem to project a degree of power; for example, the leading academic expert on drug shortages, Erin Fox of the University of Utah, discloses in slide presentations that her information comes from market-leading GPO Vizient. Zweig also points to a daylong November 2018 conference in Washington on the root causes of drug shortages, put together by the Duke Margolis Center for Health Policy. This came months after the FDA revoked a no-bid $4.2 million grant to Duke Margolis, in part because its director, former FDA commissioner Mark McClellan, is also a paid board member of Johnson & Johnson, one of the world's largest drug companies. Nevertheless, the Duke Margolis event was convened through a cooperative agreement with the FDA, and then FDA commissioner Scott Gottlieb gave a keynote address.

Speakers at the event included Blair Childs, senior vice president of public affairs for Premier, the number two GPO; David Gaugh, a former marketing executive at Vizient who now lobbies for drugmakers; and Erin Fox, who has a data relationship with Vizient. While Gottlieb had previously cited GPO middlemen as a factor in drug shortages, it didn't really come up in his speech. "We don't have a lot of very good answers, and we certainly don't have easy solutions, or we would have fixed this problem a long time ago," Gottlieb said.

This set Zweig off. He stewed as panelists repeated familiar claims about the unclear rationale for drug shortages. Finally, in a question-and-answer period, he stood up. "Listening to these folks today, one would get the sense that the shortages of these medications are among the great unsolved mysteries of the universe," he began. "They're not. This is a very simple matter, it's about money." He went on for several minutes as panelists squirmed in their seats. Finally, as there was no question coming, the moderator, Gregory Daniel of Duke Margolis, tried to cut him off. "I came down here at my own expense, I'm going to finish!" Zweig said, his voice rising. "The only solution to this problem is to restore open competitive markets . . . by eliminating the kickbacks, the bribes, the rebates, the payola." Applause followed. Zweig told me that people came up to him after his remarks, thanking him.

There was one other interesting slide from the panel. It was labeled "Sources of Shortages: Natural Disasters," punctuated by a picture of a hurricane bearing down on the Caribbean. But the text below was very telling: "IV fluid shortages *which began in 2014* [emphasis mine] were worsened due to Baxter facility impact in PR [Puerto Rico]."

Bags of saline, which have been available for commercial use since 1931, typically cost around a dollar for hospitals, and they use them incessantly. Hanging an IV is typically the first action nurses take when dealing with a sick patient. Baxter, the leading producer, ships over a million units every day. That requires constant manufacturing of a low-margin product. The FDA's drug shortage database first posted a shortage in IV saline solution in January 2014. Bags of dextrose—sugar and water—have also been in chronically short supply. The United States was actually importing saline IV bags—which, as I've mentioned so much that you're mad at me, is salt and water in a bag—from Spain, Norway, and Germany. And of course the shortages were leading manufacturers to raise the price as much as five- and six-fold. "We're not supposed to have shortages in a market economy," said Phil Zweig.

Some chalked up the lack of saline to an increase in demand, especially around flu season (which creates lots of need to replenish fluids). But the simple fact remains that three companies—Baxter, ICU Medical, and B. Braun—make around 86 percent of the nation's saline solution. And any problems, whether a recall or a manufacturing plant closure, can reduce the already tight supply. ICU's saline division, at the time known as Hospira, recalled an entire lot in 2015 after finding one human hair in one bag. Other findings of particulate matter have shut down plants, and even routine maintenance disturbs supply.

Clearly, producing a medical product that will be injected into human veins must be 100 percent sterile, and made to exacting specifications. There are hundreds of regulatory checks, which manufacturers of course complain about. But there's a bigger problem here. Each company producing saline contracts it to hospitals through a GPO. And the GPOs do not allow a second supplier to step in when a manufacturer runs into trouble. So hospitals don't really have three sources of saline; they have one.

Indeed, as Zweig explained in the *Wall Street Journal* in 2018, market-leading GPO Vizient has held an "extended single source award for IV solutions" with Baxter since 2007, when the GPO was still called Novation. Any hospital using Vizient has no other opportunity to find saline if Baxter runs into a supply problem. Moreover, new suppliers of saline don't pop up anyway, not only because of the barriers to entry but also because GPOs eat away at already thin margins. Plus, the high fees companies like Baxter pay to secure GPO contracts make it more difficult for them to invest in building new plants to make more saline.

There are also allegations of straight-up anticompetitive conduct. Months before the hurricanes in Puerto Rico, the Justice Department began investigating Baxter for antitrust violations, related to whether it colluded with other producers to artificially create saline IV supply shortages, in order to demand higher prices. A federal grand jury had been impaneled in Pennsylvania, and hospitals weren't waiting for the outcome, suing Baxter and ICU over collusion. Separately, the Federal Trade Commission and the New York attorney general's office were investigating whether Baxter illegally tied purchase of saline to other medical supplies, forcing hospitals to order higher-margin products like pumps and tubes in long-term contracts or risk being unable to obtain a steady supply of IV bags.

While these critical investigations were going on, Hurricane Maria struck Puerto Rico on September 20, 2017. And it certainly made a bad situation worse. All of Baxter's small-volume IV bag production, equaling roughly half of the bags used in the United States, comes from the island. On September 22, Baxter told hospitals and customers that it had lost "multiple production days" from the storm, affecting its production of dextrose and saline. The next day it told hospitals it would have to ration release of IV solutions to conserve its supply. "We regret this disruption to your daily operations and appreciate your patience as we re-establish our supply pipeline," Baxter wrote in a letter to customers. Months later, Baxter got clearance to import saline from Brazil and Mexico.

In a way, the hurricanes got companies like Baxter, and the GPO sellers of its products, off the hook. Now they could point to the storm as causing the shortages, instead of to a system designed to create shortages for profit. All the news headlines—CBS News, the *Washington Post*, the Associated Press, the *Wall Street Journal*, even local outlets in Minnesota and Philadelphia and Ben Boyer's hometown of San Diego—referenced Puerto Rico as a proximate cause of the shortage. Most of them included a to-be-sure paragraph noting that supplies had been low prior to the hurricane but never explained why. The media appropriately conveyed the sense of crisis; flu patients were going to die if they didn't get the fluids they needed. But overall, the coverage gave the impression that the shortages were an unfortunate case of bad luck, not a business model.

Ben Boyer didn't know any of this when the nurse told him about injecting his wife, Xenia, directly with chemotherapy medication instead of using an IV drip, because the IV bags weren't coming in from Puerto Rico. Incidentally, the increased use of syringes to mimic the IV process led to shortages in that product. It also kept the nurse from attending to other patients for a half hour, an effective manpower loss. But the immediate effect of this, given Ben's family history with Puerto Rico and his general anger at the mismanaged response to the hurricanes there, was a social media firestorm.

"My wife's nurse had to stand for 30 mins & administer a drug slowly through a syringe because there are almost no IV bags in the continental U.S. anymore," Ben tweeted. "See, they were all manufactured in a Puerto Rican factory which still isn't fixed. Meanwhile that stupid swollen prick golfs." (We can assume that last bit referred to Donald Trump.)

This was not a normal tweet for Ben. He had just moved back to San Diego with Xenia from London, after working for the BBC and then Sky News as a writer and producer. Xenia had been diagnosed with inoperable brain cancer in 2009 and did a round of chemo in Britain. She needed more treatment when the couple moved to the United States, forcing Ben to rustle up stateside insurance coverage. "I didn't know anybody in the city, so I spent an even more unhealthy amount of time on social media than most people," he told me. "Especially during chemo, my wife would be sleeping, and I would be endlessly scrolling stuff." But normally Ben's posts were apolitical, mostly jokes and gags, perhaps to release tension.

"It really was off the cuff," Ben said. But it started to get traction, particularly among some friends in television who had large followings. Within a day or so it had over 100,000 likes and 62,000 retweets; fury directed at Trump moves pretty well online. Reporters from *Newsweek* and Snopes picked up the story, which devolved into the usual political back-and-forth of charges and countercharges. "It was definitely pretty fascinating. I've never had anything like that happen before or since," Ben said. But he eventually figured out that his rage about IV saline, while partially accurate, had a huge backstory attached to it. "It very much felt that way once you zoomed out," Ben said. "That this is an insane side effect of a larger issue."

Two weeks after Xenia's Christmas-week chemo session, she and Ben returned to the hospital; the IV shortage was ongoing. They were told that since Xenia had had to deal with the syringe the week before, now she'd get a machine. Xenia never experienced the manual process again. But the ravages of cancer finally became too much. She died on Mother's Day 2018, leaving behind Ben and a daughter.

"The entire experience of going through my wife's illness and death is the sort of thing you don't wish on anyone," Ben said. "But if you have to deal with the health care system, you can't hold the opinion that everything's working, or that there's not enormous improvements to be made."

The question is how you get to those solutions without addressing the concentrations of power and double-dealing schemes in the industries that supply and administer medical treatment. Neighborhood hospitals are among the biggest opponents of single-payer health care, and politicians feel constrained from going after them, because they heal the sick and employ large numbers of people. "I've talked to politicians. I've said if you just have engineers around a table with the devices used in a hospital, and figure out what it costs to make and what it would cost to buy, it would change everything," said Lillian Salerno, who was on the team at Retractable Technologies and later worked in the Obama White House and ran for Congress. "I think the public deserves to know, we can have single payer if we get the costs down." But nobody wants their ox gored, and when it comes to hospitals, suppliers, and the middlemen in between, it's a pretty big ox.

I do a lot of reading, but it took me a minute to notice the capital red letters on my bottle of Listerine. "THIS FORMULA IS NOT SOLD TO ANY RETAILER AS A STORE BRAND," it exclaimed.

Mouthwash is a concentrated industry, and Listerine—or rather its parent company, Johnson & Johnson—is the established leader, with about 41 percent of all sales. Procter & Gamble comes next, and then Colgate-Palmolive; those three control about 64 percent of the market. But Listerine's container declares something important: that when you go into a supermarket or drugstore and pick up a store brand of mouthwash, you will not find Listerine in the bottle.

You might think such a disclaimer wouldn't be necessary. Listerine is the leading mouthwash brand; why would Johnson & Johnson allow Target or Walgreens to sell it under their own brands and compete with Listerine at a lower price point? But then you have to think about it a second longer. Does Walgreens own a manufacturing plant where workers dutifully place Walgreens's special concoction of mouthwash into branded bottles? No. Groceries and drugstores are not independent manufacturers, generally speaking. Walgreens licenses someone else's product for use as its store brand. So do most other retailers.

That licensed store brand could be sitting right next to the name brand at your local retailer. A few smaller companies specialize in making store brands, but well-known brands are in this game as well. Retailers acquire products they can put into generic store-brand packaging from large companies. Costco's Kirkland brand batteries come from market leader Duracell, Costco CEO Craig Jelinek admitted in 2016; Kirkland coffee is roasted by Starbucks; Kirkland canned tuna comes from Bumble Bee. Walmart's Great Value brand includes foods manufactured and packaged by Sara Lee and ConAgra; product recalls for each company gave this away, the same way a produce facility stricken with listeria had to recall Trader Joe's store-brand vegetables along with Green Giant and Signature Farms. Most of Trader Joe's beloved store-brand products secretly come from outside companies like PepsiCo, ConAgra, Wonderful Pistachios, and Snack Factory. Sometimes there are trivial changes and sometimes there aren't.

Everybody wins in this scenario. The retailers get a lower-priced product that can pull people into their stores. The manufacturer gets to capture two audiences at once—those loyal to their brand and those who shop for value. Consumers enjoy the illusion of selecting between different options: in reality one has a brand name and the other is essentially or even literally the same product with a different name.

I called Listerine last year and asked the cheerful customer care specialist why Listerine felt the need to put that disclaimer on its bottle. "It's very very common for store brands to put 'compare to' or 'same as' on their bottles," she explained. "So we're just saying that this is not used in any store brand." I asked her what brands might sell their mouthwash to retailers to use as store brands; she did not seem to know. She seemed like a nice lady, and I take her at her word.

One enterprising science podcaster who knows a lot more about mouthwash than normal people compared the Listerine mouthwash with the Walgreens store brand and found that the four major active ingredients in Listerine (eucalyptol, thymol, methyl salicylate, and menthol) matched the Walgreens mouthwash to within .001 percent. This is also true of Walmart's Equate brand. The alcohol concentration is slightly different, but that's relatively trivial. There's no reason that one of Listerine's competitors, if not Listerine itself—though again, I trust the nice consumer care lady—couldn't ever so slightly tweak the mouthwash, throw it into a different bottle, and sell it as one of the many options on retail shelves.

Large food and household goods producers have entire departments licensing products for use as store brands, for which they earn money from consumers who spurn their products. There's an entire website for obsessives called storebrands.com, dedicated to these generic-label items. There's a store brand lobby, the Private Label Manufacturers Association, fighting in Washington for the right to sell broadly similar goods at slightly reduced prices.

It introduces what shoppers read as choice into the system, the same way the dozens of products made by Unilever, Nestlé, Procter & Gamble, Kraft Heinz, and other conglomerates give the impression of alternatives. In 2017, the consumer goods sector saw its most mergers in fifteen years. You couldn't always tell from the label.

CHAPTER 10

Monopolies Are Why a Woman Found
Her Own Home Listed for Rent on Zillow

Dana Chisholm didn't know anything about private equity. All she knew was that after two years of commuting twice a week from her home in San Diego to Biola University, an evangelical Christian college two hours away in La Mirada, she was tired. The driving was exacting a toll on her mental health. She needed to move.

Bounded by freeways and littered with transport trucks and warehouses, La Mirada sits in a clutch of endless sprawl southeast of Los Angeles, just north of Orange County. Biola had a block of apartments available to students, and in February 2016 Dana moved in. She was completing her PhD in intercultural education, had studied and taught abroad in China and Thailand, and maintained ties to international students and researchers. Often she would help out friends, or friends of friends, with a place to stay. On top of the apartment being too small, Biola frowned on having multiple tenants in its properties. Only something with more room and fewer restrictions would do. Like a rental house.

Dana's search would take her to San Feliciano Drive, a cul-de-sac in the middle of a quiet neighborhood of one-story houses. The house was sandy-colored, with a reddish brown roof, and ten palm trees were scattered in the front yard. The neighborhood looked solidly middle class and well maintained, but as you drove around you would find hints of dilapidation—a house without siding on the front, a broken fence, a water heater sitting on a front lawn.

The first time Dana saw the house, "it was destroyed," she told me. But the location was so desirable that she dropped in a couple of weeks later and discovered that all the cabinets had been replaced. It looked good enough for Dana to make an offer; she signed the lease in June.

The house on San Feliciano Drive was a foreclosed property that Starwood Waypoint, a private-equity-backed real estate company, picked up in 2014. "I thought it was a leasing company. I had no idea it was a corporate

landlord," Dana told me. She later learned she was the third or fourth renter in the home since Starwood Waypoint acquired it; the neighbors asked
her why tenants constantly turned over. Dana soon found out. The dish-
washer was broken, the refrigerator's temperature would shift wildly and
spoil food, there was no running water in the sink, the pool leaked an inch
a day, rats and roaches scurried in and out of the home. The problems took
months to fix, with Dana continually calling to demand repairs. The company's own maintenance manager, Steve (Dana is the kind of person who
tells you the first name of everyone she's ever met), told her that any pretext
would be employed to avoid completing repairs. "Steve said to me, 'We
have really good lawyers. If there's a way to get out of it, these guys will.'"

The constant complaints may have changed some minds back at Starwood Waypoint. In July, just a month after moving in, Dana got a call from
Gilbert, the leasing agent (like I said, Dana tells you everyone's name). "He
said, 'Dana, we just had a meeting, they were talking about renting your
house, I thought you were staying in it a year.' I said, 'I am. I just paid my
rent.'" A month later, Dana got an email alert she had set up through Zillow when she was looking for houses, informing her of a new property on
the market: hers. "I got a Zillow alert in my email for my own house. I was
like, 'What the hell is going on?'" she said. "I live here! They didn't serve
me, they didn't do anything. They just started trying to rent my house."

Rental horror stories like this have become widespread since a new breed
of landlords, backed by Wall Street money, arrived on the scene after the
foreclosure crisis. The biggest is Invitation Homes, created by Blackstone,
the world's largest private equity firm. In 2017, Invitation Homes merged
with Starwood Waypoint, then number three in the market, creating a
combined company with over 82,000 properties nationwide, focused in
areas hit hard by foreclosures. Invitation Homes is the largest landlord in
Sacramento, and Atlanta, Houston, Phoenix, Charlotte, and several cities
in Florida have high concentrations of private-equity-owned rental homes
as well. Tenants across the country, many of them previous foreclosure
victims, have complained about jacked-up rents, lagging repairs, ruthless
evictions, and "charge-backs" for routine maintenance.

Dana Chisholm documents many of these tales at a Facebook page she
created for Invitation Homes tenants. She hopes to bring the industry to
heel. "I raised my boys with consequences, equal consequences for whatever you do," she said. "We regulate energy, water, everything. We broke

up the railroads, we regulated steel mills, factories. Why are we not step-
ping in on this housing thing?" It sounds like a typical response from a
California woman—until you learn that Dana is a hard-core Trump supporter. She was active in the pro-life movement for decades and maintains
her roots as a dedicated conservative. Meanwhile, the CEO of Invitation
Homes' creator, Blackstone's Steven Schwarzman, is one of the president's
closest allies. "I still support Trump, but I'm angry at him," she said. "My
pitch is, 'I'm your biggest supporter. Why aren't you supporting me?'"

Only private equity can bring together left and right during one of the
most politically polarized eras in our nation's history. The industry has
driven an inordinate amount of monopolization while mastering the art
of extracting value from corporate carcasses, harming workers, customers, and the overall economy. More than Amazon, private equity can be
blamed for the death of retail; more than Walmart, it's responsible for
widespread grocery closures. Examine any insidious business that nobody
with a modicum of self-respect would touch, and you're likely to find private equity. It's a business model that has engineered customer loyalty and
even success out of the equation. The greed-stuffed titans fattening themselves off this financialized doom loop are the architects of the modern age
of monopoly.

Initially, private equity deals were called leveraged buyouts, rising out of
the junk-bond craze of the 1980s. Michael Milken's scheme to skim profits from high-yield securities attracted corporate raiders, who made hostile bids for established companies. Milken's Drexel Burnham Lambert
financed the takeovers with subordinated debt. The media nicknamed
Drexel's annual junk-bond conference the "Predator's Ball."

Raiders used borrowed money (the "leverage" in the leveraged buyout)
to accumulate shares in asset-rich, low-debt companies. They would either
grab a controlling stake or use the shares as a wedge to buy the company
outright. Sometimes the targeted company would pay the raider to go away;
the business press called that "greenmail," in an inversion of blackmail.
Other company tactics, like writing massive "golden parachute" payouts
into executive pay packages in the event of a takeover, were envisioned as
poison pills but actually encouraged bids by spreading the riches around.

The largest buyout of this period came from Kohlberg Kravis Roberts
(KKR), which purchased the conglomerate RJR-Nabisco for $25 billion in

1988, nearly doubling the previous record. Only $15 million of the money belonged to KKR; the rest was debt. The RJR-Nabisco deal, memorialized in Bryan Burrough and John Helyar's book *Barbarians at the Gate*, gave KKR control of Camel, Winston, and Salem cigarettes; Life Savers, Baby Ruth, and Butterfinger candies; Planters peanuts; Del Monte canned goods; Ritz crackers and Triscuits; Shredded Wheat; Oreos and Animal Crackers. At one point during the period, KKR also owned Safeway and Stop & Shop, the stores where Nabisco products were sold, along with Samsonite luggage, Tropicana orange juice, Duracell batteries, and more.

When a corporate raider gained control, he (and usually it was a he) would transfer debt onto the company's balance sheet. The company, known as a portfolio company because it existed as one of many in the raider's briefcase, suddenly had large borrowing costs to manage, in addition to paying management fees to the new owner, meeting payroll, and running the business. Advisors, bankers, and fund managers ushering the deal through also took their cut. Often portfolio companies couldn't handle the financial burden and went bankrupt. To the corporate raider, this *did not matter.* They purchased the portfolio company with someone else's money, and took out enough fees and assets that, by the time the reckoning arrived, they'd already covered their nut. Through financial engineering, corporate raiders devised a mass asset transfer, shifting value into their friendly arms. Bank robbers would call it looting; raiders called it the leveraged buyout.

The only way for companies to protect themselves from corporate raiders was to either load up on debt to make their balance sheets unpalatable or build a fortress that couldn't be scaled. So leveraged buyouts not only pulled companies under the roofs of corporate raiders but also drove monopoly in other areas of the economy by making dominance the only antidote to a takeover.

Before too long, the whole game went south. The media and the public recoiled at the dazzling displays of greed amid flurries of corporate bankruptcies. Milken got busted for running an insider-trading ring that profited off information about future leveraged buyouts. Ivan Boesky, who speculated on the timing of corporate takeovers to win stock rewards, was also prosecuted for insider trading. Both served time in jail. By the end of the 1980s, the junk bond market crashed, with Drexel Burnham Lambert heading into bankruptcy in February 1990. With seed funding for buyouts drained and associated criminality exposed, the raiders slipped away. But they didn't disappear; they rebranded.

Leveraged buyouts became known as private equity, a gentler-sounding version of the same maneuver. Private equity firms use closed-end funds to raise money investors cannot withdraw, though they get paid through special dividends and "dividend recapitalizations" that increase debt loads on portfolio companies. Fund managers take "2 and 20," a management fee of 2 percent of total capital deployed and 20 percent of any profits in the fund. These fees have gone up recently in some funds to 2 percent of capital and 30 percent of profits. The same players, like KKR, TPG Capital, and Nelson Peltz's Triarc, returned to the stage for the private equity boom. Even Milken rehabilitated himself after prison; he now runs an economic institute that throws a giant annual conference in Beverly Hills for business elites.

Like its practitioners, the private equity scheme remained the same: buy companies with borrowed money, load them up with debt, force them to cut costs through layoffs and liquidation, and cash out with management fees and proceeds from the asset fire sale. Private equity managers insist that they help struggling companies fix management problems and grow. But the cost cutting usually comes at workers' expense; you can see private equity as a direct transfer from labor to capital. After a few years, the portfolio companies get spun out or taken into bankruptcy; either way, private equity firms win. The actual returns for investors are middling, but managers hope that nobody with money figures that out.

Led by global pacesetters KKR, Blackstone, Apollo, and Carlyle, private equity surged to a record $2.5 trillion in raised funds by mid-2019, double the figure in 2012. The unspent cash is called dry powder, taken from pension funds and the investment resources of sovereign nations. Workers, in other words, have helped fund the modern bonanza of deal-making. Despite those prodigious sums, private equity buyouts remain largely financed through debt, because of the tax advantages (interest is typically deductible) and the benefits of leverage in juicing returns. If a private equity firm borrows $80 to make a $100 investment and the investment goes up 10 percent, they've made $10 while risking $20 of their own money, a 50 percent gain. But if they borrow $95 for that investment they make $10 while risking only $5, a 200 percent gain. Scale that up and you can see how borrowing is much more lucrative. "Debt is the lifeblood of the leveraged buyout model," said Eileen Appelbaum, author and private equity expert.

It's hard to find a sector of the economy where private equity doesn't play. Many of the monopolized industries discussed in this book, from health care to journalism to prisons, contain a strong role for private equity. And there are many more. Casinos? Private equity. Crunch Fitness, the gym chain? Private equity. Smarte Cartes, those baggage carriers at the airport? Private equity. Election Systems & Software, the largest manufacturer of electronic voting machines? Private equity. The ski resorts at Squaw Valley, Alpine Meadows, Mammoth Mountain, Aspen, Steamboat, Deer Valley, and a dozen others? One private equity firm gobbled up all of those by 2017. Global rugby leagues? Private equity has been fighting for control of that industry. Even Taylor Swift's back catalog got bought by a private equity firm in 2019.

Often the sleaziest industries in America have private equity firms at the helm. The industry owns many of the biggest payday lending firms, which prey on vulnerable borrowers needing everyday expenses, trapping them in a cycle of debt. MoneyGram International, which has been dinged repeatedly for abetting money laundering and scams against Americans over sixty, is private-equity-owned. Warburg Pincus, a private equity firm run by former Obama treasury secretary Timothy Geithner, orchestrated a shady loan operation through the company Mariner Finance, which mailed people checks that locked them into high-interest loans.

Private equity firm DC Capital Partners owns what once was the only for-profit detention camp for migrant children, in Homestead, Florida. America is one of only two places in the world with a cash bail industry (the other is the Philippines), compelling suspects to avoid jail by paying high fees to bail bond agencies. Private equity has a stake in that market. Endeavour Capital, which owns the nation's largest bail agency and its dedicated insurance underwriter, even raised funds for a ballot measure to overturn a California law banning the practice. The same company, Endeavour, ran a network of for-profit colleges and loan services that churned out worthless diplomas while saddling graduates with debt. Private equity has a large stake in predatory for-profit colleges.

Even in more respectable business corners, the private equity business model leads inevitably to pain. The New England Confectionary Company, known popularly as Necco, has made Clark bars, Sweethearts, and Necco wafers since the nineteenth century. Private equity firm American Capital bought Necco for $57 million in 2007. Losses mounted, $150 million over a decade, as American Capital rained debt upon Necco while snatching assets, according to the company's bankruptcy trustee. The subsequent cost cutting included reduced exterminator visits. Rats took over the Necco factory, with one worker finding 112 over one weekend. "I wouldn't eat the candy," he said. Another private equity firm bought Necco in 2017, split off the buildings, and rented them back to the confectioner—a common scheme to convert assets into cash, called a sale-leaseback. A year later Necco filed for bankruptcy and then closed operations. This is a familiar path; research on leveraged buyouts shows that they increase the chances of corporate bankruptcy by ten-fold.

Private equity giant Carlyle took over the 25,000-patient HCR Manor-Care nursing home chain, and short-staffing led to unconscionable neglect: patients breaking bones while falling out of bed, others soiling themselves while waiting for assistance to the bathroom, a rising number of health code violations. Investors extracted $1.3 billion from the company. Among other things, ManorCare was forced to—wait for it—sell all its real estate and rent it back. "I compare private equity to an otter," said Congressman Bill Pascrell (D-NJ), who has called for stronger private equity oversight for years. "It tears open a clam, takes the meat, and throws away the shell. It's people being tossed away."

I wouldn't say that private equity firms never nurture companies back to fiscal health; success is in fact irrelevant, so it's certainly possible. But we can say that private equity's financialization of the economy has trended it toward monopoly and concentration, whether by agglomerating the competition into a giant or destroying the competition through attrition.

According to the financial data analyst Pitchbook, private equity firms were responsible for one-quarter of all mergers and acquisitions from 2010 to 2015, rising to one-third by 2018. The deals were larger as well: the median private equity M&A deal was $140 million in 2018, almost triple the value of non-private-equity counterparts, with many of them megadeals of over $10 billion. And this is all before that $2.5 trillion in dry powder gets deployed. In a real sense, the merger boom reflects a private equity boom.

Acquisitions reflect a slight change in strategy for private equity. Typically they have bought companies with the expectation of revamping management and spinning them back out into the private market within a few years, and that's still true. But the buy-and-build strategy has become another way for private equity managers to extract profits; portfolio companies pay all transaction costs, including the time spent by managers working on the deal.

Fattened-up portfolio companies themselves often become someone else's acquisition. In 2017, 42 percent of merger targets were private-equity-backed companies. One example is the 2019 merger of McGraw-Hill and Cengage, creating the nation's second-largest college textbook company; both acquirer and target were owned by private equity. Private equity facilitates mergers on the front and back end, and it gets paid on either side.

The chain restaurant industry, much of which has been snatched up by private equity, reflects this trend. Roark Capital has a controlling stake or major investment in Arby's, Auntie Anne's Pretzels, Carl's Jr., Carvel, Cinnabon, Corner Bakery Café, Hardee's, Il Fornaio, Jimmy John's, and Buffalo Wild Wings, which Arby's took over in 2017. The new Arby's/Buffalo Wild Wings conglomerate, Inspire Brands, later bought Sonic and then Jimmy John's, which Roark Capital already owned a majority stake in, making it another example of a company effectively merging with itself.

In 2014, Burger King and Canadian coffee-and-donuts chain Tim Hortons merged for $11.9 billion. Burger King's owner, Brazilian private equity firm 3G Capital, executed the deal, staked with $3 billion in capital from Warren Buffett's Berkshire Hathaway. The merged company later bought fried chicken chain Popeyes. 3G also teamed up with Buffett to tie up Kraft and Heinz, creating the nation's third-largest food company. (Check your condiment packets from Burger King; guess the brand.) 3G also brought together Anheuser-Busch and InBev, now the world's largest beer company. Burgers, cheese, ketchup, and beer; that's an entire Fourth of July menu from one private equity firm.

3G engages in "zero-based budgeting," where managers scrutinize every expense, every year. In practice this leads to relentless cost cutting and layoffs: 1,400 jobs at Anheuser-Busch corporate HQ, 600 more at Heinz (including eleven of the top twelve executives), and 350 at Tim Hortons. Entire departments can be axed from one year to the next. At its fast-food division Restaurant Brands International, 3G earns 45¢ for every dollar on the menu, a incredible profit margin available only because costs have been slashed. "Costs are like fingernails: they always have to be cut," said one of

3G's founding partners, Carlos Sicupira. Cuts have even funneled down to printer paper and trash collection.

The bottom-line focus, workers be damned, made 3G a Wall Street darling—until investors realized that none of this created any value and in fact worsened the companies involved. After proposed takeovers of Mondelez and Unilever collapsed, profits for Kraft Heinz swung to losses, as there wasn't anything left to cut. With no investment to improve the products amid changing tastes, 3G was exposed as a one-trick pony, made worse by an SEC investigation into cooking Kraft Heinz's accounting books. Ultimately, 3G sold more than 25 million shares of Kraft Heinz in September 2019. The cost-cutting imperative damaged once-legendary brands.

In the grocery sector, private equity's stranglehold has caused further suffering. Between 2015 and 2018, seven large regional grocery chains filed for bankruptcy; all were private-equity-owned. This included A&P, once the largest grocery store in America, with almost sixteen thousand stores at its height in 1930. Under private equity, it drowned in debt and dissolved. In the seven bankruptcies, tens of thousands of workers lost their jobs and saw reduced pensions, while private equity managers extracted assets and prospered. A number of the grocery chains failed after—yep—sale-leaseback arrangements, where grocery companies had to pay rent on real estate they previously owned. In perhaps the most absurd example, Haggen, a small private-equity-owned chain from Washington state, took over 146 West Coast grocery stores divested in the Albertsons/Safeway merger. Within nine months, Haggen went bankrupt, having no idea how to scale up to that size, especially when weighed down by debt. Haggen liquidated its stores in the bankruptcy, and guess who bought thirty-three of them? Albertsons, the very company forced into divesting the stores nine months earlier. Albertsons paid far less money to reacquire the stores than the original sale price.

This carnage decimated regional supermarket chains, concentrating the industry for the largest players. Today, in over two hundred regions of the country, Walmart captures 50 percent or more of all grocery sales, according to a 2019 study. At its height, A&P controlled only 16 percent of the market nationally, and that led to a series of laws and antitrust enforcement to reduce the grocer's power. Future shakeouts could emerge, with Apollo buying Smart & Final and Cerberus-led Albertsons struggling. The pathway to deeper monopolization in grocery markets lies with continued private equity debt loads and mismanagement.

But one industry perfectly exemplifies private equity's destructive power. There's even a nickname for what the industry has wrought: "the retail apocalypse."

Romerick Anderson of Ontario, California, started working at Toys "R" Us over the holidays in 2013 and got retained part-time afterward. He rose to assistant manager, helping open a new Toys "R" Us Express in May 2017. A year later, the store was shuttered and Romerick was laid off without severance. "It seems like nobody's listening," Romerick told me in 2018, after protesting with other fired Toys "R" Us workers in New York City. "Middle America is paying for everything and not reaping benefits from it. The big dogs are getting away with murder."

Many people assume that Amazon doomed the retail economy. A look at the corporate ownership of fading retailers like Toys "R" Us reveals private equity's role. "The idea that Amazon disrupted [retail]—retail is constantly disrupted," said Eileen Appelbaum. "Zara came along and changed high fashion every two weeks. The difference is that retail is traditionally low debt. That gives breathing room to catch up." Well-managed companies with cash reserves can respond to market changes. A private-equity-owned retailer loaded down with debt lacks resources to reinvest in stores or build an e-commerce platform. The structure of these companies, forced upon them by private equity, signaled their downfall, especially when sales shriveled during the Great Recession. Meanwhile, private equity managers and investors, enriched through management fees, dividend recapitalizations, and asset stripping, came out ahead.

A 2018 report by the website Retail Dive looked at all private equity retail transactions since 2002, finding that more than 15 percent of them ended in bankruptcy. Of the largest buyouts since 2007, more than half wound up in default, bankruptcy, or deep financial distress. More than two-thirds of retail bankruptcies in 2016 and 2017 came from companies owned or controlled by private equity. A 2019 report from United for Respect, a union-backed group that represents retail workers, found that private-equity-owned failures in the past decade destroyed 597,000 retail jobs directly and another 728,000 jobs indirectly. "They have no interest in creating viable retail businesses," said Lily Wang, an organizer with United for Respect. "Their interest is short-term profits, at the expense of working families having to suffer, and communities losing their malls and stores."

Casualties include Linens n' Things (Apollo), Sports Authority (Leonard Green), H. H. Gregg (Freeman Spogli), rue21 (Apax), The Limited (Sun Capital), True Religion (TowerBrook), Claire's (Apollo), Nine West (Sycamore), Wet Seal (Versa), and Brookstone, twice, in 2014 (J. W. Childs) and 2018 (Sailing Power). Charlotte Russe, owned by Advent International, and Sun Capital's Shopko both filed for bankruptcy last year.

Dual bankruptcies, nicknamed "Chapter 22" (11 + 11), have become a trend. Payless Shoe Source hit bankruptcy in 2017 under Golden Gate and Blum Capital, who paid themselves $700 million in dividends in 2012 and 2013 while the company teetered. Payless was sold to Alden Global Capital and then hit bankruptcy again two years later, closing all its stores. The company altered its severance policy right before announcing the closures, capping it at a week per year. After the bankruptcy, Alden Global converted severance into an unsecured claim, leaving workers to fight it out with other creditors for their share.

Gymboree also had a double-dip bankruptcy, first under Bain Capital's leadership in 2017 and then one that dissolved the company in 2019 after an unwise decision to completely retool the children's clothing line. On the same day as the bankruptcy filing, Gymboree triggered a self-destruct provision in its severance policy, allowing it to terminate severance "at any time and in any respect." Days earlier, eight members of Gymboree's executive leadership team received paper checks with a "retention bonus" equal in value to their severance. The board, which included representatives from hedge funds and private equity firms, told executives to deposit the checks immediately. Two vice presidents with equal titles to the executive leadership team lost their severance entirely. "Me and this other woman were the altar sacrifices for the others to get paid," said Mera Chung, a vice president of design, intimating that canceling her severance freed up funds for the payoff to the other executives. Days after the bankruptcy filing, Chung learned that four bonus recipients jetted off to the Sundance Film Festival, despite major decisions being made about the company's future at that time. "It's like a B-grade Netflix movie," she said. "If they were so needed for retention, why were they able to go to Sundance?"

Store clerks never had a severance to begin with, and for months weren't told when their last day would be. "For five months I never knew if I was going to show up and my store would have a notice to vacate on the door," said Nichole Schorer, a former manager who finally had that moment in April 2019. "Shame on those higher-ups who ruined the brand and the clothes us moms came to love."

Sears, the company that pioneered the twentieth-century version of e-commerce—the catalog—reflects how financial engineering destroyed retail mainstays. An investment fund manager and former Yale roommate of treasury secretary Steven Mnuchin, Eddie Lampert of ESL Investments, occupied the unusual simultaneous roles of Sears's CEO, board chairman, transaction partner, landlord, and banker. Critics argue that rampant mismanagement led to Sears's demise: Lampert drastically reduced investment in stores and formulated the bright idea to pit three dozen management divisions against each other, a competition that proved disastrous. Sears made it through bankruptcy after closing hundreds of stores; Lampert remains chairman and primary owner. But the bankruptcy ended the careers of hundreds of thousands of workers and stripped Sears suppliers of their life savings, as they were stiffed for inventory.

The logic of capitalism insinuates that someone who obliterates so much wealth and investment would personally suffer. But Eddie Lampert sucked plenty of cash out of the business along the way. He personally lent Sears $2.6 billion, about half the debt load as of the October 2018 bankruptcy. This produced interest cash flow of $200 million to $225 million per year. Much of this debt was secured, putting Lampert first in line to be paid back in bankruptcy. He also sold off longtime Sears brands like Craftsman tools and Lands' End, a clothing line that went to a consortium that was two-thirds controlled by ESL. In 2015, Lampert executed a sale-leaseback, splitting off 235 of Sears's most profitable stores and 31 other Sears real estate holdings into a trust called Seritage, primarily owned by Lampert's hedge fund. Lampert serves as the chairman of Seritage. Sears paid Seritage nearly $400 million in rent and other expenses from 2015 to 2017. When Sears terminated leases, a decision that Lampert as CEO and chair had a hand in, Seritage redevelops the properties. With attractive locations across America, those properties are worth billions. Asset sales were also used to pay down debt . . . to Lampert. He remains a billionaire after all this, while over 250,000 Sears workers lost their jobs. The former Sears holding corporation sued Lampert in 2019 over $2 billion in relentless asset stripping, as well as the board who approved it—including Treasury Secretary Mnuchin.

And then there's Toys "R" Us, a venerable retailer subjected to a leveraged buyout in 2005 from three investment giants: Bain Capital, KKR, and Vornado Realty Trust. The transaction force-fed the retailer $5.3 billion in debt, which translated into $450 to $500 million annually just in interest payments, on top of management and advisory fees. Toys "R" Us actually grew operating income in its last three years of operation, increasing net profits if you set aside the debt burden. In 2017, it was responsible for one out of every five toys sold in the United States. But even market share couldn't provide salvation from the debt mountain. After refinancing several times, while cutting staff and underinvesting in stores, operations, and information technology, Toys "R" Us filed for bankruptcy in September 2017. Six months later it closed all eight hundred U.S. stores. The company might have been able to keep going after restructuring, but two leading creditors, hedge funds Angelo Gordon and Solus Alternative Asset Management, demanded liquidation, deciding it was "worth more dead than alive," as the *Wall Street Journal* put it.

In other words, it was a classic private equity bust-out. Bain and KKR made back their investment in fees, deductions, and tax write-offs, placing losses on investing partners. And like with Sears, executive bonuses were paid out before the bankruptcy. But 33,000 retail workers lost their livelihoods, including Romerick Anderson and Debbie Beard, an assistant manager who worked for Toys "R" Us for twenty-nine years. Beard explained to me how, unlike prior downsizings, nobody was offered severance pay. "We are the ones who built the company, been the backbone," Debbie told me. "I always felt that retail and food-service workers have been considered second-class citizens. We become numbers to the people running the companies." Maryjane Williams, a mother of five from Waco, Texas, and a twenty-year employee, told me she loved working at Toys "R" Us. "I carry the medical benefits for my family," she said. "I have life insurance to take care of. I just turned fifty, I don't have a job. You can't have Wall Street buy up these stores."

Romerick, Debbie, and Maryjane participated in mass actions throughout 2018, demanding severance from the private equity owners. They set up a mock gravestone in the offices of Bain Capital, reading "Here Lies Geoffrey [the Toys "R" Us mascot], Killed by Wall Street Greed." The protests, bolstered by pension fund criticism, did pay off somewhat: KKR and Bain set aside $20 million for severance, a portion of the $75 million workers say they were owed. Later on, workers won $2 million more as a creditor in the final settlement. But Toys "R" Us added a final indignity: the new hedge fund owners brought the brand back for global licensing agreements, and opened a half dozen new physical stores. Workers would of course not share in any of the benefits and had no guarantee of getting their old jobs back. Those who supported Toys "R" Us for decades watched financiers try to milk a few final dollars out of its carcass.

Private equity financiers have turned one of the largest occupations in America into an unstable mess, concentrating the market amid rapid-fire bankruptcies and ripping asunder countless workers. "I can't tell you how many women I've met who said, 'This is the only job I've had,'" said Carrie Gleason, another United for Respect organizer. "They just want people to know what they're going through."

Dana Chisholm did not quietly leave her rental house when Starwood Waypoint put it on the market in August 2016 without her knowledge. She found out that the property management company had been hiding her rent checks, using lack of payment as an excuse to evict. She surmised that the company grew tired of hearing her constantly ask for repairs and therefore sought to get rid of her. Dana filed a small-claims case to rectify the situation. "The judge threw it out because I owed them too much in rent, but they refused to take my money," Dana told me. "The judge said, 'Why would a landlord refuse money?' I said, 'These are not normal landlords.'"

Dana claims she was charged a host of other fees throughout that year. "They charged me an entire year for a lock that was never on my house," she said. During this fight, the next-door neighbor moved out and a new tenant replaced them. As it turned out, that property was also a private-equity-backed single-family rental, owned by Invitation Homes. One of the new tenant's dogs broke the fence between the two houses, and Dana appealed to get Invitation Homes to fix it; it refused. A few weeks later the dog came over the broken fence and injured Dana's dog. She called Invitation Homes, Starwood Waypoint, city code enforcement, animal control, everyone; nobody offered assistance. For $700, the cost of repairing the fence, "this could have all been over," she said. "If they hadn't injured my dog I would have been out of there and done."

At that point Dana began researching the history of these companies.

Starwood Waypoint and Invitation Homes had capitalized on the pain of the foreclosure crisis, something Dana knew about firsthand. She'd bought a house in 2005, when the bubble was inflating, and lost it a few years later after funding for her nonprofit, which got government grants for abstinence-only education, dried up.

Dana joined roughly 9.3 million American families who lost homes from 2006 to 2014. Private equity firms looked past the human toll and saw real estate inventory that could be converted into profits. They raised large sums of capital to buy up the houses, focusing on areas where the foreclosure crisis inflicted the most pain. "In some ways they were very smart," said journalist Aaron Glantz, author of the book *Homewreckers*, which covers the scheme. "They were not the people making the predatory mortgages. They sat on the sidelines waiting to pounce when it all went bad. It ends up being this massive wealth transfer."

The firms targeted cheap, often damaged homes that they could buy with borrowed cash. They would rapidly renovate the properties and turn them into rental housing, promising investors annual returns of anywhere between 6 and 10 percent. It was a $40 billion flurry that has put over 240,000 homes in the hands of investors, mostly private equity firms.

Concentrating purchases in distressed markets was critical; those were the cheapest homes, and controlling significant supply in a region could help drive rents. Blackstone, then the parent company of Invitation Homes, spent $1 billion in the Tampa Bay area alone in 2012. In 2011 investors made 27 percent of all home purchases; in Oakland that number swelled to 42 percent. In Atlanta, a major target because local rental laws are so lax, 90 percent of homes sold in one zip code in an eighteen-month period from 2011 to 2012 went to private investors. This frenzy changed the character of neighborhoods from homeowners to more transient renters. It boosted housing prices due to investors taking supply out of the market, locking out younger families. And many of the renters, reports indicate, were former homeowners, forced by foreclosure back into the rental market after financiers scooped up the homes they lost. Poor communities would be the testing ground for this mass experiment.

Government officials initially saw private equity as a savior, bailing out the market by putting a floor on housing prices and reducing blight in foreclosure-scarred neighborhoods. In fact, the Federal Housing Administration and quasi-public mortgage giants Fannie Mae and Freddie Mac gladly sold off foreclosure inventory to the industry. But before this point, the typical landlord was a mom-and-pop business with a stake in the neighborhood, not a Wall Street investor thousands of miles away with no history of property management and a rigid bottom line to meet.

Problems with the model emerged right away. It takes real effort to convert a substandard foreclosed property into a livable rental, but investors limited expenses, making just enough superficial changes to draw an offer. After tenants move in, they find it hard to get anybody on the phone, and even harder to get repairs made. Private equity landlords place call centers far from the homes they own, don't staff property management units adequately, and simply can't cover all the problems that need fixing. One former tenant in the Atlanta area told me about her rental, which had a leaking upstairs shower that flooded the inside of the house through to the foundation. The combination of water, mice droppings, and mold made the house uninhabitable. "I lost twelve bags of clothing and other items, have not been able to use my bedroom in over eight days," she said. Another Atlantan found black mold in her Invitation Homes rental, causing health problems; a home in California was deemed unsafe by city building inspectors.

Plumbing problems, leaks, mold, and animal infestations are fairly common problems for houses left vacant for months after foreclosure. But Wall Street landlords slap on a coat of paint and try to bulldoze through it, leaving the worst problems for tenants to discover. Their empire of homes is rotting, and their solution is studied ignorance. According to a 2019 *Atlantic* article, supervisors at one management company instructed line-level staff to ignore repair requests and not call tenants back.

In 2014, I went to South Los Angeles, a hotbed of Wall Street rentals, to a community meeting with renters. Already by this point, the strains were showing. "You can't reach anybody, it's very hard," said Ursula, a South Los Angeles renter. "But when you owe them money, they call you, harass you on the phone, put a note on the door, email you constantly." Fine print in the standard rental contract makes the tenant responsible for water bills, utilities, and landscaping costs. Partial payments trigger large late fees, along with smaller fees for pets or electronic payments. Tenants talked of paying higher rents for a short-term lease and being charged security deposits that were more than twice the monthly rent (a violation of California law). One renter named Jeanette, a single mother of four, said she had to take out multiple payday loans to cover surprise charges. "I just feel like I'm sinking deeper and deeper into debt, and not getting much for my money," she said at the meeting.

Renters also pointed to language in the lease allowing Invitation Homes to "evict the tenant without warning" if the property needed to be sold. The Federal Reserve Bank of Atlanta found in 2016 that institutional investors evicted tenants at 18 percent higher rates than mom-and-pop landlords. A young Invitation Homes staffer posted a joke on Facebook of a "Happy 30 Day Eviction Notice" cake, adding the comment, "Technically, an eviction notice *does* have to be presented in writing." After Dana publicized it the staffer was fired, though Dana thought the episode revealed something significant about the culture private equity landlords have built.

Often eviction notices were meant not to remove the tenant but to generate eviction-related fees. That's a major profit center, with the companies' own investor calls touting automated fees and charges (coded as "other property income" in earnings reports) as driving revenue. "What I've observed is if you live in one of these homes, then you're not even a person," said Aaron Glantz. "You're an economic unit."

In marketing materials to investors, private equity firms promise "competitive rents" to maximize returns; in a 2018 report by three advocacy groups, some tenants reported spikes of hundreds of dollars a month. In an eerie parallel to the mortgage-backed securities that created the financial crash, private equity firms created and sold bonds backed by the stream of rental revenue. As of 2018 there were $17.5 billion in outstanding bonds on the market. The duty to pay back investors drives the harassing attempts to collect and increases in rent and fees. Homes, and the lives of the people inside them, were just another tradable asset, like pork bellies.

Inevitably, the market consolidated. Colony American Homes, a product of private equity kingpin and Trump ally Tom Barrack, merged with Starwood Waypoint, and that company merged with Blackstone's Invitation Homes. The other big player, American Homes 4 Rent, acquired American Residential Properties in 2015. Those two, created by private equity and later spun out as public companies, now control 60 percent of the investor-owned rental market. Advocates question how renters will cope during another downturn. "For the tenants, the same thing will happen that happened to homeowners," said Julia Gordon of the National

Community Stabilization Trust. "Even if you get to talk to a person, the rental security is now obligated to a Norwegian pension fund. Who do you negotiate with?"

Blackstone finally cashed out of Invitation Homes in November 2019, earning more than twice its initial investment on the stock. And the firm has expanded the rental model to the Czech Republic, Denmark, Ireland, Spain, and Sweden. The experience in America should spark caution elsewhere. In 2019, the Philadelphia Federal Reserve blamed investor-owned rentals for driving up rents and reducing homeownership rates. The same year, the United Nations special rapporteur on adequate housing, Leilani Farha, formally accused Blackstone of violating international human rights laws by concentrating rental markets and "pushing low-income, and increasingly middle-income people from their homes." This financialization "has disconnected housing from its core social purpose of providing people with a place to live in with security and dignity," Farha wrote.

By the time Dana Chisholm had her run-in with Wall Street rentals, the industry had been in business for half a decade. The idea that they had worked the kinks out after early struggles didn't scan. Her small-claims case took a year to resolve. A scheduled four-day jury trial got preempted the night before, with the landlord offering a settlement. "They did try to get me to sign a nondisclosure agreement, I said no and hell no," Dana told me. "I want to be able to sue you anytime I want to." At the end of the one-year lease in June 2017, Dana left the house, though she hadn't paid anything for the year during the legal wrangling. Yet the home was still being listed on investor reports as occupied.

Dana didn't walk away after getting out of her lease. She started a Facebook group for tenants, a support space that boasted over 1,400 members as of October 2019. Members share an array of horror stories: landlords keeping security deposits for damages that didn't exist when renters moved out, tenants spending months trying to get Invitation Homes to make repairs, Invitation Homes putting tenants into collections to recoup fees. Dana forwards these stories directly to top executives like Invitation Homes chief operating officer Charles Young, demanding relief for tenants. One of the first people Dana heard from was the tenant at her old house, who relayed all the same problems she experienced—the leaking pool, broken fence, rats and roaches. When he told Invitation Homes about it, Dana said, it replied that it had never heard such complaints.

In May 2018, Dana's work led to a proposed class-action lawsuit against Invitation Homes over its late-fee policy. Invitation Homes has a flat late fee of $95, according to the lawsuit, even if the rent is one minute late, due to the company's own creaky online payment portal. One ledger of payments Dana showed me had five late fees within four months, three of which were eventually removed. Invitation Homes also structures incoming payments and sends out eviction notices to "stack" additional late fees, the complaint alleges. Invitation Homes has in general denied allegations of misconduct and pointed to favorable tenant reviews.

It's hard to square the fact that the same person who savages Wall Street greed and condemns MIT for accepting a $350 million gift from Blackstone's Schwarzman as "funds confiscated from working families" also tweets from her Tenants of Invitation Homes Twitter feed, "Stop your petty fighting and build the fence to secure our borders." I pressed Dana on this. Her enemy Schwarzman chaired President Trump's economic advisory council, contributed to his inaugural, and advises the president on China policy. "I email the White House every day," Dana told me, as well as officials in the Trump organization. "I put together ten stories of Trump supporters that are tenants, former homeowners that are now having to rent. Someday one of them is going to see the right story."

But that seems implausible. Trump himself is a real estate magnate. In the 2017 tax law, private equity actually got socked with a limitation on how much interest could be deducted from taxation. This directly attacked their business model, which relies on tax advantages for debt. But there was a loophole: the deduction limitation does not apply to real estate. So schemes like the single-family rental play are *incentivized* in the tax deal. And companies like Schwarzman's Blackstone—which created a $20 billion real estate fund, the largest in history, shortly after the tax law's passage—are poised to take advantage. Private equity firms raised $8 billion for distressed real estate in the first quarter of 2019 alone, and have started to build their own homes and apartment buildings for the rental market; they currently own at least one million apartment units. If you think it's a good idea for Wall Street to become your landlord, just wait until the tax code pushes more money in that direction.

Blackstone's rental play has shifted from buying homes directly to staking funds for other landlords to do the purchases, staying one step removed from any negative consequences. "It's going downstream and downmarket," said Julia Gordon. "Blackstone is enabling nonpublic companies that are less subject to reputational risk to go into at-risk neighborhoods. We seem to have decided as a country that we don't care."

Blackstone has joined another clutch of private equity firms on a separate real estate play: trailer parks. Private equity provided one out of every six dollars traded in the sector in 2018. Residents of manufactured homes, who are mostly poor, own their homes but not the land under them; private equity firms can raise lot rents on people with little ability to move, earning steady profits. Like with single-family rentals, Fannie Mae is helping this along, providing $15 billion in no-strings loans to purchasers of mobile-home sites. Like with single-family rentals, it has resulted in a wave of rising rents and mass evictions. Blackstone, TPG, Carlyle, Apollo, Centerbridge, and Brookfield Asset Management have all piled into the sector in recent years. Interestingly, before this point the manufactured home sector was very concentrated, with companies owned by Berkshire Hathaway—there's that guy Warren Buffett again—controlling half the market.

When Dana hears all this, and I connect Schwarzman to Trump, she nods. "There are no good actors in this," she said. According to her, only a broad movement will stop the pain. "I'm really looking at how social movements get created, how they move and evolve," she said. "I tell Schwarzman, 'I'm not in control anymore. They're breeding activists.'" I acknowledged to her that it's not out of character for a conservative to argue to break up big companies and let competition flower. I told her that Theodore Roosevelt was the first president to earn the moniker of trustbuster, and she smiled. "I need to remember that. I am a Roosevelt Republican."

For my job I have to read a lot of press releases, being a member of the, er, press. At first glance, the one I came across in January 2019 from the Consumer Financial Protection Bureau (CFPB) was not particularly notable, until I put on my monopoly decoder ring.

Sterling Jewelers was fined $11 million by the CFPB and the New York state attorney general's office for opening credit card accounts for customers and enrolling them in payment protection insurance without their knowledge. Sterling also misrepresented how much these products would cost. It was a depressingly perfunctory example of penny-ante scamming on financial transactions. And bad behavior wasn't out of character for Sterling Jewelers, which for more than a decade has been mired in a legal odyssey with tens of thousands of its female employees over pay and promotion discrimination and allegations of a culture of sexual harassment and assault.

But what did interest me was this section of the press release, right at the bottom:

> Sterling is headquartered in Akron, Ohio, and does business throughout the United States. Sterling operates over 1,500 jewelry stores under several names, including Kay Jewelers, Jared The Galleria of Jewelry, JB Robinson Jewelers, Marks & Morgan Jewelers, Belden Jewelers, Goodman Jewelers, LeRoy's Jewelers, Osterman Jewelers, Rogers Jewelers, Shaw's Jewelers, and Weisfield Jewelers.

That comes out to eleven different jewelry stores that are all just Sterling Jewelers, including some pretty well-known brands with insidious earworm jingles ("Every kiss begins with Kay," "He went to Jared"). But the CFPB wasn't done dropping bombs. It turned out that Sterling Jewelers is itself part of a larger conglomerate:

> Sterling is a wholly owned subsidiary of Signet Jewelers Limited, the largest specialty-jewelry retailer in the United States, Canada, and the United Kingdom.

That's a lot of history in one footnote! And it sent me down a rabbit hole. First of all, CFPB didn't list all of Signet's stores in the United States, only the ones associated with Sterling Jewelers, which is kind of a Russian nesting doll inside the bigger Signet figurine. Signet bought out the Sterling family of jewelers in 1987. Later, Signet swallowed up British firms Ernest Jones and H. Samuel, and in 2014 it bought the Zale company, which includes Zales, Peoples, and Piercing Pagoda.

CFPB mentioned 1,500 stores associated with Sterling specifically, but according to Signet's 2019 annual report, the brand operates 3,334 store-fronts in three countries. According to the National Retail Federation's 2017 figures, that's nearly twice as many stores as Home Depot, Target, or Lowe's, and roughly the number of Sonic restaurants or ExxonMobil gas stations. This makes Signet the largest jeweler in the country and the world, with total annual sales checking in at $6.25 billion. And that doesn't count James Allen, the online retailer Signet bought in 2017 for $328 million.

Does this make Signet a monopoly? Actually, no. Jewelry is still generally speaking a mom-and-pop business. About 14 percent of brick-and-mortar jewelry stores in America are associated with Signet, according to Labor Department statistics, and in terms of revenue, Signet claims its market share is more like 7 percent. IBISWorld, the industry intelligence firm, puts Signet's share at 15.3 percent. (The other three big companies? Tiffany, now part of a conglomerate that includes Louis Vuitton, Dior, and Bulgari; a Swiss conglomerate named Compagnie Financière Richemont that owns the brands Cartier and Van Cleef & Arpels; and Warren Buffett's Berkshire Hathaway, which has around three hundred jewelry stores under three brands nationwide.)

But the point is that all these well-known national brand names emblazoned on storefronts, all these outlets I remember walking past in shopping malls when I was a kid, are now part of the same company. People are given the illusion of choice. There was once a history attached to each jeweler: Harriet Samuel (H. Samuel) opened her shop in Manchester, England, in 1862; Kay began as a department store in Reading, Pennsylvania, in 1916; Zales came out of Wichita Falls, Texas, in 1924; Henry Shaw founded LeRoy's Jewelers (why not Henry's?) near Akron, Ohio, in 1910. But a series of leveraged buyouts, acquisitions, combinations, and tie-ups washed away all that history, regional variation, and personal touch, until all you have is the cold corporate stare of Signet.

CHAPTER 11

Monopolies Are Why a Family Has Seen Only the Top of Their Loved One's Head for the Past Two Years

The rain was pouring down in sheets that day in Charlotte, North Carolina, and Jennifer Hamilton was late. The only available parking spot nearby had a sign in front reading "Staff." Jennifer parked there for a moment and dashed inside, asking if she could stay in that spot, what with the rain and all.

"No, you have to park across the street," was the reply.

By the time Jennifer made it back, drenched and surly, she had missed her scheduled time by about five minutes. The county sheriff's Administrative Services Building looked just as generic as the name implied. Metal dividers separated the room, with uncomfortable-looking stools in front of metal boxes covered with a plastic screen. "I'm looking at this screen and it's tiny," Jennifer told me. "All the pictures in the ads, it's funny to see what they show, these big screens, very clear pictures."

Jennifer sat down to video-chat with her partner, Jeremy, the father of her child, from his cellblock in the Mecklenburg County Jail across the street. Instead of visiting Jeremy personally, instead of looking into his eyes, studying his facial expression, feeling his hand, her only connection could take place through this tiny metal box. The visit would be free, unlike the 50¢-per-minute video calls she had placed from home. But Jennifer wasn't at the Administrative Services Building because of the expense; she was there because she hoped the damn video would actually work. After all, Jeremy was only steps away, and this building was optimized for video chatting.

That didn't matter. Unlike a phone call, which begins when you dial and connect, incarcerated families start their video visit—and, in most cases, start paying—whenever the scheduled time dictates. So Jennifer was five minutes in. After connecting, Jeremy's mouth started moving several seconds before Jennifer could hear his first words. The videophone was bolted to the wall in the middle of the cellblock; Jennifer could barely hear over the background noise of other inmates and jail doors slamming shut. And the picture would stop and start, break up, and fuzz out. It looked like a constantly buffering video on a dial-up modem in the days before You-Tube. "This place across the street where they set up to do these calls made the experience no better," she told me.

A company called Global Tel*Link, or GTL, owns the contract with Mecklenburg County to run video visitation for the county jail, a growing national trend. That GTL runs it abominably hasn't stopped the company's rise into one of two major prison communications and money transfer companies (Securus is the other); combined, they supply phone and video for 80 percent of the nation's lockups. You could say the poor quality enhanced the monopoly, since all the money not wasted on actually providing good service could be put toward the more lucrative task of lobbying for additional contracts.

If you want to witness the logical endpoint of our age of corporate power, take a trip to a correctional facility. Prisons and jails contain literal captured audiences, inmates with no choice whatsoever for food, banks, health care, telephone providers, internet services—nothing. And here's what that leads to: terrible quality, rank exploitation, endless corruption, avoidable deaths, and a lack of transparency about all of the above. In the case of phone and video communications, it has the effect of incarcerating people twice: once by locking them in a cell, and again by cutting off contact with the outside world, unless their families give tribute to a toll booth operator. "I think 'isolation' is a really great word," said Bianca Tylek of Worth Rises, a nonprofit that works on prison justice issues. "We've heard from people who have said, 'I haven't seen my kids in two years.'"

This can eliminate the only escape valve from the rigors of prison life. It breeds loneliness and alienation. And it weds people to the criminal mindset, subverting the very function of rehabilitation that the system is theoretically intended to promote. Which, of course, suits prison monopolists just fine, because an inmate who rotates back into the system can again be subjugated for earning potential. We've turned caging humans into a for-profit business, so we shouldn't be surprised that the business tends to keep humans caged. And the families fed into this machine, disproportionately people of color, are the poorest and most vulnerable in the country.

But we should all watch out. Maybe you think that people who commit crimes deserve punishment and not a country club. Maybe you don't care that prison food isn't great and phone rates are high. But the reason inmates and their families suffer through this abuse and despair has plenty to do with monopoly; the lack of choice creates the opening for mistreatment and the cycle of despair. And since we're living in an increasingly monopolized world, the circumstances in prisons may signal an early warning to what our life could be like someday, maybe soon.

Once upon a time, public employees ran prisons, though the first state penitentiary in America was a private prison. In 1790 the Quaker religious sect took over a city jail in Philadelphia called the Walnut Street Prison and reimagined incarceration as a means for rehabilitating prisoners. Somehow they got the idea that the best way to do this was through near-total solitary confinement in individual cells. The solitude was intended to focus the mind—the word "penitentiary" is derived from the Latin for remorse—and ready the penitent for a return to the outside. It didn't work because solitary confinement makes people insane, and an influx of prisoners turned Walnut Street into the same kind of filthy, overcrowded facility the Quakers wanted to reform. It's now a library.

A small lockup in Auburn, New York, countered the "Pennsylvania system" of criminal justice by envisioning prison as a work camp. Inmates took ten-hour shifts six days a week; officials believed it would build self-worth and discipline. The Auburn system succeeded mainly because private corporations saw it as an opportunity to hire cheap labor.

In the South this led to something called convict leasing, where states rented out prisoners to mine coal or construct railroad tracks. Thanks to the Thirteenth Amendment's allowance for involuntary servitude "as a punishment for crime whereof the party shall have been duly convicted," companies could enslave with impunity, reserving their deadliest jobs for prisoners to tackle. Convict leasing accounted for nearly three-fourths of Alabama's state revenue in 1898. The prisoners, of course, got nothing, and the grisly conditions, social unrest, and periodic rebellions from convict leasing caused states to eventually phase it out.

I guess I should say "phase it out." Today inmates still work in prison kitchens, laundries, warehouses, and metal shops, but also as farmworkers for Whole Foods, as firefighters and customer service reps, as Microsoft packaging specialists and Victoria's Secret lingerie makers. They slog along for as little as 2¢ an hour. There's even a Justice Department program for federal inmates called Unicor, which solicits clients to lease its 20,000-strong prison labor force at rock-bottom prices; they call it the "onshore advantage." I guess there's an appeal there: if we just lock up the entire domestic workforce, we can bring jobs back to America after all.

But a few corporations realized that borrowing incarcerated slaves was not as lucrative as directly targeting prisoners and their families for profit, especially after the prison population jumped five-fold within forty years to over 2.2 million. Desperate government officials burdened with tough-on-crime sentencing laws needed assistance to house, clothe, and feed an exploding number of inmates.

Private companies had already wedged their way into the criminal justice system, winning contracts for lower-security facilities. The Reagan administration invited them to manage prisons as well, in a 1988 report from the President's Commission on Privatization. Contracting out prison management "could lead to improved, more efficient operation," the report said, and conservative organs like the Heritage Foundation echoed the sentiment, asserting that private companies could run prisons for as low as $25 per inmate per day, as opposed to $40 when run by government.

Within a decade, private prisons were a billion-dollar business, with operations in twenty-seven states. And providing continuing evidence that anything run at scale in Second Gilded Age America trends toward monopoly, by 1997 two companies, Corrections Corporation of America and Wackenhut Corrections Corporation, managed 75 percent of all private prisons in America. Perhaps because they take so much pride in their work, both companies would eventually change their names: CCA became CoreCivic, and Wackenhut became GEO Group.

Alex Friedmann first learned about private prisons while he was incarcerated in the 1990s. "They recruited people to private prisons, and the big draw was a rumor that they had free soft drinks in the dining hall. When you're in prison, small things make a big difference," Friedmann told me. He served ten years for armed robbery and attempted murder, became a jailhouse lawyer and writer, and now, twenty years after his release, runs *Prison Legal News*, a monthly magazine about criminal justice. "Sure enough, when I got there, soft drink machines in the chow hall. But what are soft drinks? Sugar water, cheaper than healthier alternatives. There was lots of soda, not much milk, and no juice."

Friedmann's new home, the CCA-run South Central Correctional Facil-

ity in Wayne County, Tennessee, extended the concept of cheap amenities across the prison. Instead of two blankets, inmates got one. Instead
of unlimited toilet paper, it was rationed. Instead of adequate heating, ice
formed on the cellblock windows—on the inside. Instead of four guards in
the chow hall, there were two. This is consistent with how private prisons
lower operations costs while still extracting a layer of profit: they cut back
on everything, making life on the inside both terrible and dangerous.

Wages for private prison guards are well under those for public corrections officers—as low as the $9 an hour *Mother Jones* journalist Shane
Bauer received when he went undercover for four months at a CCA facility in Louisiana. That level of pay attracts inexperienced employees,
increases turnover, and expands the likelihood of corruption, like accepting money to truck in contraband. Reduced training and insufficient
equipment, in addition to fewer officers—1 for every 176 inmates at Bauer's
facility—magnifies these problems. In 2012, a state audit in Idaho found
that guards at a CCA facility in Boise were outfitted with empty cans of
pepper spray and told to "just fake it" when breaking up disturbances.
The facilities are treated no better than the officers: reports detail mold
infestations, broken doors and locks, and even no working toilets in one
case. Accumulated misery fosters anger that understaffed personnel cannot handle. A common technique has been to just throw prisoners into
solitary. A 2014 ACLU report with interviews from hundreds of prisoners
documented the practice; even asking for new shoes could get you tossed
in the hole.

Public prisons aren't models of excellence either: a Justice Department
report into Alabama's indicated a "flagrant disregard" for constitutional
rights. But private prisons transform the horror into profit for corporate
executives, dividend-loving shareholders, and cities, which enjoy kickbacks known as "intergovernmental service agreements" worth millions of
dollars. Plus, we know less than we should about private prisons, because
of a helpful feature of privatization: they can more easily fight disclosure
under public records requirements.

GEO Group and CoreCivic were teetering at the end of the Obama
administration after the Justice Department agreed to end their use for federal prisons. The companies responded by placing a bet on Donald Trump
and winning. A GEO subsidiary gave $225,000 to a pro-Trump super PAC,
violating laws barring federal contractors from making political donations.

After Trump's victory, CoreCivic pushed $250,000 into Trump's inaugura-
tion fund. GEO Group hired two former Jeff Sessions Senate aides, David
Stewart and Ryan Robichaux, to lobby on their behalf. As attorney general,
Sessions revoked the Obama-era guidance.

But private prisons cover only around 8.5 percent of the state and federal
population. While CoreCivic and GEO take most of the heat from activists, monopoly service providers are a far bigger menace in prisons.

"Typically, prisons sign monopoly contracts," said Alex Friedmann at a
Waffle House in Nashville, where we met for breakfast. He cited Tennessee, CoreCivic's home state, as a good example. "You get your medical care
from Centurion, your mental health from Corizon, your food services
from Aramark, your money transfer from JPay, your phone service from
GTL," Friedmann said. The entire life cycle of the criminal justice system
has become a profit-taking opportunity. And it starts right after arrest.

The median bail in America is around $10,000, or eight months' income
for the average defendant. Most pay a commercial bail bond agency to float
the amount and guarantee appearance at trial. Bail agents enjoy tremendous power to exploit defendants, charging them for pretrial supervision
or monitoring. If defendants fall behind on payments or violate release
conditions, the agency can even force them back to jail. Such violations
trigger a higher bail amount and more money for the bail agent; the system incentivizes extortion. Bail companies are seemingly mom-and-pop
operations, but nine insurance companies underwrite most of the $14 bil-
lion in bail bonds in America. They have structured the business so they
never take a loss: forfeitures are put on bail agents, who pass them through
to defendants. It's a pure profit play for large insurers.

Prisoner Transportation Services (PTS), the largest inmate transporter
in America, takes convicts into lockups, transfers them between prisons,
or sends them off to work release. They're paid per prisoner per mile, and
the inexperienced, low-wage drivers must cover hotel rooms out of their
own pockets, motivating them to take no breaks, travel through the night,
and pack vans tightly. Crashes, sexual assaults, defecation in the vans, and
several inadvertent deaths (including from untreated illnesses as inmates
roll down the highway) have been reported.

Once in the prison, inmates learn a dirty secret: corrections facilities,
whether public or private, subcontract practically everything out to sepa-

rate monopolies. According to a 2019 Worth Rises report, over half of the $80 billion in annual spending on incarceration goes into the hands of private vendors. The private equity industry looms large over the space. "They can operate in areas where companies not palatable to the public work," said Bianca Tylek of Worth Rises.

Consider HIG Capital, the prison monopoly's "man behind the curtain." Transformer-style, it constructed the largest food and commissary giant in the prison world, Keefe Group. HIG bought Trinity Services Group, grew that through acquiring Swanson Services Corporation, then merged *that* with Keefe. More than half of all revenues at prison commissaries, which sell food, clothing, and sundries like deodorant and shampoo, flow through Keefe. The prices vary widely from the outside world. "A bag of coffee is $10–$11," said Jennifer Hamilton, whose partner has spent time in federal prisons in Virginia and Florida.

Commissary revenue often depends on the company running kitchen services. Often the same company runs food service and the commissary, and that can be rewarding for the contractor. "If the food is terrible, people go to commissary," said Bianca Tylek. "If the food is good, you can run it into the ground to move people into commissary. It doesn't matter if the food is bad, because that's a fixed payment."

Aramark is the largest company for kitchen service inside prisons, serving more than one million meals every day. Though it runs a large food service business on the outside, at hospitals, colleges, stadiums, and cultural attractions, inside prisons high quality isn't Aramark's priority. In Michigan, Aramark took over for a state-run prison food service in 2013, vowing to save money. The company stocked kitchens with spoiled food and used equipment infested with maggots. Workers constantly substituted with inferior ingredients, like making hamburgers out of peanut butter. In St. Louis, Michigan, workers covered a cake partially eaten by rats with frosting and served it to inmates. In Saginaw, workers reheated and served meat that had been thrown in the trash before they realized there were more inmates to feed.

The Michigan Department of Corrections cited Aramark for 2,945 food quality and sanitation violations over a seven-month period in 2014. In that time, Aramark had to ban seventy-four employees from Michigan prisons for misconduct, like acting as contraband couriers; cutting salaries in half probably played into that. Prisoners also staffed kitchens, with Aramark profiting from free labor. Inmates protested chow hall conditions with sit-down strikes and other disruptions. Michigan terminated the Aramark contract within two years, giving the contract to Trinity Services Group, a division of . . . private equity firm HIG Capital. And Trinity's effort to charge more for kitchen services led Michigan to end its dalliance with privatization.

In New York State, Aramark runs kitchen, commissary, and a third source of food for prisoners, care packages. The days of loved ones being able to send Mom's banana bread or other personal comforts into prisons are largely over. Aramark got New York State to ban all outside care packages, requiring that they come from approved vendor catalogs, like Aramark's iCare. Other care package vendors include Union Supply Group and Keefe Group's Access Securepak. The impersonal, standardized care packages were pitched as a security measure, like most things in prisons. But price gouging has been a nice side benefit. The heavily processed foods (almost nothing fresh can be included because all packaging must be tamper-proof) and other options are marked up significantly; a pack of oatmeal going for $2.79 on Amazon can cost over $7. Shipping and handling fees get tacked on. "If you order a $29.99 ramen noodle special, with your fee you end up paying $36 and change," said Jennifer Hamilton. "The more expensive the package, the fee gets higher. It's a racket, it's all to take advantage."

To use the commissary or other services, prisoners need money, and they make almost nothing working. JPay leads the market in electronic money transfers, serving around 70 percent of all U.S. inmates. For Jennifer, a $200 transfer to Virginia included a $13 charge, and perusing JPay's fee schedule reveals that even $20 transfers can incur $5.95 in fees. If a prisoner finishes their sentence with a balance on their account, they get a JPay release card, with charges like "account maintenance fees" of $2.50 a week, even if the card goes unused. Another release card giant? JPMorgan Chase.

Health care is particularly profitable in prisons; inmates even have to cough up co-pays, which they often cannot afford. Born from a merger in 2011 and owned by private equity firm BlueMountain Capital, Corizon Health provides medical services in 220 facilities in seventeen states, but that number has shrunk amid canceled contracts and thousands of lawsuits alleging short-staffing, broken equipment, and substandard treatment so awful that an Idaho special master in 2012 found it to constitute cruel and unusual punishment. In Arizona, an inmate died after screaming for help as lesions all over his body were "swarmed by flies." In Georgia, delays in getting an inmate eye drops led to his going blind. Much of the brutality in Alabama's public prisons comes from Corizon's unconscionable health care, which supplied just one doctor for every 1,600 inmates.

Canceling Corizon contracts often matters little given industry concentration. New Mexico dropped Corizon in 2016 and shifted to Centurion, its chief competitor. "If you don't like Corizon because people are dying, you bring in Centurion, which also has a terrible track record," said Alex Friedmann of *Prison Legal News*. "Because the business model is the same. If you want to make money providing medical care to prisons, don't provide as much medical care." The newest big player, Wellpath, is another concoction of HIG Capital, which merged Correct Care Solutions and Correctional Medical Group Companies. Unsurprisingly, it too has fielded a large number of lawsuits—at least 1,395 since 2003, although many of them were dismissed—including ignoring one dying patient whom staff allegedly accused of faking illnesses, giving pregnant inmates tranquilizers, and forcing one woman in Florida to give birth alone in her jail cell. We surely don't know the extent of this: subcontractors are even more insulated from public records requests.

States don't hand over prisons to financial predators just to save money; they're in on the take. Nearly all subcontractors send back commissions to prisons, in some cases incredibly high percentages of revenues. To earn profits, subcontractors must charge exorbitant rates, and mostly the payers are families in no position to endure such financial stress. According to a 2015 Prison Policy Initiative report, an inmate's average income before entering prison is around $19,000. Removing that person from the family income stream typically increases the family's hardship.

The profit taking continues once inmates rotate out of prison, as our old friends CoreCivic and GEO Group recognized. The duopoly has branched out into "community corrections" like halfway houses, probation, reentry services, and drug treatment facilities, growing the business through acquisitions. For example, GEO Group bought BI Incorporated, the largest provider of electronic monitoring and house arrest products. Often ex-cons pay for such monitoring directly. As legislators produced "smart on crime" policies to reduce the prison population, the same companies slid over to build the treatment-industrial complex, profiting from incarceration and alternatives to incarceration simultaneously. "It's where the industry is headed," said *Prison Legal News*'s Alex Friedmann.

All of this is supercharged when it comes to immigration detention, the real growth area for monopolists, given the stalemate over the undocumented and the political arms race to prove toughness on border security. While only 8 percent of jails are privately run, that number rises to 72 percent for Immigration and Customs Enforcement (ICE) detentions, according to a Worth Rises study. Three private companies also run an immigrant-only prison system for noncitizens convicted of federal crimes (which has been criticized as deadly, particularly for the sick), as well as massive family detention facilities in southern Texas that have been compared to Japanese internment camps. GEO Group also holds the contract for immigrant electronic monitoring.

Nearly everyone in a migrant shelter sits in a privately run facility, run out of shuttered Walmarts or empty office buildings by firms like Southwest Key. And all the food, health care, and transportation services are parceled out to the same giants who run them in prisons. One private company charters deportation flights under the "ICE Air" brand. All those border camps, the tent cities, the human cages with no showers or blankets, the children covered in lice, the forced medication, the inedible food, the reliance on solitary confinement, the breeding grounds for rampant sex abuse and premature child deaths: people in nice suits profit off that. That's who we get to do our dirty work in America. Without these monopolists, the immigration machine would seize up and sputter.

The most exploitive, socially damaging private-equity-influenced practice in prisons comes from the communications monopoly, dominated by two companies, Securus and GTL. This includes phone, video, email, and digital services for inmates. And to understand what this does to prisoners and their families, you have to talk to someone who has experienced it.

Jennifer Hamilton met Jeremy Lemmond at a coffee shop in Charlotte. She worked in home health care, and he built houses. They both had bluish gray eyes. They exchanged phone numbers, and one thing led to another. "I loved him. I always loved him," she told me.

But the Great Recession was a terrible time to be a home builder. On top of that Jennifer lost her job, and her health insurance along with it.

Among other things, this meant that Jennifer had to go off birth control. And within a few months, she got pregnant with Caleb. "He changed my life forever. I'm so happy that he's here," Jennifer said. "But it was a very difficult time because of what was happening."

Jennifer didn't know how difficult. Around this time, Jeremy had started using cocaine. The combination of desperate financial straits and a drug addiction can lead to ideas that seem righteous in your head but less so in practice. That's what robbing a bank looked like to Jeremy. He was caught and put in a holding cell in the Mecklenburg County Jail in 2009 to await trial and sentencing. Jeremy had never seen his son, who was born after the arrest. Our broken wheels of justice, along with changes to North Carolina sentencing guidelines, kept him there for two years.

During that time, Mecklenburg County allowed visitation behind glass, which you've probably seen in movies. The visitor uses a phone to communicate with the inmate through a glass barrier. "To be honest, there's something about seeing a person face-to-face," Jennifer said. "To make eye contact, see the details of their face, hold a conversation. We needed to have lots of conversations because of what just happened." Jennifer didn't often bring Caleb, who was born after Jeremy was arrested, but when she did, Jeremy could see him through the glass. "I don't think I would have waited on him or supported him if I would have had video visits for two years," Jennifer confessed. "I needed that connection with him."

When he was finally sentenced, Jeremy was shipped five hours away, to a federal penitentiary (the bank robbery was a federal crime) in Lee County, Virginia. Traveling was expensive and arduous, between hotels, gas, and the meager food options on visiting day (just a vending machine). Jennifer made the trip a few times, once with Caleb, the first time father and son met without a glass obstruction in the way. "It was incredible to see, because I had talked to him so much about the good in his dad," Jennifer said. "He ran to him, as a toddler, ran straight to his dad. To be able to even touch his hand was something that most people take for granted."

United States Penitentiary, Lee houses a violent population: rapists and murderers, gang members and white supremacists. The environment changed Jeremy, Jennifer said. "Literally every day your life is in survival mode. Your brain starts functioning on a different level." Jeremy lived on a hair trigger, trying to keep away from the fights, the intimidation, the perceived slights that can burst out into fury. "He was exposed to things that made him a worse human being than when he went in there," Jennifer said. "When you're treating a person like an animal they start acting like one."

Jeremy's only respite from this environment was Jennifer's voice, and the monopolists controlling phone lines knew it. GTL managed phone service in Lee County, and unlike most of America in an age of unlimited calling, the company still charged for long distance. Jennifer was resourceful, creating a local Google Talk number and forwarding calls to her cell phone. But the service, which required a special account funded through wire transfers, still cost around three bucks for a fifteen-minute call.

Jennifer got off easy. Today a fifteen-minute call through the federal Bureau of Prisons will set you back $3.75, putting it ahead of market-leading Kentucky, where the price is $5.70. Inmates and their families worked for two decades just to get rates that low, assisted by state laws and rate caps from the Federal Communications Commission (some of which were rolled back by an appeals court in 2017). But even today, in local jails prices can range as high as $24.82 for fifteen minutes in Arkansas. Plus the rates don't include fees to open or close an account, place money into it, or receive a paper bill. As with all other things in America, for immigrants this is worse: members of Congress complained in 2018 that parents separated from children at the border had to pay $8 a minute to speak with them.

The high prices again stem from the commission model. With corrections departments earning large kickbacks from the contracts, companies must jack up the price to make their cut. And poor families pay the price. In 2015, Amsani Yusli submitted her phone bill for testimony in a legal trial: $130.20 for one month of calling. "This amount translates to groceries for the month," Yusli wrote. "When you don't have much, you have to choose between feeding your kids . . . and allowing your kids to know their father." Yet she and thousands of others paid, because that human spark gave their loved ones a light in darkness, a link back to their communities, to hope. "The support I had from my family throughout my incarceration made such a difference," wrote longtime prison phone activist Ulandis Forte in 2019. Forte's late grandmother Martha Wright-Reed filed the original lawsuit that led to the FCC's rate caps. But activists shouldn't expect help from the government today: FCC chair Ajit Pai's old law firm counted Securus as a client.

Oh, all the calls are monitored, too. "Sometimes we'd kind of joke about it, we're like 'Heyy . . . ,'" said Jennifer Hamilton. "You have to laugh instead of cry." But also cry, because prisons are using digitized phone calls to produce voice prints and feed them into biometric databases, a new form of lasting surveillance.

The architects of this price-gouging machine once again lead back to Miami and the offices of HIG Capital. In 2002, HIG acquired two prominent prison telecom firms, Evercom and T-Netix, themselves the product of dozens of smaller mergers. Two years later, HIG merged them to form Securus. More acquisitions followed, as well as a couple of sell-offs to other private equity shops. Today Securus is in the hands of Platinum Equity, whose founder and CEO, Tom Gores, also owns the Detroit Pistons.

Securus serves over 1.2 million inmates throughout North America. GTL, also a private equity portfolio company (American Securities owns it), has an even bigger share, 1.8 million inmates at 2,300 different facilities. Like Securus, GTL grew through acquisitions, including the prison phone affiliates of Verizon, AT&T, Qwest, and MCI. Where Securus or GTL don't win the contract, Securus often wields patents to force agreement with smaller rivals on expensive licensing agreements that commandeers the business in all but name. If the rival doesn't like it, Securus will happily sue, making it monopolist and patent troll.

Bianca Tylek estimates the total market share between the two companies at 80 percent. That could have grown to 90 percent in 2018, when Securus attempted to buy Inmate Calling Solutions, the third-largest provider (and a division of the Keefe Group, which is part of . . . HIG Capital), for $350 million. The usually cowed FCC managed to avoid shame by blocking that merger.

Still, Securus and GTL's efforts at monopoly are relentless. "If you look at the market over the last ten years, and you see who bid and who got the contracts, the only people bidding would be those two," said Tylek. She explained a bizarre situation in New York State where GTL held the phone service contract for over a decade without ever winning the bid. "They kept acquiring the company that won the bid," Tylek said, walking me through a spreadsheet on her computer. MCI won the contract in 2001, and later was folded into Verizon. In 2005 Verizon sold off its prison telecom business, and in 2007 GTL acquired it. In 2008, New York awarded the contract to Unisys, which partnered on the front end with a company called Value Added Communications. The following year GTL acquired

Value Added Communications. In 2017, GTL met its match by losing the contract to a company it couldn't buy: Securus.

Since 2012, Securus has acquired seventeen different companies, diversifying its product line in the wake of activist pressure for prison phone justice. It took over a surveillance monitoring company, candidly called Satellite Tracking of People (STOP), which includes electronic monitoring, alcohol testing, and a phone monitoring service that police departments have employed to track non-inmates without court orders. But Securus's biggest acquisition targets prison families' wallets.

Remember that company JPay, which manages money transfers? Securus bought it in 2015. The same year GTL bought TouchPay, JPay's biggest competitor. "They could own the business and charge rates to put money on people's accounts," said Bianca Tylek. "They got the two largest payment processing companies in less than a year. It's hard to believe there was not a conversation had somewhere, 'You're going to take one and we take the other.'"

JPay offers a range of communications and digital options. The business model leverages the knowledge that a mother will pay any price to make contact with a son, will bear any burden to brighten that child's day. Prisoners and their families are the only people in America who need a stamp to send an email. Each page of a JPay e-message requires a 35¢ stamp; so does each picture or video. And prices go up around key dates, like Mother's Day. Inmates read these emails on kiosks around the cellblock, or on special JPay tablets where they can download books, music, podcasts, and games, each for a fee larger than comparable downloads in the real world (an album can cost $46). The tablets occupy prisoners with diversions instead of educational material that could further rehabilitation, and enable another profit opportunity for monopolists.

Colorado's contract with GTL for tablets allows the company to increase prices on any of these services at any time, and to terminate the contract if it doesn't earn enough money. Paying for any services requires deposits in GTL accounts that trigger more fees. The hustle extends the monetization of prisoners, a godsend for private equity managers. The tablets are sometimes "free," in the way that drug pushers offer a free hit; usually free tablets translate into higher rates for emails and other services. "It's a vehicle to their wealth building," said Tylek. "The states are so convinced by the narrative that they're being done a favor. But why are you trading a onetime fixed cost for a lifetime of high rates?"

Like the good monopolists they are, Securus and GTL restrict as much competition to their services as possible, with help from corrections departments. In Indiana, prison officials in 2017 banned greeting cards, colored envelopes, and typewritten paper, supposedly for security reasons (you can lace colorful paper with fentanyl, allegedly). Similar restrictions popped up in Michigan and Idaho, all of which made email greetings more attractive. In 2018, Pennsylvania banned the delivery of books and magazines, again using the security excuse. All reading material had to be chosen from GTL's 8,500 ebook titles, available with the purchase of a $147 GTL tablet. *A Hole at the Bottom of the Sea* by Joel Achenbach would set you back $24.99 plus a "digital download tax." Other full-length titles were similarly priced well above ebooks for Kindle. GTL not only gouges inmates but also controls the means of communication, avoiding anything so "radical" that prisoners might get the idea of thinking for themselves. After public outcry, Pennsylvania's Department of Corrections rolled the policy back. But other states have been pushing out bans on used books, which lead to similar profit opportunities.

The worst story came, fittingly, from Florida, where prisoners could buy an MP3 player from Access Corrections, a small supplier, and download high-priced music and ebook files. Florida then switched service providers in 2018, bringing in JPay. Prison officials confiscated the old players, stocked with $11.3 million in music (for which the prisons took $1.4 million in commissions), and forced prisoners to start all over. They said the files couldn't transfer over because JPay's system was more than just an MP3 player (meaning it could sell prisoners email too) and therefore incompatible, which any tech-literate sixth-grader could sniff out as bullshit. Prisoners filed suit in February 2019, alleging that the prison system "has effectively stolen millions of dollars of digital music and books from the prisoners in its custody." The case is still pending, because in America the best way to get away with stealing is to run a prison.

Jennifer Hamilton's partner, Jeremy, was transferred to a correctional facility in Florida, released to a halfway house in 2017, and eventually returned to his family. But it didn't last. "He received no rehab in prison and his drug problem got worse," Jennifer told me. After several months out of prison, Jeremy relapsed, as a routine drug screen showed. That violated his probation, and Jeremy was sent back to the Mecklenburg County Jail, the place where he'd initially spent two years awaiting sentencing.

"When he went back in there, I was told they don't have any in-person visits," Jennifer said. "That's when I did the video calls."

Advocates generally support video visitation if it complements in-person visits and is inexpensive. Contemporary theories for rehabilitating the incarcerated place a premium on getting them as much family contact as possible. Every major study of prisoners reveals that "feelings of being welcome at home and the strength of interpersonal ties outside prison help predict postprison adjustment," according to criminal justice expert Joan Petersilla's book *When Prisoners Come Home*. A 2011 Minnesota Department of Corrections study found that just one visit from a family member reduced recidivism by 13 percent. While video may be inferior to live visits, it allows families far from prisons to get extra time face-to-face.

But in practice, of the over six hundred correctional facilities in forty-six states using video visitation systems, the main practitioners are local jails, the most accessible incarceration site for families. And around three-quarters of the jails that have installed video visitation dropped in-person visits. Time after time, local jails block access to in-person visitations, making video visitations the substitute. Even if families arrive at the jail, they cannot see their loved ones on anything but a video screen. And the cost can be prohibitive, as much as $1 a minute. In Mecklenburg County, the former sheriff who signed the contract went above its terms to eliminate face-to-face visits, with two free calls a week, but only if you come to the facility. "So you still have to travel," said Bianca Tylek of Worth Rises. "The thing it's supposed to solve for isn't even the thing it solves for."

County corrections again frame the switch to video as a security issue, a way to prevent contraband trafficking during visitations, prevent inmate movement around the facility, and transfer guards from visitation rooms to other duties. "Let me just shoot it straight to you," Jennifer said. "First of all, you talk through a phone through the glass, and it's bulletproof glass there, nothing can get through that. Second, what is getting inside of prisons and jails comes mostly from the officers. They get paid by the inmates large amounts of money, and they're bringing it in." The security excuse masks how corrections departments save money on staffing and earn money on commissions with video visitation.

But most important for Jennifer, the video, which at Mecklenburg County is supplied by GTL, just doesn't work. "In my mind I thought it would be like Skype," she said. Then she tried it and experienced a tremendous lag in the video signal, constant freezing up, and video and audio going out of sync. "I'm thinking this is maybe a Wi-Fi problem, but I have the best internet you can get," she said. "When you talk to other people, they were all having the same problem." Since video visitation companies sign monopoly contracts with prisons and jails, there's no reason for them to ensure that the system works well.

Jennifer would schedule calls for twenty-five minutes at $12.50 a pop, and on one occasion the signal was so bad she hung up after three minutes. Customer service for GTL was as frustrating an experience as the video itself. "Their whole thing was, 'You started the video,'" Jennifer told me. "I said, 'Yes, in order to see that the visit was bad I had to start the visit!' They didn't want to know about a twenty-five-minute block that I used for three minutes."

Even if Mecklenburg County's video worked in pristine fashion, video visits would be problematic. The videophone in the men's cellblock is in the middle of a hallway, and there are three phones side by side, affording zero privacy. The microphones pick up all the background noise of the jail, making it difficult for families to hold a conversation. "We did a video explaining the system and talking to inmates about it," said Tylek. "One of the guys, his major grievance is that the screen is too high. His kids can only see the top of his head." The screen is angled upward, and for the two years that individual has been in the county lockup, his children have only been able to talk to their father face-to-forehead.

The videophones in the women's unit in Mecklenburg County are positioned directly in front of the officers' station, making it easier for officers to listen in. Calls are monitored; if some form of abuse by guards is mentioned, officers will intervene and tell the participants to change the subject. Unlike in-person visits, video can be recorded, downloaded, and sent to data centers—and potentially sent to the district attorney's office.

Perhaps most important, replacing in-person visits with video robs prisoners of human contact with the only people in their lives rooting for them and their future. Combined with everything else, paying for communications, especially ones that don't work, is a luxury many families dealing with incarceration cannot afford. A 2015 report from the Ella Baker Center for Human Rights found that about half of families couldn't afford the costs associated with convictions, and one in three families went into debt to pay for phone calls and visits. Given who gets incarcerated in America, the vast majority of those paying for phone and video calls are women, and usually women of color. "Those least able to pay are the ones afflicted. It's like a regressive tax," said Alex Friedmann. Cost aside, the digital divide can be a barrier: if you don't have a computer or broadband connection, video visits aren't an option.

In practice, video-only visits approximate the deprivation of the old Walnut Street Prison, cutting off inmates from direct social interaction with their support network. We know that healthy family relationships reduce recidivism rates, but it's nearly impossible to conduct them exclusively over buggy video chats. Without visits, prisoner psychological trauma deepens, and despair grows. Life on the inside becomes the only life they know. Profiteering is making it more likely that prisoners return to prison, to the benefit of the profiteers. Millions of able-bodied men and women recirculate into prisons when they could make a life for themselves. Society loses when Securus and GTL win.

While Securus perversely sells video visitation in promotional videos as a method for "staying connected with your children," Bianca Tylek's group Worth Rises has done surveys with prisoners in the Mecklenburg County Jail about the systems. "When we ask about what it would mean to prisoners to have in-person visits, they say, 'I could really know my kids were OK.' On video you don't know. It was one of the most common responses."

Communities nationwide have fought the elimination of in-person visits, with bans on the practice in Massachusetts and Texas. California has required in-person visits since 2017, but jails that switched to video visits before that time got grandfathered in. Other campaigns have sought to drive down prices. Texas cut the price of inmate phone calls by 75 percent in 2018, and San Francisco and New York City made all calls free. After the New York triumph, Worth Rises reported that call volume increased at the notorious Rikers Island prison by 38 percent overnight, revealing the financial hardships imposed by the normal rates. Connecticut was about to follow suit and make calls free in 2019, but Governor Ned Lamont, a

Democrat and former telecom executive, wavered on supporting it, amid lobbying from Securus. State lawmakers planned to try again in 2020.

Knox County, Tennessee, has been protesting video-only visits with public rallies and through litigation for years. "It's a form of what I consider to be slavery, just extracting out of people's desperate need to have human contact because they're locked up in the penal system," said Julie Gautreau, an assistant public defender in Knox County who leads Face to Face Knox, a grassroots organizing group advocating for in-person visits. "This is morally reprehensible to any decent human being, in my view. Anyone who interacts with prisoners at a personal level will tell you the devastating effects." Gautreau pointed out to me that Terry Wilshire, a captain at the Knox County sheriff's office, left to go work for Tech Friends, a subsidiary contractor for Securus.

To truly restore justice, the scattered successes with phone rates would have to be replicated with every effort to pickpocket inmates and their families. Prison life is monopolized beyond any other facet of society, and the accumulated horrors of monopolization are all present behind bars. "I often say that nobody gets sentence[d] to being beaten or being raped," said Alex Friedmann. "It's just part of the carceral experience. Being used as a cash cow, and exploited by monopolies because they don't give a damn about you, that's another part."

Mecklenburg County got a new sheriff in 2019, and he immediately reinstated in-person visitation once a week, as well as two free on-site video visits at the Administrative Services Building. Any other video calls cost $10 for twenty-five minutes or $4 for ten minutes, down from the previous rates. But you need an Android phone, or a webcam and a broadband connection, to execute the calls.

Jennifer, who has her own caregiving business now and is doing pretty well, doesn't bother with the video calls anymore, considering them a waste of money. And she doesn't come to see Jeremy at the county jail anymore, either. "I need something more proven to me to put my life on hold," she said. "I do not want to positively reinforce his behavior. I feel like conversations through the phone are good enough." They still talk nearly every day, but the relationship is strained. "I see the good in him, but it's hard to accept that addiction has taken it all away from you."

Jennifer realizes that her decision isolates Jeremy even more, taking away that flicker of outside support he could use to get by. It saddens her, but she feels she has to move on. And she reserves her anger at the situation for GTL and the other companies who preyed on her at a low point in her life.

"They take advantage of the need for you to have human contact," she said. "You are taking families and you are punishing them for what their loved ones did. It feels like that when you transfer that money for a phone call." I asked Jennifer what she would like to say to the executives at GTL. "I'm just a normal southern girl," she replied, her voice shaking. "I believe in treating people the way you want to be treated. I just would say, 'I hope you never have to experience what you do to families. I hope you never have to experience that with anybody that you love.'"

If after reading all this you comforted yourself with the thought that the sweet release of death would at least emancipate you from the burdens of life under corporate power, allow me to introduce you to the burgeoning death monopoly.

A company with the bland name Service Corporation International (SCI) owned 1,478 funeral homes and 481 cemeteries nationwide as of summer 2019. Over half of their facilities are in just seven states; their business model lies in concentrating the market. Founded in 1962, SCI grows through acquisition; a flurry of activity in the 2000s, culminating with the 2013 purchase of Stewart Enterprises, created a death industry monster. The Dignity Memorial, Advantage Funerals, Neptune Society, Funeraria del Angel, and National Cremation brands are all part of the SCI family. Right now SCI handles more than one of every five dollars of profit from funeral services in the United States.

There's reason to grow, as SCI has expressed ghoulishly in its annual reports, where it revels in being "poised to benefit from the aging of the American population . . . the Baby Boomers are already impacting our business today." More "strategic acquisitions" are in the future, so expect an SCI funeral home in a city near you, if it's not there already. Investor concerns about changing desires for cremation led SCI to bulk up the cremation side of its business.

Grieving families have likely never heard of SCI, because those letters appear nowhere in the name of the facilities they use. Every time SCI makes a purchase, it retains the original name of the funeral home or cemetery. For example, after an SCI purchase, Geo. H. Lewis & Sons Funeral Directors was renamed Geo. H. Lewis & Sons Funeral Directors, a Dignity Memorial Provider. Since no customers know what Dignity Memorial means, they continue to believe that they're dealing with a family-run business and not a corporate conglomerate.

SCI earns more than five times the gross profit per funeral home than its smaller counterparts. Part of SCI's business strategy is that virtually no prices for burials, embalming, or caskets appear in the real world until the funeral director hands families a piece of paper at the moment of sale. Those stricken by the loss of a loved one aren't typically inclined to shop around. The Consumer Federation of America found that SCI's prices range 47 to 72 percent higher than the typical funeral home's.

Standard burial prices are elevated as it is, buoyed by concentration in the manufacturing side of the death business. Two companies, Hillenbrand and Matthews, make 82 percent of all coffins and caskets in the United States. But SCI takes this to a higher level, habitually loading on bogus "second interment fees" and other add-ons. Perhaps more important to loved ones, a monopoly doesn't have to care about quality. A 2018 lawsuit in Brownsville, Texas, is instructive. Mary Ruiz used an SCI facility to bury her brother Ernesto Eguia. Ruiz approached the casket the day of the funeral and found her late brother "covered with what looked like gnats but could have been small flies." Insects had infested the facility, which had no air-conditioning, and a haze of them buzzed around the deceased. After the burial, Ruiz learned that Eguia's organs had been mistakenly set aside and not returned to his body. Ruiz sued over this and then found that SCI stacks its consumer contracts with arbitration clauses to block access to courts. An attempt to overturn the arbitration clause failed.

In 2019 the Federal Trade Commission announced plans to review the Funeral Rule, the only main regulation on funeral providers; the current rule is routinely flouted. Advocates endorse more price transparency, so loved ones have a sense of how much a burial might cost before walking in the door. But SCI has skillfully slipped by regulation in the past; the company evaded a California rule mandating the posting of funeral prices on the internet by securing a loophole allowing it to substitute the language "price by request."

It's oddly fitting that for many of us, our final moments aboveground on earth will involve being gently placed in a monopolized box by a monopolized funeral director and dropped into a hole at a monopolized cemetery. Might as well die the way we lived.

CHAPTER 12

Monopolies Are Why I Traveled to Chicago and Tel Aviv to Learn How to Stop Them

We know how to handle monopolies.

You restore the interpretation of the antitrust laws to cover the full spectrum of harms, beyond just consumer welfare. Then you break up dangerous concentrations of economic power, block mergers that would excessively consolidate markets, regulate natural monopolies as public utilities, structurally separate functions where necessary, intervene in the public interest so citizens are protected and empowered, and vigilantly examine markets to prepare for monopolies to emerge again.

Maybe that sounds impossible in the abstract. But it's entirely possible under existing law that either hasn't been enforced in decades or has been misinterpreted for decades. We have over a century of experience with both successfully preventing unnecessary concentration and failing to do so. The mechanisms are clear; getting the political class to enforce them is the stumbling block.

For example, we know that laws preventing "supermarket"-style banks kept us safe from financial disaster for fifty years. We know that the 1936 Robinson-Patman Act, which required wholesalers to sell goods to retailers at the same price regardless of the retailer's market power, kept price discrimination in check and promoted competition. We know that the Civil Aeronautics Board ensured the benefits of air travel nationwide. We know from current-day experience that a state-run bank and local ownership of pharmacies in North Dakota, public wireless companies in Chattanooga and elsewhere, and restrictions on dollar stores in Tulsa, Oklahoma, protect communities from monopoly's worst instincts. We know that the antitrust authorities' guidelines before Robert Bork's revolution carved out a prominent role for robust competition in industry (with specific market-share thresholds that couldn't be exceeded) and helped produce a more equitable distribution of the economy's benefits.

We know that the 1956 Bell Labs consent decree, which forced AT&T's

research and development arms to license all its patents, created the electronics industry in the United States, rather than hoarding innovations
inside a monopoly. "This is what started Silicon Valley," said Jon Taplin,
author of *Move Fast and Break Things*. We know that a similar lawsuit
against IBM led to the dominant computer company of the age unbun-
dling its software options, creating another giant industry. We know that
the U.S. government's antitrust case against Microsoft changed the culture
inside a monopolist company, which allowed early startups like Google
and Amazon to thrive from visits off their browser. "They could have killed
Google in the cradle, but they didn't, and the reason why, according to
Microsoft people, was they had this public trial," said Gary Reback, whose
legal work led to the Microsoft case. Jay Himes, a lawyer who as part of the
New York attorney general's office helped monitor Microsoft, agreed. "I
don't think realistically you can go through a multiyear period of monitoring and think it doesn't affect a company's operations."

The monopolies who want to maintain a lucrative status quo know this
history as well, which is why they've worked assiduously to stack the system with allies who they know won't fight. "I think we can talk about a corrupt process," said financial consultant and author Jonathan Tepper. "The
worst thing is, it's totally legal and more effective because of that. People
buy into the system."

Two federal agencies primarily enforce existing antitrust laws: the antitrust
division of the Justice Department and the Federal Trade Commission.
Corporate lawyers dominate these agencies, regardless of which party
occupies the White House. They carry the philosophy of their former clients, a set of ideas about competition policy that resists aggressive action.
They're rewarded after mustering out of the agency with a warm seat in the
legal defense practices of Big Law, with the government service operating
as a résumé item that can be used to persuade former colleagues to go easy
on corporate clients. It's a "retrospective bribe," as Tepper calls it—not an
overt transfer or even a conscious one, but a powerful obstacle to breaking
up monopolies.

It's a sad postscript to the life of Thurman Arnold, the head of the
antitrust division under President Franklin D. Roosevelt and perhaps
the most aggressive antitrust enforcer in history, that the law firm he
co-founded, Arnold & Porter Kaye Scholer, now runs the most prominent

corporate-defense-to-government pipeline in Washington. The current roster of Arnold & Porter's antitrust group includes "the former Assistant Attorney General for Antitrust at the US Department of Justice (DOJ), two Directors of the Bureau of Competition at the Federal Trade Commission (FTC) . . . Deputy Assistant Attorney General for Civil and Criminal Operations of the Antitrust Division, Deputy Director in the Bureau of Competition at the FTC, two Chiefs of Staff at the Antitrust Division [and] Assistant Director of the FTC's Bureau of Competition." The list would be longer, but Arnold & Porter alum and former FTC chair Robert Pitofsky died in 2018. Former Antitrust Division chief *and* director of the FTC's Bureau of Competition William Baer has had multiple stints at Arnold & Porter, as has former Bureau of Competition director Deborah Feinstein, who routinely overruled lower-level FTC staffers to pursue settlements, which in a 2013 speech she called "a remedy that is as good as or better than what could be achieved from litigation."

At Arnold & Porter, Feinstein represented General Electric, NBC Universal, Unilever, Pepsi, and most recently NxStage Medical, a company trying to merge with dialysis duopolist Fresenius. Joseph Simons, the current FTC chair, represented Microsoft, Sony, Sharp, and MasterCard at the law office of Paul, Weiss, Rifkind, Wharton & Garrison. Christine Wilson, a Republican commissioner, worked at Kirkland & Ellis, representing Northwest Airlines in its merger with Delta; she later became Delta's in-house counsel. Andrew Smith, the current director of the Bureau of Consumer Protection, toiled at Covington & Burling for an incredible 120 different corporate clients, including virtually all of the nation's major banks, Facebook, the pharmaceutical lobby PhRMA, drug distributor Cardinal Health, Uber, Equifax, payday lenders, and—to cap off his service to some of the most hated brands in America—the limited partners that built the stadium for the Dallas Cowboys. (Go Eagles.)

Josh Wright, a former Republican FTC commissioner, hooked on with Google's main law firm and now writes papers defending Google on antitrust. Makan Delrahim, the head of the DOJ's antitrust division, worked for Pfizer, Qualcomm, Anthem, CVS, and Google at Brownstein Hyatt Farber Schreck; Simons's Democratic predecessor Edith Ramirez joined Hogan Lovells after her tenure and repped YouTube in 2019; former Democratic commissioner Terrell McSweeny is now at Covington & Burling while serving as a key advisor to 2020 presidential candidate Joe Biden.

Other Democratic and Republican former enforcers have worked for Comcast, Syngenta, Procter & Gamble, Facebook, Microsoft, IBM, Uber, Oracle, AT&T, Dollar General, General Electric, Boeing, and more.

Government economists also move from the DOJ and FTC into consulting firms, a perch from which they can serve as expert witnesses in antitrust cases. ProPublica estimates that George W. Bush–era Justice Department economist Dennis Carlton, of the University of Chicago and consultant Compass Lexecon, has made over $100 million billing corporate clients. An adversary, Democrat Carl Shapiro, went from DOJ to consultant Charles River Associates. The AT&T/Time Warner case was a battle between Shapiro's economic models and Carlton's; arguing for AT&T, Carlton won, though where citizens stood in an economic-model fight was unclear. "Seven professors on Compass Lexecon's payroll have served as the top antitrust economist at the DOJ, while Charles River Associates has three," Tepper wrote in 2019.

If that stone wall doesn't work, monopolists can appeal to politicians. A 2017 Harvard Business School study showed that firms headquartered in the districts of members of the House and Senate Judiciary Committees get favorable outcomes in merger cases. Administration officials held meetings with members of Google more than once a week throughout Obama's presidency, and over that period nearly 250 people shuttled from government service to Google employment or vice versa. Google has academics on the payroll, too, and augments its millions in formal lobbying by underwriting hundreds of "independent" papers backing its positions.

Finally, the judiciary has been indoctrinated into pro-merger thinking through decades of consistent opinion shaping. Conservative Supreme Court justices like Neil Gorsuch, an antitrust scholar, side with big business routinely; liberal Stephen Breyer was the one who convinced Ted Kennedy to deregulate the airline industry. A seminar put on by the Heritage Foundation from 1976 to 1999 called the Economics Institute for Federal Judges taught at its peak over 40 percent of the federal bench; a recent working paper showed that it succeeded in creating antiregulatory and pro-business rulings. Ruth Bader Ginsburg attended and praised the seminar. At a separate series for law professors run by similar interests, Elizabeth Warren met her husband, Bruce Mann.

This is how you get antitrust agency funding falling at a time of record merger activity. This is how you get the Justice Department and the Federal Trade Commission using the antitrust laws to go after organists, ice skating coaches, physical therapists, and other small coalitions of workers for colluding together to raise their incomes, while giving the biggest monopolists in America a free pass. This is how you get enforcement agencies supporting Uber over Uber drivers and Apple over Apple customers in official court briefs. This is how you get a president taking every opportunity to savage Amazon and Google even as his antitrust division slobbers over tech giants and writes appeals on their behalf. This is how you get, in the space of a few months in 2012 and 2013, the FTC denying the recommendation of its own staff and declining to prosecute Google for exploiting its monopoly power, and declining to block the Facebook/Instagram merger when they had documents from a high-level executive openly stating that Facebook sought to eliminate a competitor.

The antitrust apparatus—in government, in academia, in the establishment—has built a fortress around itself, a cloistered world where nothing is inherently wrong with the economy, where there's been no rampant inequality, stunting of innovation, degradation in quality of service, or concentration in political power, and where there aren't even any monopolies around that could have possibly instigated such bad outcomes.

There's only one way to surmount this phalanx of official power, arrayed to affix monopolies in cement, casting a shadow over American life. And to fully understand how, I had to travel across the Atlantic Ocean.

I met Guy Rolnik at a bistro a couple of blocks off the beach in Tel Aviv, amid the white Bauhaus-style apartment blocks. A couple of years earlier he'd written to me out of the blue, asking if I would participate in a conference he was preparing at the University of Chicago, the heart of the pro-corporate beliefs that hijacked American democracy, about the concentration problem. It turned out that the conference, first presented in 2017, became the launching pad for a new and important movement in our economics and politics. Every movement needs seeds and saplings to grow, and the early planting for this one occurred in Israel.

Rolnik started out not as an academic but as a journalist at *Ha'aretz*, the oldest and most respected daily newspaper in Israel. *Ha'aretz* maintained a strong left-wing voice on Palestinian issues and other facets of Israeli society. But Rolnik was a financial journalist, an area where *Ha'aretz* carried limited weight. By 1997 Rolnik was running the finance page and the internet was just emerging as a means of communication. "I thought it was a great opportunity to start something new, to focus on the bigness," Rolnik told me.

Through two years of compulsory service at Israel Defense Forces radio and eight years covering financial markets, Rolnik had developed a theory about societies that he applied to Israel. "If you control the banks, or the insurance companies, and you also control the media, you have a lock on democracy," he said. To the extent we hear anything in America about Israel, it's about war and peace, the West Bank and Gaza. But it also happens to be a land of what Rolnik calls tycoons.

In Israel, the elites made their move in the 1980s, during the era of the Washington Consensus, when the World Bank and IMF encouraged emerging nations to privatize and deregulate their economies. In 1983 Israeli banks collapsed, and one major reform involved pension privatization. "I call it closed-circuit money," Rolnik said. Five big pension funds came into control of 97 percent of Israelis' savings. This money got lent out to the largest banks and insurance firms in the country, as well as monopolies like Israeli Electric Corporation. And these firms all lent out to each other as well, financing with pension money the takeover of the economy, and denying this funding to anyone on the outside.

The Histadrut labor federation previously owned Bank Hapoalim, the nation's largest bank. After the 1983 collapse it was nationalized, and then sold during the privatization wave to an investor group led by the Arison family. They made Danny Dankner chairman; his cousin Nochi Dankner ran IDB, the largest conglomerate in Israel, including the airline Israir, cell phone provider Cellcom, cement monopoly Nesher, supermarket chain Super Sol, and Clal Insurance, the second-largest insurer. In all, twenty large business groups controlled half the stock market, typically with a "pyramid" holding structure that filtered up to one controlling shareholder. The economy was deeply and seemingly impenetrably concentrated.

Bank Leumi and Bank Hapoalim controlled 60 percent of the market. They made loans to the largest newspapers in the country, and in Rolnik's telling, they knew that the papers were insolvent and could not pay them back. "The threat went both ways," said Rolnik. "You have loans to media outlets, and those outlets give you favorable reporting. It's great for both sides." Media tycoons flexed their muscles politically as well. Audiotapes produced later revealed Arnon Mozes, owner of news giant *Yedioth Ahro-*

noth, telling prime minister Benjamin "Bibi" Netanyahu that he could remain as leader as long as he wanted if he restricted competition in media.

The government bought into this elite backscratching through the revolving door. Four straight government bank supervisors became high-level executives at Israeli financial institutions. Four straight finance ministers took the same route, as did four straight accountants general of the Finance Ministry. Antitrust chief Yoram Turbowicz became the chairman of the gas monopoly Delek Energy, owned by tycoon Yitzhak Tshuva. His replacements rotated into the industry as well. Rolnik portrayed it as a club of billionaire families, all looking out for one another's interests and their own, firmly in control of Israel's economy and its democracy. "Corruption is not tied to the right or left. Corruption is corruption," said Rolnik. "Below the table, everybody is cooperating."

Rolnik wanted to report on tycoon control of Israel, and he thought the internet could serve as the venue. At age twenty-nine he raised $4 million to start TheMarker, a financial journalism website; eventually *Ha'aretz* agreed to assist him. "I faced very aggressive opposition from the entire business sector and the incumbent newspapers," Rolnik recalled. "I was a little naive. I thought they don't like competition. As time goes by, I realized they wanted to make sure news media is aligned with the interests of the banks and the conglomerates."

Nonetheless, as a first mover on the internet, Rolnik and TheMarker achieved some success. The site's journalists had no limits and could explore issues of business and power in Israel. Its target audience was not shareholders and executives but consumers and citizens. Five years after its 2000 entry, TheMarker was profitable and launched a print supplement to *Ha'aretz*, though it had a more modest focus. "The first stage, it was reform-oriented," said Asher Schechter, a former reporter for TheMarker. "But also I think it was still a newspaper in the classic sense. It had certain values and a mission, but to report the news, not so much to shape it."

TheMarker switched its strategy as concentration rose in Israel, and the strains of corruption could be more easily seen. Rolnik had come to see himself as a campaigner, using the conventions of journalism to make real change in Israel. An initial foray, attempting to alter the fee structure of companies to increase competition, failed. "I was trying to be objective," he said. "And then came the next thing, breaking the stranglehold of the banks on the economy. I said, 'Do I have to play the British gentleman? No!'"

Rolnik ran a special weekend edition with a cover photo of Louis Brandeis, the antimonopolist who advised U.S. president Woodrow Wilson's 1912 campaign. He was seen differently in Israel, as the first Jewish Supreme Court justice and an ardent Zionist. Rolnik wrote the issue's lead editorial: "In taking on power-hungry tycoons 100 years ago, Louis Brandeis became the social conscience of the most capitalist country in the world. Who will be Israel's savior from the oligarchs?" He used Brandeis's ideas to attack the tycoons and their monopolization of the Israeli economy, sector by sector. Writers showed how this translated into political power, capturing the politicians. Everyday news stories were set into context, with articles explaining how the system works, how things fit together. This was a completely novel avenue of reporting within Israel, and it began to activate society there. The readership wasn't enormous, but it was influential; TheMarker reached the right people, and because it was internet-native its stories spread virally.

The first campaign earned quick success, as the government forced Israeli banks to sell off their asset management businesses. Because of this Israeli banks were less prone to collapse during the financial crisis; decentralization helped stabilize the banking system. Later, the minister of communications challenged incumbent telecom owners, a cartel of three tycoon-run conglomerates that charged as much as $500 a month for cell phone service. TheMarker backed this campaign as well.

The tycoons struck back, with the largest conglomerates boycotting advertising in the site's print edition, something that almost bankrupted TheMarker. The Dankner family bought *Ma'ariv*, the country's second-largest newspaper, and offered writers for TheMarker large salaries to switch sides. *Ma'ariv* would devote page-one coverage to "TheMarker gang," and fellow tycoons piled on with threatened litigation and lawsuits against unfavorable articles. "They did an investigative piece about Guy's dad," said Asher Schechter. "It's like, why would he ever be a cover story? So the reaction was very violent. But prices started rising very fast in Israel, which led to a social protest movement."

In 2011, oil, gas, water, food, and housing prices surged, in some cases doubling. The economy was strong in aggregate, but the benefits weren't reaching ordinary Israelis, particularly the young. The tycoons, meanwhile, cut dividends for shareholders while hoarding the proceeds for themselves, which TheMarker reported on. In July, a young Tel Aviv film-maker named Daphni Leef, perhaps nodding to the Tahrir Square protests in neighboring Egypt, posted a Facebook message calling for Israelis to get in the streets. Schechter, who was writing about the plight of young people in Israel at the time, watched the small group set up camp in Habima Square, close to the national theater on Rothschild Boulevard. "I could see from the first night, it blew up completely," Schechter said. "It became a national news story in an hour." The mayor of Tel Aviv visited the camp, and protesters kicked him out. Within a couple of weeks, the square and the surrounding medians of the boulevards were covered with tents, with hundreds of encampments eventually pouring out all over Israel. "Living here has become impossible, and we will not accept it," said the chair of the National Union of Students in one speech.

The protest leaders were a bit inchoate in the first month, with general antigovernment sloganeering and calls for a stronger welfare state. This was a deliberate strategy; leadership knew that the key to getting coverage in the tycoon-run media was isolating the protests to the political leadership. But at the street level, there was awareness of the tycoons and the antimonopoly campaign; one tent declared itself "Dankner's Barbershop," after the haircuts the tycoons gave shareholders. By August, as protests swelled as large as 430,000 (incredible for a country of only 8 million; it represented nearly 10 percent of Israel's entire adult population), protesters more frequently used the language of TheMarker, railing against the tycoons and oligarchs controlling Israel. Protesters affixed articles and statistics from TheMarker on their tents; a giant sign in the shape of a pyramid, showing the specific media holdings of the tycoons, was ubiquitous. Another sign featured Netanyahu next to Nochi Dankner and Yitzhak Tshuva with the caption "The Servant of Two Masters."

As soon as sentiments turned from the government to the tycoons, major news outlets stopped covering the protests. If protesters were mentioned at all, it was to describe them as unserious anarchists. Later journalists for these news outlets admitted that they had been instructed to stop coverage and to underestimate crowd sizes. Only TheMarker remained, primarily Schechter, who was embedded with the protesters. "We had an outlet that could very much direct the protests to the issues, where they otherwise might not have been as knowledgeable," he said.

That August Rolnik got a call at his office; it was Bibi Netanyahu. He wanted a personal meeting, and Rolnik agreed, but only if he could bring his editors. "We sit in this office in this crazy meeting," Rolnik told me. "Netanyahu says, 'What do I have to do?' We say, 'Come on, you know what to do.'" The next morning, at a press conference, Netanyahu urged a concentration committee, which had been quietly formed a year earlier, to move rapidly to complete its work. As some of the tycoons were Netanyahu's political enemies, the antimonopoly forces lucked into an exploitable wedge.

The interim report of the committee admitted, for the first time in an official context, that Israel had a problem with concentration. The telecom law was implemented in 2012, driving prices down 90 percent from the $500 per month peak. When I was there in 2017, I saw cell phone ads in Tel Aviv promoting $15 monthly fees for full service. The slashing of cell phone rates damaged one of the most profitable business lines in Dankner's IDB conglomerate. Schechter described it as like a chain reaction: several tycoons soon went bankrupt, and pressure for additional reforms arose. By 2013, an anticoncentration law passed the Knesset unanimously. It sharply restricted the pyramid holding structure and separated significant banking institutions from commerce (no major owner of a financial company could also control a large entity in the real economy). The effect was dramatic; whereas in 2010 the tycoon holding groups controlled 55 percent of the Israeli economy, by 2017 this was down to 37 percent, according to a report from the Israel Securities Authority.

Later the Knesset approved a cap on executive pay and an antidiscrimination law meant to aid smaller suppliers in food markets. TheMarker campaigned for both laws. IDB turned insolvent and Dankner lost control of the company. Other tycoon-run conglomerates were dissolved. Both Dankner cousins were sentenced to jail, Danny for bribery and Nochi for stock fraud; the original source of the information in Nochi's case was TheMarker. Even Netanyahu, who switched sides back to the monopolists, would be indicted for corruption. "The untouchable class is either in jail or on the way," Rolnik said.

Rolnik won the Israeli version of the Pulitzer Prize. He said the most important lesson he took from the Israeli campaign was the power to set the agenda. TheMarker discussed monopoly in a way Israelis had never heard before. While he and his band of journalists were demeaned as crazy and radical, they were the only ones telling a story that connected to people's lives. And they could mainstream an issue that was ripe for reform.

Narratives can help create a political environment, and then a movement can use them as fuel to rebuild democracy.

As his campaigns bore success, Rolnik started to look outside Israel. "I thought America was this great country that's so competitive," he told me. "What I see now, the level of competition is worse here than in Israel."

The University of Chicago conference on antitrust and competition, inaugurated in March 2017, came out of the Stigler Center, named after one of the leaders of the Chicago School of economics, which poisoned the country by persuading the political class of the benefits of monopoly. As *The Economist* wrote, "Until recently, convening a conference supporting antitrust concerns in the Windy City was like holding a symposium on sobriety in New Orleans." (In fact, *The Economist* expressing sympathy with antimonopoly sentiment is just as incongruous.)

Rolnik had just joined the university as a professor. Teaming with Luigi Zingales, a heterodox economist, they sought to expose these questions to rare scrutiny inside the ivory tower, particularly at Chicago. They may not have realized how quickly the ideas would spread. The first conference, entitled "Is There a Concentration Problem in America," brought together many who have come under the banner of the New Brandeis movement: journalists, think tank fellows, historians, academics who had been softly challenging the antitrust status quo and now had backup in the wider world. Barry Lynn, who at the New America Foundation had assembled a group of writers and thinkers to condemn the monopolists and those who sheltered them, was there. One of his colleagues in attendance, Lina Khan, had just authored one of the most well-known law review essays in recent history, "Amazon's Antitrust Paradox," arguing that the online retailer represented a leviathan that the modern practice of competition policy couldn't adequately confront. Authors and authors-to-be of major books addressing corporate power in the Second Gilded Age were on hand.

The old guard was there too. I wrote for *The Nation* about how the conference became a pitched battle of ideas. "America was founded to provide people the wherewithal to protect ourselves from enslavement," Lynn characteristically thundered. "The notion of blocking mergers because of political power has just melted away," replied Carl Shapiro, adding that Walmart's low prices were a big boon for consumers. "Concentration is actually low," asserted Dennis Carlton, adding, "I can't believe that's causing a problem." The keynote speaker, former appeals court judge Richard Posner, was blunt: "Antitrust is dead, isn't it?"

You could have walked away thinking that a bunch of intellectuals arguing, while citizens slowly sank under the weight of monopoly, wasn't getting anybody anywhere. And yet two years later the conference had changed its format from wondering whether there was a concentration problem to writing a platform to deal with the concentration problem plainly before their eyes. Indeed, just challenging the Chicago School ideas, for the first time in decades, had the effect of weakening them, making them seem less like iron law and more like a constructed set of conjectures, all too human and fallible.

The New Brandeis movement, meanwhile, had surprising momentum. It caught a wave of public anger about a rigged economy, and a desire to understand the underlying forces. In the years leading up to the conference, figures as varied as Senator Elizabeth Warren, appointees to the Obama administration's Council of Economic Advisers, and members of the Republican-run Senate Judiciary Committee had expressed concern about creeping monopoly asserting its dominance over our lives. When Lynn got ousted from New America after sending an approving press release about a fine against Google in Europe—Google is a major donor to New America, and the main conference room in its Washington offices is named the Eric Schmidt Ideas Lab, after Google's former executive chairman—the power of monopolies to stifle unwanted ideas became clearer. More dissidents came out of the woodwork, in parallel to a series of scandalous reports about Big Tech's carelessness with user privacy and its role in the 2016 elections. Roger McNamee, an early tech funder, called for breaking up the platforms; so did Chris Hughes, a co-founder of Facebook. BuzzFeed's Ben Smith famously declared that there was "blood in the water" in Silicon Valley in one of seemingly dozens of articles about the new pushback on monopoly.

Because the whole world uses tech platforms, there's a temptation to conflate the antimonopoly movement solely with an attack on Big Tech. But New Brandeis adherents were really talking about a broad restructuring of the economy, letting markets serve people instead of oligarchs in agriculture, finance, health care, and more. They were unveiling the latest sickness in society, with rising inequality and diminished opportunity. And because the statutory mechanisms to fight monopolies were already in place, this recharging of will had the effect of bursting through a dam.

The 2020 Democratic primary featured more discussion of monopoly than any since 1912, with even candidates who are openly antagonistic toward each other—from Bernie Sanders to John Hickenlooper—agreeing that something must be done. On the right, Josh Hawley, a senator from Missouri, has proposed a "do not track" opt-out against targeted advertising, part of a burst of antagonism against tech platforms. The House Judiciary Committee, with bipartisan support, is studying the effect of tech concentration on society, the first considered investigation of monopoly at the congressional level in decades. Congressional queries forced Amazon to take down special ads for its house brands in space denied to competitors. Pressure from citizens at the bottom has forced the political system to respond.

Stocked with corporate law and economics expats and their allies, the antitrust agencies initially paid lip service to enforcement, holding meaningless field hearings and giving lighter-than-air speeches. Makan Delrahim even came to the Chicago conference in 2018 and argued for an antitrust apparatus barely better than the status quo. Meanwhile, regulators waved through huge mergers like CVS/Aetna and Amazon/Whole Foods. But the agencies did sort out jurisdictional issues on the dominant technology platforms, with the Justice Department taking responsibility for Google and Apple investigations, and the FTC taking Facebook and Amazon. Pressure to act on Big Tech could bear some investigative fruit. Blocking a merger of the two main companies that print magazines and books (like this one), LSC Communications and Quad/Graphics, would be routine for any decent antitrust enforcer. Yet when the parties abandoned the merger in 2019, after the Justice Department announced a lawsuit, it was a pleasant surprise. Maybe the movement had summoned the flickers of a decent agency out of the darkness.

The courts were listening, too, occasionally. A judge sided with the FTC against Qualcomm, ruling that the chipmaker must license its patents to competing suppliers. The Supreme Court heard the case of *Apple v. Pepper*, where app developers asserted that Apple's control of the market for iPhone apps gouged suppliers and raised consumer prices. Apple tried to argue that it wasn't responsible for the charges; it was just the host of a virtual mall. But while Supreme Court justices may not know every technicality of business structure, they do have smartphones. "The first sale is from Apple to the customer," said Justice Sonia Sotomayor. She joined the majority ruling that the case could go forward.

The movement had help abroad, where India prevented Amazon from selling products in competition with third parties on its platform, and Germany outlawed Facebook's invasive targeted advertising business. In the states, investigations against Big Tech have gone forward, as has pursuit of pharmacy benefit manager middlemen that increase drug prices. A bipartisan coalition in Virginia is breaking up the longtime monopoly energy company Dominion; Arizona has also taken aim at its utility monopoly. State attorneys general forced fast-food giants to stop enforcing noncompete clauses that barred workers from changing jobs within the industry, a key wage suppression tactic. When the Justice Department waved through the Sprint/T-Mobile merger, reducing major cell phone carriers in the United States from four to three, states banded together to sue to block it, as is their right under the Sherman Antitrust Act. Private litigants have increasingly used the same power: it was a trial attorney who brought the Apple App Store case that won at the Supreme Court.

Even the markets agreed with the public, if on crass terms. Every so often an analyst's report or activist investor comes out recommending that a company would be worth more in parts than agglomerated. Sometimes the companies act on it. United Technologies split into three companies in 2018, a prelude to its merger with Raytheon but a signal that conglomerates had fallen out of favor with investors.

Most important, the people have realized their own power. Google employees marched out to demand better treatment and more humane products, despite scant history of worker solidarity in that industry. In a few areas they won. Citizens organized long-shot initiatives that succeeded in beating giants—like the supporters of public Wi-Fi in Fort Collins, Colorado, who were outspent $1 million to $15,000 and still won.

Another story is instructive. Over the past few years, the private equity industry has taken over Hollywood talent agencies, investing billions into the Big Three firms responsible for 70 percent of film and television writers' earnings. Where agents once operated in the best interest of clients, the new goal is "packaging fees," putting writers, directors, and actors from an agent's stable into the same show and earning a direct commission from the studio. In addition to excluding writers not attached to a particular agency from that agency's packaged deal, the packaging fees come out of the production budget, the same pot of money as writers' pay. This puts agents in a cash grab against their own clients. Because the studios want talent for future projects, the agent has the advantage. Median television writers' pay has fallen in an era of "peak TV," while agencies are getting into the production business, taking more control over entertainment dollars and serving as their own clients' bosses, at the urging of financiers seeking big returns.

Usually private equity jumps into sectors of the economy where workers have no bargaining power. But the Writers Guild of America (WGA) was unified. Seven thousand writers fired their agents. And the industry didn't fall apart. "In one of our last writers' surveys, 75 percent of our members had reported that their most recent job did not come from a contact from their agent," said Laura Blum-Smith, the WGA West's director of research and public policy. The union set up tools for writers to submit work to showrunners, and promoted meetups for writers to make contacts. Shows continue to be staffed. The profit-extracting middleman monopolists, it turns out, weren't entirely necessary.

Only when people are awake can such visions become reality. When the blinders come off and we expose our economic and political structures to scrutiny, we can start to imagine better alternatives. There is practically no problem in our country—war and peace, immigrants and the border, health care for all, financial stability, an economy of broadly shared prosperity—that doesn't interact with monopoly in some form. It's the ur-problem, the problem of power, and solving it will allow us to solve everything else.

Once again: we know how to deal with monopolies. What we've lacked for forty years is a social movement, based in self-respect and desire for more than just pity. The madness of the wealth gap, the worsening of our options and cheapening of our goods, the inability of entrepreneurs to gain a foothold, the shame of middle America's abandonment—these have combined to put energy into a clarion call to rebalance our economy. "I had a sense that people were frustrated with institutions," said Congressman Ro Khanna, a leader on these issues. "There was a sense that they didn't have agency over their own lives."

As much as we wish that we could walk away and put our lives in someone else's hands, great men and women will not sustain resistance alone.

They are too small and too outnumbered. Richard Hofstadter once asked, in a speech in 1964, "What happened to the antitrust movement?" He wondered why antimonopoly sentiment had ceased to be a vital topic of public agitation. When the public gets engaged, America can do great things in their service. When attentions wander, the relentlessness of monopolists hold sway. Hofstadter was prescient: not long after his question, antitrust waned, and dominance regained its throne.

What will happen to today's antitrust movement? Will it sustain the bold talk on the campaign trail and congressional hearings, brighten the glint of recognition in courts and regulatory agencies? Only if public indignation grows, and people recognize who has taken their power, so they can take it back.

ACKNOWLEDGMENTS

In 2015, Robert Kuttner of *The American Prospect* called me up and asked me what I might like to contribute for the next issue of the magazine. I don't remember exactly why, but I said I'd like to do something about monopolies. The story, "Bring Back Antitrust," appeared in the Fall 2015 issue, and was the longest piece of writing I had published to that point. (My book *Chain of Title* came out a year later.) It gave me entry into a world of journalists and thinkers that had spent years toiling on the monopoly problem, which I sheepishly thought I had personally resurrected out of obscurity. That community, which unbeknownst to me was on the cusp of breaking through with their ideas, would become the heart of the New Brandeis movement. The book you're reading draws on five years of work launched from that initial reporting.

I also didn't know then that I would become the executive editor of *The American Prospect*. I wrote this book in the midst of preparing to take that job, which I don't recommend as a time-management strategy for authors! But I must thank the *Prospect* family, who has worked tirelessly to build a nationally recognized and respected magazine about ideas, politics, and power, including corporate power. We celebrated our thirtieth year in 2020, and we're striving to bring this outpost of the populist left to the next generation. Let me single out co-founders Bob Kuttner and Paul Starr and editor at large Harold Meyerson for their wisdom and encouragement; our publisher Ellen Meany and board chair Mike Stern; and our staff—Jonathan Guyer, Gabrielle Gurley, Susanna Beiser, Alexander Sammon, Marcia Brown, Brittany Gibson, Jandos Rothstein, and Steven Whiteside.

I must also thank the other editors who I worked with on several of the stories that I drew from in writing this book: Ryan Kearney, Ryan Grim, Steven Mikulan, George Zornick, Jessica Stites, Yuval Rosenberg, Betsy Reed, Matt Taylor, and many more.

The list of those who have helped me understand the monopolies lurking in every corner of our economy is almost innumerable, and I'm sure I'll miss some. I will start with those who were so obliging on that very first story: Barry Lynn, Allen Grunes, Maurice Stucke, Joseph Stiglitz, Zephyr Teachout, John Kwoka, Diana Moss, and Thomas Shaw of Retractable Technologies. They opened the door to this world and I haven't shut that door since.

More recently, people like Lina Khan, Matt Stoller, Teddy Downey, David Segal, Shaoul Sussman, Eileen Appelbaum, Austin Frerick, Guy Rolnik, and Sarah Miller have been invaluable to my thinking about monopolies. Rohit Chopra is always a source of brilliance. Frank Foer and Jonathan Taplin and Tim Wu are terrific writers who made it easy for me to pick my way through a complex subject. The new stirrings of antitrust thought on Capitol Hill has leaders like David Cicilline, Ro Khanna, Elizabeth Warren, Bill Pascrell, as well as the stalwart members of their staffs. I had so many endnotes on this book that we moved them to the web, a symbol of how many great journalists and writers and academics are doing work in this space. They all have my gratitude.

The above names make up only a portion of the people I spoke to, bounced ideas off, and were enlightened by through the creation of this book. Anything that spans this much territory requires a team effort. I'll single out a few of the most critical team players: Paul Stephen Dempsey, Paul Hudson, Jason Kint, J.Ed Marston, Dean Baker, Gordon Adams, Paul Rafelson, Phil Zweig, Julia Gordon, and Bianca Tylek. That's just a sampling. Others shared their experiences with me off the record, and I'll honor that while also thanking them for their candor.

This was a book about people living through monopoly. So most important to me were those who gave of their time and told me their stories. They are the backbone of this book and what gives it value. Thanks to Kate Hanni, Chris Petersen, Jamie Pearson (pseudonym), Carolyn Horowitz, Travis Bornstein, Dawn Neiderhauser, Murray Sanderson (pseudonym), Cynthia Stine, Jeff Schick, C.J. Rosenbaum, Chris McCabe, Ben Boyer, Dana Chisholm, and Jennifer Hamilton. They made reporting this story a pleasure, and I'm in debt to them for their trust in me. We need to hear more from all of us who manage the burdens of monopoly, day by day, and I hope these narratives can serve as a guide.

I was fortunate enough to work again with my editor Carl Bromley and the entire team at The New Press. Carl's guiding hand was immensely important as usual, and he's a joy to work with. I appreciate the support from Ellen Adler, Maury Botton, Derek Warker, and Brian Ulicky. My early readers Hal Singer, Jared Blank, and Andy Ross really assisted me in getting the draft into shape. Andy Ross is also my agent, who took a chance on me when nobody else would. This is our second book together, and I look forward to many more. Thanks to you.

My parents Neil and Dara and my sister Jessica deserve to be recognized for their contributions to who I am and the values I hold.

For my first book, I told my wife Mary that I would thank her by using some awkward metaphor associated with the subject. In that case it was "to Mary, who foreclosed on my heart." It would be incredibly lazy to try to make this gimmick work a second time with something like "to Mary, who has monopolized my heart." And yet, there I go again. Monopolizing is actually a good way to describe the amount of time I spend on this and other projects, and Mary has shown endless, unreasonable patience with me. With this chapter closed, I look forward to taking her and our dog Sophie on an extremely long walk that I hope never ends.

SELECT BIBLIOGRAPHY

A Note on Sources

This book drew on an array of work on monopolies and corporate power: beat reporting, business news, in-depth features, Congressional testimony, audio and video material, academic studies, think tank papers, government reports, full-length books, and more. We decided to place the voluminous source notes for the book online, where they are fully searchable. You can find these notes at monopolizednotes.tumblr.com.

But I did want to acknowledge in print some of the work that helped me the most as I put together *Monopolized*.

Books

Eileen Appelbaum and Rosemary Batt, *Private Equity at Work: When Wall Street Manages Main Street* (New York: Russell Sage Foundation, 2014).

Robert Bork, *The Antitrust Paradox: A Policy at War With Itself* (New York: Free Press, 1978).

Franklin Foer, *World Without Mind: The Existential Threat of Big Tech* (New York: Penguin Books, 2017).

Mark Gerchick, *Full Upright and Locked Position: Not-So-Comfortable Truths about Air Travel Today* (New York: W.W. Norton and Co., 2013).

Aaron Glantz, *Homewreckers: How a Gang of Wall Street Kingpins, Hedge Fund Magnates, Crooked Banks, and Vulture Capitalists Suckered Millions Out of Their Homes and Demolished the American Dream* (New York: Custom House, 2019).

John Kwoka, *Mergers, Merger Control, and Remedies: A Retrospective Analysis of U.S. Policy* (Boston: MIT Press, 2014).

Barry Lynn, *Cornered: The New Monopoly Capitalism and the Economics of Destruction* (New York: John Wiley & Sons, 2010)

Edmund Morris, *Theodore Rex* (New York: Random House, 2001).

Paul Starr, *The Creation of the Media: Political Origins of Modern Communications*, (New York: Basic Books, 2004) 186–187.

Matt Stoller, *Goliath: The 100-Year War Between Monopoly Power and Democracy* (New York: Simon & Schuster, 2019).

Brad Stone, *The Everything Store: Jeff Bezos and the Age of Amazon* (New York: Little, Brown and Co., 2013).

Jonathan Taplin, *Move Fast and Break Things: How Facebook, Google, and Amazon Cornered Culture and Undermined Democracy* (New York: Little, Brown and Company, 2017).

Jonathan Tepper and Denise Hearn, *The Myth of Capitalism: Monopolies and the Death of Competition* (New York: Wiley, 2018).

Tim Wu, *The Curse of Bigness: Antitrust in the New Gilded Age* (New York: Columbia Global Reports, 2018).

Academic and Think Tank Research

Penelope Muse Abernathy, "The Expanding News Desert," University of North Carolina Hussman School of Journalism and Media, 2018.

David Autor, David Dorn, Lawrence F. Katz, Christina Patterson, and John Van Reenen, "Concentrating on the Fall of the Labor Share," National Bureau of Economic Research, January 2017.

José Azar, Ioana Elena Marinescu, and Marshall Steinbaum, "Labor Market Concentration," Social Science Research Network, December 10, 2018.

José Azar, Martin Schmalz, and Isabel Tecu, "Anticompetitive Effects of Common Ownership," *Journal of Finance*, 2018.

Simcha Barkai, "Declining Labor and Capital Shares," University of Chicago, November 2016.

John C. Coates IV, "The Future of Corporate Governance Part I: The Problem of Twelve," Harvard Public Law Working Paper, September 20, 2018.

Zack Cooper, Stuart Craig, Martin Gaynor, and John Van Reenen, "The Price Ain't Right? Hospital Prices and Health Spending on the Privately Insured," Health Care Pricing Project, May 2015.

Colleen Cunningham, Florian Ederer, and Song Ma, "Killer Acquisitions," Yale School of Management, November 2018.

Jan De Loecker, Jan Eeckhout, and Gabriel Unger, "The Rise of Market Power and the Macroeconomic Implications," November 22, 2018.

Paul Stephen Dempsey, "Flying Blind: The Failure of Airline Deregulation," Economic Policy Institute, 1990.

Marie Donahue and Stacy Mitchell, "Dollar Stores Are Targeting Struggling Urban Neighborhoods and Small Towns. One Community Is Showing How to Fight Back," Institute for Local Self-Reliance, December 6, 2018.

Brent D. Fulton, "Health Care Market Concentration Trends In the United States: Evidence and Policy Responses," *Health Affairs*, September 2017.

Claire Kelloway and Sarah Miller, "Food and Power: Addressing Monopolization in America's Food System," Open Markets Institute, April 2019.

Lina Khan, "Amazon's Antitrust Paradox," *Yale Law Journal*, January 2017.

Lina Khan and Sandeep Vaheesan, "Market Power and Inequality: The Antitrust Counterrevolution and Its Discontents," *Harvard Law and Policy Review*, February 22, 2017.

Robert R. Litan and Hal J. Singer, "Broken Compensation Structures and Health Care Costs," *Harvard Business Review*, October 6, 2010.

Stacy Mitchell, "Walmart's Monopolization of Local Grocery Markets," Institute for Local Self-Reliance, June 26, 2019.

Shaoul Sussman, "Prime Predator: Amazon and the Rationale of Below Average Variable Cost Pricing Strategies Among Negative-Cash Flow Firms," *Journal of Antitrust Enforcement*, March 25, 2019.

H. Trostle and Christopher Mitchell, "Profiles of Monopoly: Big Cable and Telecom," Institute for Local Self-Reliance, July 2018.

Elizabeth Warren, "Reigniting Competition in the American Economy," Remarks at New America's Open Markets Program Event, June 29, 2016.

Council of Economic Advisers, "Benefits of Competition and Indicators of Market Power," April 2016.

Department of Defense, "Assessing and Strengthening the Manufacturing and Defense Industrial Base and Supply Chain Resiliency of the United States," September 2018.

Department of Defense Inspector General, "Review of Parts Purchased From Trans-Digm Group, Inc.," February 25, 2019.

Economic Innovation Group, "Dynamism in Retreat: Consequences for Regions, Markets, and Workers," February 2017.

Government Accountability Office, "DRUG INDUSTRY: Profits, Research and Development Spending, and Merger and Acquisition Deals," November 2017.

Office of Attorney General Martha Coakley, "Investigation of Health Care Cost Trends and Cost Drivers," January 29, 2010.

Open Markets Institute's concentration data, 2019, concentrationcrisis. openmarketsinstitute.org. Much of the data is derived from IBISWorld, which tracks market shares.

Private Equity Stakeholder Project, "Private Equity-Owned Firms Dominate Prison and Detention Services," December 2018.

United for Respect, "Pirate Equity: How Wall Street Firms Are Pillaging American Retail," July 2019.

Worth Rises, "The Prison Industrial Complex: Mapping Private Sector Players," April 2019.

Websites and Journalists

ProMarket, a production of the University of Chicago, covers corporate concentration superbly.

The *Washington Monthly* (washingtonmonthly.com) and reporters like Mariah Blake, Daniel Block, Brian Feldman, Lina Khan, Phillip Longman, and Barry Lynn have been on this subject of monopolies for longer than almost anyone.

Food and Power (foodandpower.net) from the Open Markets Institute is an excellent source of information on agricultural monopolies. The New Food Economy (newfoodeconomy.org) is also stellar.

Publications like *The Verge*, *Motherboard*, *Recode*, and *Ars Technica* are among the best for news about digital media, advertising, Big Tech, and Big Telecom.

Stat News is terrific for all things health care.

Prison Legal News (prisonlegalnews.org) covers the business of criminal justice.

Business beat reporters at the *New York Times*, *Washington Post*, *Wall Street Journal*, *Reuters*, CNBC, Axios, and *Bloomberg News*, among others, are invaluable.

Articles

Eileen Appelbaum and Rosemary Batt, "Private Equity Pillage: Grocery Stores and Workers At Risk," *The American Prospect*, October 26, 2018.

Jeff Bailey, "An Air Travel Activist Is Born," *New York Times*, September 20, 2007.

Lenny Bernstein and Scott Higham, "'We feel like our system was hijacked': DEA agents say a huge opioid case ended in a whimper," *Washington Post*, December 17, 2017.

The Capitol Forum, "Military Revenues at Risk from Promised Trump Administration Crackdown on Military Contract Costs," January 17, 2017.

Josh Dzieza, "Prime and Punishment: Dirty Dealing in the $175 Billion Amazon Marketplace," *The Verge*, December 19, 2018.

Eric Eyre, "Drug firms poured 780M painkillers into WV amid rise of overdoses," *West Virginia Gazette*, December 17, 2016.

Robin Harding, "How Warren Buffett Broke American Capitalism," *Financial Times*, September 12, 2017.

Allan Holmes, "How Big Telecom Smothers City-Run Broadband," The Center for Public Integrity, August 28, 2014,

Robert Kuttner and Hildy Zenger, "Saving the Free Press From Private Equity," *The American Prospect*, December 27, 2017.

Josh Marshall, "A Serf on Google's Farm," Talking Points Memo, September 1, 2017.

Stacy Mitchell, "Amazon Doesn't Just Want to Dominate the Market—It Wants to Become the Market," *The Nation*, February 15, 2018.

Tim Requarth, "How Private Equity Is Turning Public Prisons into Big Profits," *The Nation*, April 30, 2019.

Guy Rolnik, "Democracy or Economic Concentration. Your Choice," *Ha'aretz*, July 6, 2010.

Alana Semuels, "When Wall Street Is Your Landlord," *The Atlantic*, February 13, 2019.

Matt Stoller and Lucas Kunce, "America's Monopoly Crisis Hits the Military," *The American Conservative*, June 27, 2019.

Jonathan Tepper, "Why Regulators Went Soft on Monopolies," *The American Conservative*, January 9, 2019.

Phillip L. Zweig and Wendy Zellner, "Locked Out Of The Hospital," *Businessweek*, March 15, 1998.

My Own Work

"Amazon Is One Step Closer to Taking a Cut on Literally Every Economic Transaction," *In These Times*, July 10, 2018.

"Big Tech: The New Predatory Capitalism," *The American Prospect*, December 26, 2017.

"Bring Back Antitrust," *The American Prospect*, November 9, 2015.

"Contractor Whose Business Model Is Price Gouging the Pentagon Has Powerful Wall St. Backers," *The Intercept*, April 13, 2017.

"Google's Remarkably Close Relationship with the Obama White House, in Two Charts," *The Intercept*, April 22, 2016.

"The Hidden Monopolies That Raise Drug Prices," *The American Prospect*, March 28, 2017.

"How Sears Was Gutted by Its Own CEO," *The American Prospect*, October 17, 2018.

"Obama's Agriculture Secretary, Now Working for the Dairy Industry, Urges 2020 Democrats to Be Nice to the Dairy Industry," *The Intercept*, May 6, 2019.

"Special Investigation: The Dirty Secret Behind Warren Buffett's Billions," *The Nation*, February 15, 2018.

"This Budding Movement Wants to Smash Monopolies," *The Nation*, April 4, 2017.

"Thousands of Amazon Delivery Drivers Won't Be Eligible for the $15 Wage," *In These Times*, October 12, 2018.

"The True Cost," Talking Points Memo, June 2016.

"Unfriendly Skies," *The American Prospect*, November 3, 2017.

"Your New Landlord Works on Wall Street," *The New Republic*, February 11, 2013.

INDEX

ABOUT THE AUTHOR

David Dayen is the executive editor of the *American Prospect*. His work has appeared in *The Intercept*, the *New Republic*, *HuffPost*, the *Washington Post*, the *Los Angeles Times*, and more. He is the author of *Chain of Title*, winner of the Studs and Ida Terkel Prize for a first book in the public interest. Dayen lives in Venice, California.

PUBLISHING IN THE PUBLIC INTEREST

Thank you for reading this book published by The New Press. The New Press is a nonprofit, public interest publisher. New Press books and authors play a crucial role in sparking conversations about the key political and social issues of our day.

We hope you enjoyed this book and that you will stay in touch with The New Press. Here are a few ways to stay up to date with our books, events, and the issues we cover:

- Sign up at www.thenewpress.com/subscribe to receive updates on New Press authors and issues and to be notified about local events
- Like us on Facebook: www.facebook.com/newpressbooks
- Follow us on Twitter: www.twitter.com/thenewpress

Please consider buying New Press books for yourself; for friends and family; or to donate to schools, libraries, community centers, prison libraries, and other organizations involved with the issues our authors write about.

The New Press is a 501(c)(3) nonprofit organization. You can also support our work with a tax-deductible gift by visiting www.thenewpress.com/donate.